Women's Stories of Strength and Empowerment,
Accompanied by Actionable Strategies on How to Thrive

She GROWS STRONGER

HANNA OLIVAS
Along with 31 inspiring authors

© 2025 ALL RIGHTS RESERVED.

Published by She Rises Studios Publishing **www.SheRisesStudios.com.**

No part of this book may be reproduced or transmitted in any form whatsoever, electronic, or mechanical, including photocopying, recording, or by any informational storage or retrieval system without the expressed written, dated and signed permission from the publisher and co-authors.

LIMITS OF LIABILITY/DISCLAIMER OF WARRANTY:

The co-authors and publisher of this book have used their best efforts in preparing this material. While every attempt has been made to verify the information provided in this book, neither the co-authors nor the publisher assumes any responsibility for any errors, omissions, or inaccuracies.

The co-authors and publisher make no representation or warranties with respect to the accuracy, applicability, or completeness of the contents of this book. They disclaim any warranties (expressed or implied), merchantability, or for any purpose. The co-authors and publisher shall in no event be held liable for any loss or other damages, including but not limited to special, incidental, consequential, or other damages.

ISBN: 978-1-960136-66-4

TABLE OF CONTENTS

INTRODUCTION 7

She Grows Stronger: A Journey of Transformation
   By Hanna Olivas 9

Breaking the Silence: Reclaiming Women's Rights and Voices
   By Adrian Gentilcore 15

My God Is Stronger
   By Allison Gabaldon 24

Breaking Free: My Journey to Empowerment and Healing
   By Amie Rich 37

Turning Pain into Power
   By Bailey Waite 47

You Are Stronger Than You Give Yourself Credit For!
   By Bec Koop 53

A Journey of Resilience and Transformation
   By Charlotte Cheetham 64

My Journey Back to Myself: Self-Empowerment Knows No Limits
   By DK Hillard 70

Rooted in Strength: Cultivating Resilience Through Actionable Intentional Living
   By Dr. Farah Jindani 78

Tragedies Can Open the Door to Our Higher Calling
   By Kerrie D. Stone 87

My Journey to Purpose: Finding Strength in Truth and Transformation

By Lynsey Mahoskey..97

Women Grow Stronger: Building a Legacy Through Real Estate
By Maureen Byers, GRI, MRE..107

Be Still and Know
By Meghan Skrepenski..114

Dear New Victim: The Survivor of Your Narcissist
By Michelle Gill...120

Coming Out of the Grey
By Molly Hurd...129

Rising Stronger with Purpose: Owning Your Future in Life and Business
By Phuoc Anne Nguyen, PharmD, MS, BCPS, FTSHP 143

Rising Above
By Roxanne Dinel 159

The Power of an Energy Burnout
By Sarah Carswell..163

Forced Paths, Found Strength: Lessons from the Road We Didn't Choose
By Shannon Addison 172

I Am Enough!
By Shanon Opp 187

Surviving the Storm: Keys to Finding Life Beyond Loss
By Sheena L. Smith..197

She Grows Stronger: She Will Not Fail
By Sherry Vinson...207

Ray of Hope
By Shirin Lakhani..222

Surviving and Thriving: The Power of Resilience
  By Sonia Rodrigues 230

Beyond Boundaries
  By Stéphane-Laure Caubet 240

Finding Joy in the Hard
  By Suzanne Andora Barron 254

I Celebrate Recovery
  By Teri Katzenberger 270

The Space Between
  By Tina Fletcher 288

The Strong Woman Myth: Redefining What It Means to Be Strong
  By Traci Powell 305

Flipping the Script: Prioritizing Passion, Purpose, and Time Freedom
  By Valarie Harris 314

Why Me, What Now
  By Wendy Harmon, PhD 319

Lettuce Talk About My Breaking Point
  By Yulia Drummond 330

INTRODUCTION

Welcome to *She Grows Stronger: Women's Stories of Strength and Empowerment, Accompanied by Actionable Strategies on How to Thrive*, a transformative journey that celebrates the resilience, strength, and boundless potential of women. Within these pages, you'll encounter stories of remarkable women—ordinary yet extraordinary in their capacity to rise, persevere, and evolve. These narratives are more than just tales of hardship and triumph; they are testimonies of the untapped power that lies within every woman, waiting to be uncovered.

As you turn the pages, you'll see how each woman, facing her own set of challenges, learns to navigate adversity with grace and grit. Their stories of personal transformation are not just inspiring—they are a testament to what happens when we embrace our struggles and use them as stepping stones toward something greater.

But *She Grows Stronger* is not merely about reflection. It is also a practical guide to living a life of empowerment. Alongside these heartfelt stories, you'll find actionable strategies that are grounded in real-world experience. Whether you're looking to cultivate unshakeable confidence, embrace change with courage, or simply navigate life's hurdles with more ease, this book offers the tools to help you thrive.

Each chapter will help you understand that strength isn't just about fighting through the storm; it's about understanding your inner power, trusting your journey, and embracing every step of growth along the way. With every page, you'll be reminded that empowerment isn't a destination—it's a lifelong journey of transformation and self-discovery.

So, take a deep breath, open your heart, and let these stories and strategies guide you to your own strength. *She Grows Stronger* is a celebration of women, a call to rise, and a promise that no matter the challenge, you can—and will—grow stronger.

Hanna Olivas

Founder and CEO of SHE RISES STUDIOS

https://www.linkedin.com/company/she-rises-studios/
https://www.facebook.com/sherisesstudios
https://www.instagram.com/sherisesstudios_llc/
www.SheRisesStudios.com

Author, Speaker, and Founder. Hanna was born and raised in Las Vegas, Nevada, and has paved her way to becoming one of the most influential women of 2022. Hanna is the co-founder of She Rises Studios and the founder of the Brave & Beautiful Blood Cancer Foundation. Her journey started in 2017 when she was first diagnosed with Multiple Myeloma, an incurable blood cancer. Now more than ever, her focus is to empower other women to become leaders because The Future is Female. She is currently traveling and speaking publicly to women to educate them on entrepreneurship, leadership, and owning the female power within.

She Grows Stronger:
A Journey of Transformation

By Hanna Olivas

Strength. What does it truly mean to be strong? For me, strength isn't simply about pushing through challenges or carrying the weight of the world on your shoulders. It's something deeper, something more personal. Strength reveals itself in the quiet moments, when you're left alone with your thoughts, doubts, and fears. It's in those moments when you choose to rise again, knowing the path won't be easy. That's where I found my strength, and that's where I know you'll find yours too.

I used to think that being strong meant always having it together, never letting anyone see my vulnerability. But the truth is, real strength is found when we allow ourselves to fall apart and then gather the pieces to rebuild—stronger, wiser, and more resilient. There's no shame in feeling broken; there's only power in getting back up.

For a long time, I believed that life's challenges were there to test me, to see how much I could handle without breaking. But now, I see that these challenges were opportunities for growth. They were invitations to evolve into the woman I was always meant to be. And the more I leaned into the discomfort, the more I grew. I've learned that we don't grow stronger by avoiding the storm but by learning to dance in the rain.

There's a personal mantra I live by: "Strength isn't in surviving the storm; it's in how you navigate through it." We often think that surviving the worst of times is where we find our power, but it's not just about getting through. It's about how we choose to respond, how we choose to rise. It's about turning the pain into purpose, the struggle into strength.

I've had my share of storms, from health battles to navigating the complexities of motherhood, entrepreneurship, and relationships. Life has tested me in ways I could never have imagined. I've been on the brink of giving up more times than I can count. But each time, something inside me said, "Get up. You're not done yet." That voice wasn't always loud, and sometimes it felt like a faint whisper, but it was enough to pull me back up.

I've come to understand that strength doesn't mean doing it all alone. For too long, I thought that asking for help was a sign of weakness. I believed that if I couldn't handle everything on my own, I was failing. But as I've grown, I've realized that "True strength lies in vulnerability, in knowing when to lean on others." There is no shame in needing support, in asking for help. In fact, it takes incredible courage to admit when we need a hand.

The women in my life—my friends, my sisters, my daughters—have been a source of immeasurable strength. We are stronger together, and there is a power that comes from lifting each other up. There's an unspoken bond between women who have faced adversity and come out on the other side stronger. When we share our stories, our victories, and our heartbreaks, we empower one another to keep going. This sisterhood is sacred, and it's where we draw our greatest strength.

I often tell the women in my community: "You are not defined by the battles you fight, but by how you rise from them." Every scar we carry, every tear we've shed, every setback we've faced—these are the marks of our resilience. They show us that we are capable of enduring more than we ever imagined. We grow stronger not by hiding these scars but by wearing them proudly as evidence of our growth. Each one tells a story of a woman who refused to be defeated.

Some days, life feels overwhelming, and I have to remind myself of my own words. I've learned that self-compassion is a critical part of growing stronger. On the days when the weight of my responsibilities—motherhood, business, health—feels too heavy, I remind myself that it's okay to slow down. It's okay to rest. "Strength is not in doing it all; it's in knowing when to pause and recharge." There's power in rest, in allowing ourselves to recover so that we can rise again.

Over the years, I've also learned that strength doesn't just come from fighting through the hard times. It comes from standing in your truth, even when it's uncomfortable. For so long, I silenced myself, afraid of being too much—too bold, too opinionated, too loud. But as I've stepped into my power, I've realized that my voice is one of my greatest strengths. "Your voice is your power; don't ever silence it." When you stand in your truth, you give others permission to do the same.

There's a particular kind of strength that comes from knowing who you are, embracing every part of yourself, and refusing to hide. We grow stronger when we allow ourselves to be fully seen—flaws, imperfections, and all. I used to think that strength meant having all the answers, always being in control. But I've learned that strength is found in admitting that we don't have it all figured out. It's in the moments when we say, "I'm still learning. I'm still growing. And that's okay."

I remember a time when I was overwhelmed by the demands of life—running businesses, raising a family, and managing my health. I felt like I was juggling too many things at once, and the weight of it all was unbearable. I reached a point where I knew something had to give. And that's when I realized that strength isn't about carrying it all; it's about knowing when to let go. "Strength isn't about how much you can carry; it's about knowing what to release." I had to release the expectations I had placed on myself, the need to do it all perfectly.

As I let go of the unrealistic standards I had set for myself, I felt lighter. And in that lightness, I found a new kind of strength—one that came from being kind to myself, from offering myself grace. We, as women, are often our own harshest critics. We expect ourselves to be everything to everyone, and when we fall short, we feel like failures. But the truth is, "Grace is the greatest gift you can give yourself. It's what allows you to rise, even when you stumble."

Another realization that came with this journey is that growth and strength aren't linear. There will be days when you feel invincible, and there will be days when you feel like everything is falling apart. But here's the beauty of it: "Strength is not about never falling; it's about choosing to rise every time you do." Each fall, each setback, is an opportunity to rise with more wisdom, more resilience, and more clarity about who you are and what you are capable of.

I've learned that growing stronger isn't just about enduring hardships; it's about transforming them. When you take your pain and turn it into purpose, you become unstoppable. For me, that transformation has come through sharing my story, through connecting with other women who are walking their own paths of growth. When we share our struggles, we remind each other that we're not alone. We give each other permission to heal, to grow, and to thrive.

As I reflect on my journey, I am reminded that strength comes from choices. Every day, I choose to show up for myself, to believe in my dreams, to trust my journey. I choose to rise, even when it's hard, even when I don't have all the answers. And in those choices, I grow stronger. "Strength is a choice you make every single day. It's not about the absence of fear but the presence of courage."

There's a mantra I hold close to my heart: "I am a force of nature, and nothing can break what's built from within." This mantra has carried me through my toughest times, reminding me that my strength comes from within, that nothing and no one can take away the power I hold inside. When you realize that your strength is inherent—that it's not something that can be given or taken away—you become unbreakable.

I want to leave you with this: "You are stronger than you know, braver than you think, and more capable than you ever imagined." Every challenge you face, every obstacle you overcome, is shaping you into the woman you are meant to be. Don't shy away from the hard times; embrace them. They are the forge that is creating your strength.

As we grow stronger, we become a beacon for others. Your strength is not just for you; it's for the world. When you rise, you inspire others to rise with you. When you speak your truth, you give others the courage to speak theirs. And when you stand in your power, you create a ripple effect of empowerment that touches the lives of everyone around you.

So wherever you are in your journey, know this: You are growing stronger every day. You are rising, even when it feels like you're standing still. And as you continue to rise, remember that you are not alone. We are all in this together, lifting each other higher, growing stronger with each passing day.

And that is how she grows stronger—each day, each moment, each choice to keep moving forward, knowing that her strength is limitless, her potential is boundless, and her journey is just beginning.

Adrian Gentilcore

Your Fairy Debtmother
Entrepreneur & Debt-Free Coach

https://www.linkedin.com/in/adrian-gentilcore
https://www.facebook.com/yourfairydebtmother
https://www.instagram.com/yourfairydebtmother
https://www.yourfairydebtmother.com
https://www.yourfairytechmother.com

Adrian Gentilcore is a seasoned entrepreneur with a 40-year career in Corporate America and a proven track record of creating successful online businesses. Now a full-time freelancer, she operates two distinct brands: Your Fairy Debtmother, where she offers her expertise as a Debt-Free Coach and popular Personal Finance Blogger and Your Fairy Techmother, where she specializes as a LinkedIn Trainer, Email Marketer, and Web Designer. In her 60s, Adrian has embraced the spirit of feminism and is interested in empowering other midlife women to step into their power and embrace their formidable abilities.

Breaking the Silence: Reclaiming Women's Rights and Voices

By Adrian Gentilcore

Election Day, November 5, 2024, changed my worldview forever. It just broke me that this country would choose a man who is everything AWFUL, including a convicted felon and twice impeached, rather than give a smart, intelligent, and kind woman a chance.

I've never considered myself a feminist, although, to be honest, I've never NOT considered myself a feminist. I just never really owned that label, because it has some negative associations. But I don't care about that anymore.

This situation made me realize how much *contempt* this country has for women. Men, women, political leaders, CEOs, Managers, Doctors, and so many others, just don't think we are worth bothering with.

It's been going on for so long, that we've gotten in the habit of overlooking it and making endless excuses for it.

But, it's like someone punched us in the face, and instead of punching back, we don't even complain much because we think we *deserve* it. Lather, rinse, repeat...

That's just crazy – we are smart, hardworking, kind, and creative. And in most other first-world countries, women have much more status, much more support, and are actually listened to and respected. Maybe not 100%, but definitely MORE than in the US.

I know some men ARE supportive and try to be helpful, but obviously, they aren't making enough noise about it to help much.

Women and Babies

Let's look at maternity leave—many companies only allow the bare minimum of leave, often unpaid. That's just uncivilized!

But as we know, in most European countries, they can get free government-provided healthcare, huge amounts of paid maternity leave, and sometimes paternity leave as well, plus extra services such as lactation support, home healthcare visits, etc.

It's just basic biology—**approximately half of the available workforce are women, and women make babies**. If we didn't, our society would die out.

However, the rules are mostly made by wealthy white men who can afford to have their wives stay home to raise their children. Why is that? Even more importantly, why are we *ALLOWING* that to be?

Why aren't we screaming our heads off about this? Why do we continue to support companies that have policies that are harmful to our families and our mental health?

I don't know if we can match European policies, but at least 4–6 months of guaranteed **PAID** leave for all pregnant women would make a big difference. And it could be done if we *REFUSED* to accept anything less. Collective bargaining works, and other countries have proven that it is possible to have humane maternity policies to help mothers navigate those difficult early months.

If you are going to work and have children, there needs to be daycare and flexible schedules. But good affordable daycares are incredibly hard to find. These days, infant care is almost as expensive as a college education. Why? Because a lot of government subsidies for daycares expired last year and a lot of them closed their doors. It's not a priority for our male, profit-driven, pig-headed leaders.

I have my own story about this. I got FIRED from a job because my son had chicken pox, and I couldn't get coverage for the 10–14 days he was going to be sick. They didn't even pretend otherwise. Your kid is sick, so you are fired!

Was I supposed to just leave my sick two-year-old on a street corner and wish him well?

I couldn't even apply for jobs because it was the 90s. We didn't have computers or online applications, and I could have been *contagious* to the interviewers! So, we just had to dig into our savings and get along as best we could.

Workplace Inequities

Let's talk about salary and working conditions. Companies **knowingly** and **willingly** underpay and overwork women. It's an epidemic throughout every industry, and if you are a woman of color or a woman over 50—you really get shafted.

I know about this first-hand. That's why I left my last job after 30 years—we had one male employee and about five women. But the advantage had been blatantly in favor of the man for years—he had much less work, a higher title, more pay, and was allowed to work from home while we weren't.

The last straw was when I was handling a triple workload, and they attempted to give me MORE rather than burden *him* with it. Nope. I don't think so. I started planning my very early retirement the next day.

Fortunately, I had a detour in the form of a successful side hustle I'd been running part-time for several years. I bailed out of a job I'd loved for 30 years because I was so tired of being disrespected, but most women aren't that lucky and don't create a backup plan like I did.

In virtually ALL businesses in the US, women get all the shit jobs, do the lion's share of the work, don't get listened to, paid well, or promoted as much as men. Why are we OK with this?

Newsflash—it's not right, and we need to speak out about it—loudly.

Imagine This Mirror Image World

In this world, men's contributions are considered secondary, if they're acknowledged at all. The workplace is no exception: women hold 95% of leadership positions, dominate boardrooms, and determine corporate strategies. A token 5% of men are given leadership positions, but are still asked to take notes, serve coffee, and be otherwise "useful."

Men are expected to thrive in caregiving roles or low-paying service jobs, and when they attempt to enter traditionally female fields, they're labeled as "emotional" or "too soft for the job."

In the financial world, men consistently face systemic barriers. To open a bank account or take out a loan, they often need a wife's approval. If they dare to negotiate for higher wages, they're labeled as "pushy" or "ungrateful."

Men, despite working long hours, are also responsible for most of the cooking, cleaning, and caring for the children. If they protest, they are told they simply need to "man up" and stop complaining. Then, when they reach midlife, they are summarily dismissed or shunted off to dead-end positions of little responsibility or initiative.

These roles are reinforced by the entertainment and media industries. Women's storylines dominate movies and TV. There are often three strong female characters for every male-speaking character in a blockbuster film. Men are often portrayed as the handsome sidekick or bumbling comic relief. Male characters are routinely sexualized and wear far less clothing than female characters, their intelligence dismissed in favor of their physical appearance.

Imagine a world where women have historically dominated every sphere of influence, and men were relegated to the background for hundreds of years.

Nearly every museum showcases art created by women, and science curricula revolve around the achievements of the great female geniuses. In school, history books celebrate the achievements of women—scientists, leaders, and artists—while men appear in the margins as footnotes or husbands of notable figures.

Sports? Women's leagues dominate college funding, 95% of media coverage, and sponsorship deals, while men's sports are relegated to an occasional mention—if they're covered at all.

If this world sounds absurd when you flip the genders, it's not surprising—but pretty much every woman in the world will recognize these as scenarios we encounter every day.

I love this quote by Ruth Bader Ginsberg— *"I ask no favor for my sex. All I ask of our brethren is that they take their feet off our necks."*

I think that sums it up—we're not asking for superiority, but we do expect a level playing field—something we haven't enjoyed in America's history. In fact, our rights are being eroded by the day, and the next four years are likely to be the most difficult for women, people of color, LGBTQIA folks, and all marginalized communities.

Is Gender Bias Improving? No, Not So Much

According to a recent study published by the United Nations, gender bias is getting *worse* rather than better.

The data, which was collected from 75 countries covering 81% of the world's population, found that 91% of men and 86% of women show at least one clear bias against women in the areas of politics, economics, education, and physical integrity.

That's pretty horrifying because it says that 9 out of 10 people worldwide—both men and women—are biased against women in vital areas that impact the world in major ways.

Even more concerning, the bias is getting stronger in younger men making them even less likely than the current generation to want to correct the situation.

Here are some tidbits from the study:

- About 50% of people—both men and women—think men make better political leaders than women *(meaning our chances for electing a female president any time soon are about zero!)*
- About 40% of people think men make better business leaders than women
- Close to 50% of men believe that men have more right to a job than women
- About 30% believe that it's justifiable for a man to beat his intimate partner

It's hard to believe a number like that, but recent controversies around physical assaults and rapes of women have shown a nearly complete disregard for women's physical safety. The fact is fewer than 1% of rape complaints result in a felony conviction.

Could you imagine if that were true about burglaries, murders, or any other type of crime?

But it's OK because most rapes happen to women, and if it's a "his word against hers" situation, the woman is unlikely to be believed due to this very real gender bias.

That's a legitimate nightmare situation. We absolutely NEED to do better in all these areas.

Planning for the Future

This is where I'm supposed to come up with some brilliant plan to fix all this, but that's where I'm struggling.

But I keep coming back to one essential fact. We are HALF the damn population. We are often the head of the household with kids to support, and we typically control the family purse strings. How can we use our dollars, our votes, and our voices to create the world we want to have?

We can make a point to support women-owned businesses and to avoid doing business with companies that won't commit to equal opportunities and equal pay for employees regardless of gender.

One thing that needs to happen is widespread awareness. Sunshine is the best disinfectant.

A lot of the problem is **unconscious bias**—people are so accustomed to these situations that they don't even notice that women are being disrespected and disadvantaged.

The #MeToo movement has raised a lot of awareness and driven a lot of change regarding sexual harassment. Sexual harassment workshops have long been a fixture in Corporate America (as they should be). Maybe we need to add workshops for unconscious bias as well—particularly for hiring managers.

This is just my opinion, but I think women would be smart to abandon ship on Corporate America altogether. **That infamous glass ceiling isn't made from glass, it's solid brick.**

It might be time to leave the sandbox to the boys and move on to start our own businesses where we can write our OWN rules and make our own opportunities for ourselves and other women.

I know so many smart, confident, capable women who are rocking it at running their own successful businesses. In fact, if I might say, I'm one of them. I've run a successful freelance business for more than a decade.

These businesses are the way to help other women rise—either by sharing our example or by hiring them into a business where they have a fair chance to succeed.

One thing is extremely clear. We can't keep going the way we're going. Supporting women in this country needs to be a daily task. We need to be LOUD about it and find ways to show the leadership how much better our society could be if everyone was treated well and given a chance to use their talents so we can all reap the rewards.

Allison Gabaldon

Founder of Dynamite Leader

https://www.linkedin.com/in/allison-gabaldon
https://www.instagram.com/dynamite_leader/
https://www.dynamiteleader.com

Allison Gabaldon is a native New Mexican and resides in the East Mountains of Albuquerque with her husband and their blended family of five children. Allison is very passionate about positive leadership and has worked in a number of leadership positions with school districts in New Mexico and the California Bay Area. Allison is the founder of Dynamite Leader where she actively works to promote the best in others and has a passion for teaching others how to shine. In her down time you can find her at home in the East Mountains spending time with her family, participating in her church community, or cooking in the kitchen.

My God Is Stronger

By Allison Gabaldon

My husband and I sat in the family law attorney's office for our initial consultation, and after reviewing our case, she looked at us both and said, "I'm sorry, but I can't represent you both." We must've had a look of utter disbelief on our faces because she quickly followed up with, "You two are going to get divorced! There is no way you will be able to get through this!" Completely puzzled, we looked at each other and then asked, "What are our options?" Representing both of us would be a conflict of interest. She told us that she could represent me and provide the name of another attorney to represent my husband. Two attorneys!

We got home that night from our legal consultation and sat on the couch in our living room in utter disbelief, not saying a word. We were both thinking about it, but my husband finally turned to me and said, "Are we gonna get divorced? Is that what we need to do?" After a few minutes of pondering this question, I turned to him and said, "No, we are going to fight." "This is adult bullying, and I refuse to be bullied by anyone." I experienced bullying throughout Elementary, Middle, and High School. I didn't tolerate it then, and I sure as hell was not going to tolerate it now as an adult.

I'm no stranger to adversity, in addition to childhood bullying, I was hit by a car a month before my freshman year of high school. I started high school in a body cast, was dependent on a wheelchair, and had to relearn how to walk all during the first semester! That was a trying experience but I got through it, learned compassion for others, and became stronger for it. I got divorced at twenty-four and again at thirty-eight. I thought that experiencing divorce twice was the lowest point of my life, but again, I overcame it, rebuilt myself, and came out stronger. In each of these situations, I handled things myself. I was raised to be an independent girl and to pick myself up and get things done because nobody was going to do it for me. So that's what I did, and that is how I lived my life. However, that was all going to change. Everything I thought I knew and believed was about to be challenged. Everything came to a screeching halt when I was completely blindsided on May 07, 2021.

At 12:30 PM on Friday, May 7th, I was at work, and I received a phone call from a man who stated that he had to officially serve me with a court summons. He said, "I know you are a principal, so do you want me to come to your school?" "Absolutely not," I replied, "I will meet you at the gas station across the street." I told my secretary that I would be right back and rushed over to the gas station. The man from the phone saw me, walked over to my car, asked me to confirm my first and last names, and said, "I'm sorry to do this to you, you seem like a nice lady. I hope this isn't too bad." He then officially served me with the official paperwork and quickly turned around, got back into his car, and drove off. Stunned, I stared down at the brown envelope that was lying in my hands. Trembling, I opened it.

Inside was a protective order. My ex-husband, Percy, had served me with a protective order on Mother's Day Weekend! I instantly began to sob! I had never been away from my nine-year-old daughter for more than a week, and now I could have no contact with her until the scheduled court date. I drove back to the school, got out of my car, and tried to compose myself. I walked into the school office, and I asked my secretary and clerk to join me in my office. When they came into my office, I closed the door and broke into tears and told them what had just occurred. My secretary asked me, "Can I pray for you?" I nodded with tears streaming down my face. They both held my hands, and my secretary began to say a prayer for me. I thanked them both, and my secretary told me, "You will get through this." I muttered, "I hope so."

Getting married three times is not typically on many people's bucket lists. I got married to my husband, Ray, in 2017. We had both been married twice before, and we had dated each other over twenty years ago in high school. We reconnected when I was planning my twenty-year high school reunion in 2015. We quickly realized that both of us were in marriages that were headed for potential divorce, and we agreed to keep communication open to be a support to one another. Before I left New Mexico, Ray said to me, "You need to come home." New Mexico has always been my home, but I had been living in California for the past fourteen years, as that was where my second husband, Percy, was from.

As I predicted, my second marriage ended upon my return to California. When I found out that Percy had filed for divorce and backdated it to the first day I left, three weeks prior. I quickly called my father and made plans to rent and drive a Uhaul trailer with all of my and my three-year-old daughter's belongings back to New Mexico. Percy and I found a legal mediator who helped us complete the required paperwork and dissolve the marriage amicably. For six weeks, we met with the mediator and came up with a plan that we both agreed to. Percy would stay in California, I would move back to New Mexico, and since he worked remotely, he would come to New Mexico to see our daughter one week a month. We would also alternate breaks from school. I was proud of us for coming up with a plan that we both agreed to without breaking the bank. In the midst of this season of my life, I had continued to communicate with Ray and let him know that I was moving back to New Mexico. Ray had filed for divorce as well, and when I returned to New Mexico in mid-October, we both were navigating the logistics of a second divorce with children.

During this time, I began looking for a church family to join. I had been actively searching for a church family since before my daughter was born. I wasn't really raised in a church family, and I felt strongly that I wanted my daughter to have that sense of community that I did not receive. Upon returning back to New Mexico, my mother had asked me to come visit her church, John XXIII Catholic Community. I was hesitant as my maternal grandmother used to drag us to Catholic church periodically as children, and she would make my brother and me feel awful. She would announce to the whole congregation each time we attended that we weren't baptized Catholic. I wanted to melt into the pew and disappear each time she said it. I looked at my mom, "Catholic church, really?" She looked at me and said, "It's not your grandmother's church anymore." I laughed, she sounded like a commercial!

My daughter and I began to attend church regularly with her at John XXIII, and I really liked the sense of belonging that I experienced from the clergy and the parishioners. I felt welcomed and embraced by the parish. The Parish Priest, Father Ark, was one of the most caring people I had ever met. I immediately had a connection with him. I appreciated his knowledge as a theological scholar, and I adored how compassionate he was. Every week during the Eucharist, he invited the children to come and stand with him, he also spoke to people instead of speaking at people.

In August 2016, I made an appointment to speak with him. We met one afternoon in his office, and I spilled my guts to him about the last thirty-eight years of my life. I thought he would judge me and tell me how wrong I had been for decisions that I had made. But he wasn't like that at all. He was understanding, caring, and loving. He told me that my generation had forgotten how to be friends and how to forgive one another. Above all, he told me that my daughter and I were welcome and loved. He suggested that I join RCIA, which is the process of converting to Catholicism. He had told me that once I completed RCIA, he recommended having both of my marriages annulled. He also recommended that Ray and I consider a civil marriage, as we had recently found out that I was pregnant.

In September 2016, I joined RCIA, and my mother was my sponsor. Ray was incredibly supportive of my conversion as he was a practicing Catholic and attended RCIA sessions with me. In October, Ray and I experienced a miscarriage, and we were both devastated. We each had children from previous marriages, and we were excited to have a child together. Per the advice of Father Ark, we had already planned to get married in February. What do we do now? Do we move forward? After consulting with our parents and Father Ark, we both agreed that moving forward with the wedding was the right thing to do. Ray said, "I have loved you for over twenty years, and that's not going to change!"

On February 19, we got married in a small wedding in Las Vegas, Nevada. In April, I completed RCIA and received the First Eucharist and Confirmation at the Easter Vigil. On Mother's Day that year, my daughter was baptized Catholic. For the first time, I felt like I was where I was supposed to be. I was proud of my new faith, and I was excited to start this new journey with Ray by my side.

My biggest concern about getting remarried for a third time was blending together five children. Ray had four children from previous relationships, and I had one. Before getting married we made sure that the children had time to be around one another as we split our time between his parent's and my parent's homes. To our surprise, the children all were very accepting of each other and loved one another right from the start. I was excited because I had prayed for more children, and I wanted my daughter to have siblings. To this day, blending the kids together has been the easiest part of our relationship. Managing the other co-parents would prove to be the hardest part.

Percy was not pleased that I had gotten remarried so quickly, but he had been in a long-term relationship with his partner, Trish, since before I left California. He continued to come to New Mexico monthly to see our daughter, and things seemed to be going pretty well. Ray's ex-wife, Vanessa, was more of a wildcard and did not like her children being around me. In the beginning of their divorce, Ray had his two children from Vanessa every other Thursday to Monday. Ray had two older boys from different relationships. The youngest of the two boys had visitation with us every other weekend while the eldest son lived with us until he graduated from high school.

In January 2020, everything changed when Percy decided to buy a house in Albuquerque and move closer to our daughter. I had told him that he wasn't going to like it in New Mexico, but he insisted that he wanted to be closer to our daughter. I have to admit when he first relocated, it was nice because he had our daughter every other Thursday-Wednesday, which was helpful as I got promoted in March 2020 from being a teacher to a school principal. In September, Percy and Vanessa met each other in front of our home when they were picking up children and exchanged phone numbers, so they could set up playdates. To be honest, I was skeptical about this but decided to just let it go. In March, Percy and I officially went to mediation a second time to change our parenting plan to a 50/50 plan since he was now living in New Mexico. This was relatively painless as we had basically been doing this on our own since January. He mainly wanted to make sure things were changed so he could pay less child support. No concerns were brought up, and one of the agreements we made was to go back to mediation if any circumstances should change before filing any motions in court.

During this time, my husband had been injured on the job as a law enforcement officer when he was hit by an individual who attempted to run him over twice while he was on duty. He had obtained substantial shoulder injuries and had gone through a couple of surgeries. We were facing the fact that he may have to retire early from a profession he loved. He was not in the best place mentally or physically and was quickly irritated with me and the kids.

On Saturday, April 10, 2021, we were sitting down for dinner as a family. He began to harp on the kids about eating their dinner, and I asked him to stop. He told me to stop, and I replied, "No." Our voices quickly escalated, and the four children, who were 7, 10, 11, and 13, all went to their rooms. After about twenty minutes of arguing, I decided to take a break and go outside to cool off. This is what I had always instructed the children to do when they were upset, walk away and cool down. I needed to cool down, so I followed my own advice and stepped outside for a few minutes and then I came back inside the house. When I came back into the house, the four children were standing in the kitchen waiting for me. They each hugged me, and I told them that it was OK and sometimes parents argue but that we always love one another. My husband was in our bedroom. I went into the bedroom, we hugged one another and promised that we wouldn't ever argue like that in front of the children again. This was the first time we had ever had an argument get the better of us in front of the children. We called the children down to the living room, and we all watched a family movie like we did every Saturday night. No one mentioned anything about our argument, and we all went to bed.

Ray's two youngest children went back to Vanessa on Monday just like they always did. On Thursday, April 15, Ray was supposed to have dinner with his children, and Vanessa sent a text message that their children were fine but that he needed to contact his attorney. Ray contacted the attorney that we had been using to help with parenting plans and custody arrangements. The attorney, Bob, informed Ray that Vanessa had filed a protective order and that Ray was not allowed to have any contact with his two youngest children until they went to court. Vanessa had reported that there was domestic violence in our home. She then filed a complaint with the Children, Youth, and Families Department (CYFD) against Ray and me for domestic violence, and they opened an investigation.

I couldn't believe this was happening, Vanessa never even called us. Sometimes, married couples argue. We had raised our voices and shouted at one another, the kids were all in their rooms with the doors closed. Our two daughters were upstairs in their room playing and laughing with their door closed throughout the entire argument. How could this even be considered domestic violence?

On Monday, April 26, I received a phone call from a caseworker at CYFD who had been assigned to the case. I was very transparent with her and answered her questions openly and honestly. I had nothing to hide. My husband and I had an argument in our kitchen. The last time I checked, it wasn't against the law to have a verbal argument with your husband. I figured she would hear what Ray and I had to say, and the whole thing would be shut down. Boy, was I wrong.

She began to ask me questions that made me feel uncomfortable, "So why did you leave the house the night of your argument?"

I said, "I stepped outside for fifteen minutes to cool down."

She said, "Are you sure you came back?"

I adamantly said, "Yes".

She continued to ask me why I would leave the children in an unsafe situation. "Unsafe?" I responded. "They were with their father. I would never leave any of the children in an unsafe situation."

She then told me that she would need to interview the children separately while they were with their other parents. I asked her if the children would be interviewed with me and Ray present as well, and she quickly shut me down and told me, "No." I asked her if it was OK for me to call Percy to let him know what was happening. She hesitated and said, "You haven't told him about this yet?

"Ummm, no, it was just an argument between me and my husband. I don't expect him to tell me when he has an argument with his partner."

She told me that I could contact Percy.

After hanging up with her, I instantly called Percy and explained what had occurred in regard to the argument between me and Ray. After I was done speaking, he said, "I already know all about this, Vanessa called me." Shocked, I said, "She called you?" He responded with, "Yes, I know all about it." Surprised, I said, "How would she know what happened? She wasn't at our house, and she hasn't spoken to Ray." Percy defensively said, "Are you calling her a liar." Taken aback, I said, "No. But if her story is different from the one I just shared with you, then it's not true." He ended the conversation with, "I'll expect a call from the CYFD caseworker." I felt so absolutely betrayed. How could this man who I had spent fourteen years of my life choose to believe her over me? He didn't even know her!

After being served with the protective order on May 7, I was completely dumbfounded and not knowing what else to do, I called the CYFD case worker looking for answers. She actually answered her phone, and I started crying. Through my sobs, I asked her what I needed to do to get my daughter back. Coldly she said, "You need to prove that you aren't a threat to yourself or your child." What was she talking about? How was I a threat to my child? I was responsible for protecting over a hundred children every day. She then went on to say, "We know your husband beats you, you need to stop defending him?" Are you kidding me? My husband does not beat me. I stopped talking to her and hung up. I called my father, who is an attorney, and his advice was for me to call a family law attorney for a consultation. I set up the consultation for both my husband and me as we both were now forced to defend ourselves.

That weekend, I lay in my daughter's bed and cried and cried. It was Mother's Day weekend, and I wasn't allowed to be around my daughter. How could Percy do this to me? We had agreed just six weeks prior in court to go to mediation, and here I was being served with a protective order! As I lay in my daughter's bed crying, I felt helpless and hopeless. Why was this happening? Was I really a bad mother? How was I going to overcome this? On Monday morning, I drove to work, and out of nowhere, I felt an urge and I began repeating, "My God is bigger than this, My God is stronger than this, My God will get me through this." Every time I said this, I felt a little stronger. I started saying it louder and louder. Before long, I was shouting it. This situation was bigger than anything I had ever dealt with before, and for the first time, I knew that I couldn't get through this by myself; I needed God. I called the Deacon of our Parish as our beloved Father Ark had passed away, and he told me to never lose hope and to continue to pray whenever I felt weak.

My husband and I went to court separately with different attorneys, and on the advice of our lawyers, we each agreed to a settlement. I wanted to fight, but my attorney advised me that the longer we dragged this out, the more likely I would be to lose my job. The settlement that I agreed to was that my husband would have no contact with my daughter for a year, that all of my visitations would occur at my parent's house, that a Guardian Ad Litem would be assigned to the case, that my husband and I would attend marriage counseling, that I would go to individual counseling, that my daughter and I would attend family counseling sessions, and that I would complete a co-parenting class. My attorney felt confident that this settlement would only last three months and that once a Guardian Ad Litem got assigned to the case, things would quickly change. A Guardian Ad Litem is basically an attorney who represents the children. In addition, my husband was ordered to pay for half of a Guardian Ad Litem for his children, attend individual counseling sessions, attend marriage counseling, and he was forced to only see his children during reintegration therapy sessions until further specified. We were now paying for four attorneys! I had no idea how we were going to pay for this or how our marriage would withstand this. So, I began to pray, "My God is bigger than this, My God is stronger than this, My God will get us through this."

My parents had recently downsized from a four thousand square foot home to a 1300 square foot mobile home in a retirement community. My daughter and I would be sharing a room and I would sleep on the couch on the weeks that I had my timesharing. I had no idea how I was going to juggle my demanding job and all of these counseling sessions that I was now required to attend. My husband jumped into action and got us set up with marriage and individual counseling through the Vet Center, and the sessions were virtual. My daughter's counselor agreed to conduct family therapy sessions in addition to my daughter's individual sessions. We began our new normal, and what we thought would end in three months took a year and a half!

Our initial Guardian Ad Litem passed away within a month of our first visit, and it took months before another one was assigned and able to start on our case. I quickly learned that the family court system is a money-making enterprise where no one wins except the attorneys. The new Guardian Ad Litem felt that I was downplaying the original argument that had occurred between my husband and me. He insisted that the argument that my husband and I had was detrimental, terrifying, and borderline abusive. I continued to stick to my story as I knew what I was saying was the truth. At one point, Percy's attorney told me that everything would be dropped if I just agreed to divorce my husband. Are you kidding me? I kept telling my husband that this was an attempt to destroy our marriage and the family that we had created. I was even more determined to get us through this and not let them win.

Every day on my way to work, I would pray in the car, "My God is bigger than this, My God is stronger than this, My God is going to get us through this." Some days I said it with tears in my eyes, thinking that this situation would never end, but unwavering, I continued to say it every day. Saying it gave me strength. I'm not going to tell you that everything changed instantly as soon as I started praying and asking for God's help. If nothing else, this experience has taught me that prayers are answered in God's time, not our time. However, I will tell you that we never gave up. There were days when I didn't know how we would pay for the legal bills that were quickly piling up, and a few weeks or months later, we would receive a low-rate credit card offer, a low-interest personal loan, or a home equity line of credit. We received a higher refund on taxes than we were expecting, and I was promoted from a school principal to a district administrator, which came with an increase in my salary. God was always there supporting us in ways we didn't even realize.

After a year and a half, I received the court order that allowed my daughter and I to return to our home. Around this same time, my husband also regained time sharing at our home with his children, and we slowly began the process of rebuilding our family. A lot of damage had been done, and during this time, I read Matthew Kelly's book, *Life is Messy*. In his book, he talks about a Japanese art called kintsugi, where broken pieces of pottery are put back together with gold making the pottery even stronger and more beautiful than before. This form of art has become a metaphor for our family. We may be broken or have imperfections, but we are stronger and more resilient than before.

After three long years, the court cases finally came to an end, and we ended up with more time than we originally had with all of the children. Ray and I never gave up. We remained strong throughout this entire ordeal with the help of counselors, friends, the veteran community, and of course, our faith. As this book goes to print we are closing this chapter in our life by getting married in the Catholic church. This is not to say that we won't be tested again, but I am confident that our faith in God, one another, and the love we share for our family will continue to help us prevail.

The advice that I have to share is that no matter what you are going through, you have to believe in something bigger than yourself. No matter how strong you are, you cannot get through all of the trials and tribulations that you will be faced with alone. Without my faith in God, I would not have been able to persevere and continue to fight for three long years. I truly believe that no matter what is thrown at me, I got this because my God is bigger than this, my God is stronger than this, and my God will get me through this.

Amie Rich

Certified Coach & Spiritual Hypnotherapist

https://www.facebook.com/profile.php?id=100094152004634
https://www.instagram.com/awakenedwithamie/
https://amierichcoaching.com/
https://amierich.com/

Amie Rich is a certified coach, spiritual hypnotherapist, and energy healer with a passion for helping overwhelmed women reclaim their confidence and self-worth. With 28 years of corporate experience and a personal journey of overcoming perfectionism and people-pleasing, Amie understands the struggles of balancing life's demands while staying true to your authentic self. Through her signature HEAL method, she guides women to break free from guilt, set healthy boundaries, and embrace their inner power. Amie's work blends mindfulness, energy healing, and spirituality to create transformational experiences that empower women to prioritize themselves and manifest the life they desire. When she's not coaching or creating inspiring resources, Amie is a wife, mom, stepmom, and Mimi to two grand babies, finding joy in the simple, beautiful moments of life.

Breaking Free: My Journey to Empowerment and Healing

By Amie Rich

Life is a journey filled with trials and triumphs, each shaping who we become. My story is no different, marked by moments of profound pain and incredible resilience. Growing up, I faced the complexities of a family fraught with emotional turmoil, but it was through these challenges that I found my path to healing and empowerment. This is the story of how I broke free from generational trauma and learned to embrace my true self.

Imagine the early 80s in Southern California, I was a little girl who loved being outside, and the imaginative playtime of playing house or school with my toys. I ran around the neighborhood playing, climbing trees, and having fun with the freedom of being young and carefree. My mom coached me in soccer and T-ball, and we kept ourselves busy. When I was around eight years old, my parents were on the brink of divorce. At that young age, I was shielded from the complexities of their unraveling relationship. And while most of my childhood is still a blur, there are certain moments that remain etched in my memory. One such moment was seeing my father sitting at the end of their bed, tears streaming down his face. As a young child, I couldn't grasp the full scope of his sorrow, but the image of my father crying is one I will never forget.

Only years later did I understand the depths of their struggles. My father was drowning in his pain, finding a temporary escape in alcohol, while my mother grappled with her own turmoil. She had grown weary of his constant drinking, but there was more to her distress. She had her own childhood trauma that had her seeking inner peace and happiness. She was discovering a side of herself that yearned for emotional and compassionate connections with women, a realization that brought her peace and validation she so wanted yet tore at the fabric of their marriage.

For my mother, the decision to end her marriage must have been incredibly difficult. She was not only leaving a long-term relationship but also embarking on a journey to find her authentic self. They decided that my brother and I would live with my dad in Missouri, while Mom stayed in California. The physical distance must have been lonely for her, going from having her family with her always, to suddenly being without us. As a child, I felt a profound sense of abandonment from her departure, a feeling that has lingered with me into adulthood. Even now, I can be triggered by a sense of loss, anxiety, and loneliness, remnants of that early separation.

Witnessing my father's heartbreak was shattering. No child should have to bear the weight of their parent's sorrow, and yet, that memory of him sobbing remains vivid, a testament to the deep-seated pain that would shape my own emotional landscape for years to come.

Fast forward to my high school years, and my father was still grappling with his demons, his drinking a constant presence in our lives. He was now a single parent, doing his best to maintain a facade of normalcy. One day, as we pulled into the driveway, he turned to me, his teenage daughter, and confessed that he was still in love with my mother. He was struggling to come to terms with her being gay, a truth that clashed with his religious beliefs. His admission was another cry for validation, a desperate need to share his pain with someone, anyone, even his child.

Reflecting on these moments now, I see the profound impact they had on me. My father's rigid parenting style was his attempt to control the chaos of his own life, to ensure everything was perfect as a single parent. Yet, this rigidity, combined with his emotional turmoil, created an environment where he micro-managed everything. My codependent patterns were instilled very early in life, and I learned to please others in an effort to maintain peace. I became a people-pleaser, a trait that would follow me into adulthood and ultimately influenced my corporate career and the way I raised my own children.

These memories, vivid and unyielding, are just the tip of the iceberg. They are the foundation of the woman I became, a woman who would later realize the importance of breaking free from these patterns and embarking on a journey of self-discovery and healing.

By the time I reached my late 30s, I found myself in a similar cycle of unhappiness, now within my own marriage. Despite my best efforts to maintain the facade of a perfect family, I was deeply unhappy. I had been living in a state of depression, desperately trying to salvage a marriage that no longer served me. My journey towards healing began with the painful realization that I needed to prioritize myself and my own happiness.

I vividly remember the moment I decided to end my marriage. It was a flash of clarity and determination, igniting what I now call my 'no-BS year.' I moved out, we sold the house, and I became a single parent. This decision, while undeniably hard, marked the first step toward reclaiming my life and choosing a path authentic to me.

As I entered the world of co-parenting, I noticed a pattern emerging, a reflection of my own childhood playing out in my parenting. I found myself meticulously striving to present a picture-perfect life, a life that looked flawless and effortless, as if everything were 'rainbows and unicorns.' I wanted my children, and everyone we encountered, to see only the brightness, to shield them from my struggles and heartaches. It was a desire deeply rooted in the image of perfection my own father had tried to uphold as a single parent—his strict, controlled approach to keep everything in line. Yet, in my efforts to create this illusion, I realized I was carrying forward the very rigidity I had once felt restricted by. The journey that began with reclaiming my life evolved into something even more profound: breaking the cycle of perfection and learning to embrace authenticity—for the sake of myself and my children.

Yet, the reality of co-parenting brought its own challenges. After 16 years of marriage, transitioning to being alone felt daunting and, at times, overwhelming. The isolation and loneliness could be debilitating, with days where the silence was almost unbearable. In those quiet moments, I recognized a painful parallel to what my mother must have experienced when my brother and I moved away. Without realizing it, I was reliving her heartache, carrying forward the echoes of a past pain that had shaped both her journey and now mine.

Though, at the time, I did not recognize the generational trauma patterns on repeat, it's important to note that this period of solitude was also a time of profound personal growth. I learned to find peace in being alone, to understand that I didn't need someone else to validate my existence or happiness. This was a critical step in my journey toward healing, as I began to recognize and break free from the unhealthy patterns I had inherited from my past.

Re-entering the dating realm after 20 years and meeting my current husband was a turning point for me. He helped me recognize the unhealthy patterns I had been repeating and the impact they had on my parenting style. I began to understand that my need to control and protect my children from any form of failure was not helping them but hindering their personal growth. I was the enabling mom who handled every aspect of life, including situations that they could have handled on their own. My actions made them feel as though they were not capable of handling tough situations. I inadvertently removed their sense of power and self-worth. I had to learn to let go, allowing them to experience life's challenges and learn from them.

My divorce, though the hardest thing I had ever done, was also the best decision. It marked the beginning of my journey toward true self-discovery and understanding my purpose in this lifetime. I learned that facing hard times is necessary to reap the benefits on the other side. Being in a healthy relationship has had a profound ripple effect on my children. They now have a father figure who loves them and shows them what healthy love looks like. They see a couple in love, unafraid to express their affection. This positive example is invaluable. It's a lesson that they will take with them when they have families of their own.

Realizing that I had been raising my children from an unhealed place made me determined to break the cycle of generational trauma. I wanted my son to see how a loving husband and wife should interact, so he can one day show the same to his children. I wanted my daughter to know her worth and feel empowered in everything she does. By sharing my story, I hope to show other women that it's never too late to heal from childhood trauma and have difficult conversations with their children. We can all do better, regardless of our age, or the age of our children. I want to inspire other women to share their stories and heal together through vulnerability.

As I worked on healing myself and transforming my relationships with my children, I began to realize that my professional achievements also played a crucial role in my journey. Professionally, I have been an executive at a major studio for 28 years. I am very proud of the accomplishments of those 2-plus decades, but I climbed that corporate ladder saddled with unhealed emotional baggage.

Throughout my career, I dedicated myself to achieving excellence and helped lead my team to success along the way, but I often did so at the expense of my personal life and emotional well-being. I see now how my people-pleasing tendencies at the office—constantly saying yes to more responsibilities, avoiding conflict, and stuffing down my own needs to meet others' expectations—only led to feelings of disappointment, resentment, and a profound loss of self. Like many women, I thought if I worked harder and stayed quiet, I could avoid rocking the boat and earn the respect I craved. But what I really lost was my voice and my sense of self.

It wasn't until I began exploring energy healing that I found the tools to truly reclaim myself. Through holistic practices like energetic cord-cutting, I was able to release the negative energy that wasn't mine and let go of the emotional ties that kept me stuck in old patterns. This process allowed me to rediscover my voice, set healthy boundaries, and find a sense of empowerment I had never known.

As I began to reclaim my sense of self and embrace my worth, I noticed a powerful ripple effect in those around me. My children started to see a version of their mom who was no longer overworked, resentful, or overwhelmed but instead confident, present, and joyful. This ripple effect extended beyond my family and into my workplace. As I stepped into my power, I no longer felt the need to carry the weight of every project or say yes to tasks that drained me. Instead, I began to delegate, speak up for myself, and approach my work with a renewed sense of purpose. Colleagues noticed the shift and often commented on how I seemed more calm, more focused, and, dare I say… even inspiring.

I realized that when we, as women, prioritize ourselves, we don't just change our own lives, we inspire others to do the same. Empowerment isn't selfish; it's contagious. It creates a ripple that spreads to our children, partners, coworkers, and friends. It shows the world that it's possible to thrive without sacrificing our well-being or losing our sense of self.

You have the power to be that ripple in your own life. When you say yes to your healing and worth, you show others, especially those closest to you, what is possible. Imagine what the world would look like if more women embraced this truth. It starts with you. By choosing yourself today, you create a better tomorrow, not just for yourself but for everyone who looks up to you and learns from your strength.

Recently, I realized that my passion and mission in life are not about working for others but about sharing my story with the world. I want to help women see their worth and empower them to overcome their own struggles. Healing is possible, and learning to release what no longer serves you, whether it's limiting beliefs, unhealthy attachments, or negative energy, is essential. You deserve to thrive, and the journey starts with believing you are worthy of it.

To further this mission, I went back to school and earned certifications in energy healing, life coaching, Reiki, and spiritual hypnotherapy. These practices became an essential part of my journey to not only heal but also rediscover my authentic self. Through neurolinguistic programming, visualization, and energy healing, I've learned that life after trauma is not only possible but also an opportunity to embrace our true potential. These modalities transformed my life and equipped me with the tools to guide others on their healing paths.

Empowerment and healing are not destinations; they are continuous journeys filled with both challenges and breakthroughs. My story is a testament to the resilience we all hold within us and the life-changing impact of prioritizing ourselves. When we share our experiences, we inspire and support one another, building a community of strong, empowered women who rise above adversity and thrive together.

Today, my children are young adults, and we have a very open and honest relationship. My healing journey has allowed me to break the cycle of generational trauma that I unknowingly continued. By recognizing how my parenting style was unhealthy, I have been able to change the way I interact with my children, setting healthy boundaries and fostering an environment of love, understanding, and open communication. My son can experience a safe space where his emotions are validated, teaching him the importance of emotional intelligence and healthy expression. My daughter can feel safe in a home where her voice matters, teaching her to advocate for herself and follow her dreams unapologetically.

In addition to these personal transformations, I have experienced a profound spiritual connection with my father since his passing. I know he guides me from the other side, offering his love and support as I continue my journey. Through countless confirmations, I've come to understand that he is a significant guide of mine, deeply aware of how my childhood experiences shaped the woman I've become. At times, I am overwhelmed by an all-encompassing feeling of love, and I know it's him. His love is so powerful that it transcends the veil, guiding me with a steady presence as I navigate life today.

We each have a divine team of spirit guides who walk with us, offering their support in ways both subtle and profound. My father is a pivotal part of mine, and their presence reminds me that even in our darkest moments, we are never truly alone. This spiritual connection has become a cornerstone of my healing, a constant reminder of the love and guidance available to all of us.

Yes, my journey has been filled with struggles and triumphs, but it has ultimately led me to a place of strength, resilience, and empowerment. There were times when I felt utterly lost, overwhelmed by the weight of life, and unsure of how to move forward. I know what it's like to feel stuck in unhealthy patterns and believe that change is impossible. But by embracing my past and taking control of my future, I have transformed my life and the lives of those around me.

I hope my story serves as a beacon of hope for other women, showing them that it is never too late to embark on their healing journey and find their true selves. No matter how deep the wounds or how long you've been struggling, you hold the power to change your life and create a future filled with genuine happiness, self-love, and fulfillment. Through this journey, I learned that the familiar and seemingly easy path of staying in an unhealthy relationship is far more damaging than the unknown path of self-discovery and empowerment. Sacrificing the life I knew, for the possibility of a healthier, happier future was the hardest yet most rewarding decision I have ever made. It is through this sacrifice and the courage to face the unknown that true healing and empowerment begin.

If my story has resonated with you, know that you're not alone, and there's a community of women cheering you on, including me. The pain, struggles, and sacrifices you endure are not in vain. They are the steps needed for a life filled with genuine happiness, self-love, and fulfillment. I invite you to follow my journey and learn more about how I can help you as your spiritual cheerleader. Whether you're ready to break free from people-pleasing, embrace self-love, or set empowering boundaries, I'm here to be your biggest advocate and guide you on your journey.

To connect with me and explore how we can work together, visit my website www.amierich.com and follow me on social media @awakenedwithamie. Let's embark on this transformative journey together and create a community of empowered women who rise above adversity and thrive. Remember, all healing is self-healing, and you have the power within you to create a life filled with joy and fulfillment.

So, as you close this chapter, remember that your strength is not defined by the obstacles you've faced but by the resilience you've shown in rising above them. You are capable of incredible transformation, and the power to create the life you desire lies within you. Whether it's setting boundaries, embracing your authentic self, or rewriting the narrative of your life, know that your greatness is already within reach—you just have to claim it.

Here's to your journey of rising, thriving, and growing stronger.

Bailey Waite

Wellness with B
Mental Wellness Coach

https://www.facebook.com/people/Bailey-Waite/100076759955174/
https://www.instagram.com/bail_nyen02/
https://www.amare.com/115371/en-ca
https://linktr.ee/bthechange902

Bailey Waite is a highly sought-after expert in Mental Health and Wellness, specializing in helping others transform their painful stories into powerful comebacks. Her journey began in 2022 after enduring immense personal loss when the father of her children completed suicide infront of her. Determined to heal and break the cycle of trauma, Bailey immersed herself in holistic practices, including breathwork, meditation, grounding, and trigger journaling, to reclaim her life and thrive in ways she never imagined.

Today, Bailey is a thriving entrepreneur, a certified mental wellness coach, and a single mother to two incredible daughters who inspire her daily. When she's not cheering at her kids' sports games, hosting events, or enjoying a ladies' night, Bailey devotes her time to mentoring women. She empowers them to find success, happiness, and healing through the online space, proving that trauma can indeed be turned into triumph.

Turning Pain into Power

By Bailey Waite

It's said that adversity builds character, but sometimes it feels as though life piles on more than anyone can bear. My story isn't one for the faint of heart and begins during childhood in a home where love was scarce, communication nonexistent and survival was my only focus. From being raised by babysitters and relatives while my parents worked tirelessly, I learned early on how to fend for myself. Again, after being submitted to watching whom I thought was the love of my life complete suicide, I learned how to fend for myself. These types of loneliness and independence, while they turned out to be a strength, came at a cost – I never learned how to process emotions or feel truly cared for and supported.

To give you some back story ; by the age of 12, I found solace in what I thought would numb my pain : addiction. It became my escape from the chaos inside me and around me. Those years, from 12 to 21, were pretty much lost in a haze. Although that was an extremely hard season, it never took away my ability to work hard, support myself & mature at an very rapid pace. I was a teenager forced into adulthood, working when I should have been studying or simply being a kid. Addiction didn't ask questions or demand explanations – it was just there, a constant companion through my darkest hours.

As i mentioned, at 29 life dealt me another blow. After enduring 11 years in an abusive relationship, the father of my two daughters, my then fiancé, cheated on me one month after proposing. The betrayal was devastating since it was with a woman who was supposed to be my friend, but nothing could have prepared me for what was about to shake my world up next.

Ten months later, my life changed forever.

I remember everything "that night" from begging and pleading with him that his life didn't need to end this way, that we had children who thought the absolute world of their father and that quite frankly, I didn't have children with him to raise them alone all the way to him, for the first time in our years of being together, physically assaulting me over and over while I tried my hardest to fight for his life. That night broke me.

That traumatic moment caused my demons to reappear rather quickly, it was the only mechanism I had for calming the chaos around me, or so I thought. Each time I went back, a different addiction would rear through and I would find myself into a deeper rock bottom then before. Lost, feeling alone, exhausted and with my nervous system on the brink of shutting down – I thought this was as bad as it could get but, I was wrong.

The turbulence was not over yet, 9 months after losing their father I allowed my addiction to become the driver of my chaotic life. I ended up losing custody of my girls and being arrested for drug and alcohol offences all within a 24-hour period. This was a new type of rock bottom, even for me. My heart shattered. My daughters were my light in an otherwise dark world, losing them felt like losing the last remnants of my humanity.

But, even in the depths of despair, there was a spark – a whisper that told me this wasn't the end; this wasn't MY end. I fought like hell for months doing all the things from counselling appointments to addiction meetings and everything in between to prove they were worth fighting for. Some days were grueling and I felt like giving up than a visit with them would happen, their smiles and light kept me going. I kept a solid support system around me so that when I felt like it was all too much they reminded me of where I was heading.

That whisper turned into a roar and finally, after a long hard road, they were placed back into my care. My life was complete now, or so I thought. Being survival mode for so many years when I felt emotions, they were intense throughout my body. I was violently ill each day due to my nervous system being so out of control.

There was one morning when my youngest daughter was rubbing my back as I was head deep in the toilet throwing up from severe anxiety and she said, "Mom, I hope one day you start to feel better so that you can help me get ready for school without having to be sick first." Her words pierced my soul.

It was then that I realized that my pain was no longer just mind to bear, it was shaping my daughters lives too. For the first time, I truly understood the weight of generational cycles and I made a vow to break them. I refused to have my children growing up with the same uncertainty and unhealthy patterns that I did.

Change terrified me. It felt like standing on the edge of the abyss, not knowing if I would fall or fly. But i knew one thing for sure, I couldn't stay where I was.

I dove into my first holistic resource pretty quickly, a mental wellness journey where I could finally start healing at a root level instead of masking all of the pain and suffering. It was all new to me so I was certainly skeptical but I was more desperate then I was a skeptic. I started to feel a peace, clarity and calm I had never realized was possible. My C-PTSD symptoms began to ease, the anger and exhaustion that had ruled my life for so long started to dissipate. This transformation wasn't just about me – it was about becoming the mother my children deserved, I was all they had.

Healing wasnt linear and it certainly wasnt east. I faced my traumas head on through therapy and EMDR, finding new ways to process the pain. I embraced many more holistic tecniques that became pillars of my recovery:

- Breath work and meditation: these practices grounded me in the present, helping me navigate flashbacks and panic attacks.

- Trigger Journaling: Writing had became my therapy. This was a way to pin point, understand and defuse triggers that once controlled me.

- Nutrition and Exercise: By fueling my body with intention, I discovered how much physical health impacts mental wellbeing.

- Grounding and Mindful living: These daily habits reminded me to reconnect with myself and the world around me.

- Prayer and Community Support: Faith and connection gave me strength on days when I felt like giving up.

Slowly but surelym I rebuilt my life. After regaining custody of my beautiful daughters, I began to see them not just as my reason to fight but as my greatest blessings. They were my anchors through the rough water, my joy in each day and the proof that even in darkness – light exists.

As I healed, I felt and undeniable pull to help others do the same. I started sharing my journey on social platforms, not out of pride but out of purpose. I wanted people to know that no matter how messy, traumatic and hopeless their pasts – THEY had the power to rewrite their story and turn it into something more powerful then ever imagined.

I joined the mental wellness movement, not just as a participant but as a leader. This is personal for me. My work now isn't just about income – its about impact. Saving those souls who felt lost and hopeless like I once did. I've seen firsthand how healing is contagious, how one persons growth can inspire a ripple effect in others.

Through my journey, I've learned that healing isnt about perfection it's about progress. Small changes over time are the ones that stick and make the biggest impact. Its about choosing everyday to let go of what no longer serves you while embracing the life you deserve.

To anyone reading this who might feel trapped by their circumstances, I want you to know : You are not your pain. You are not your mistakes or the things that happened to you. You are the choices you make TODAY and every day moving forward.

"The things you aren't changing, you're choosing."

Its time, for once, to choose you.

Although my journey is far from over, I've grown with every step. I hope my story reminds you of your strength, your resilience and your ability to rise, thrive and grow stronger.

This isn't just my story, it's OUR story. Together we can heal, grow and create a brighter future. Let's do this, together.

Bec Koop

Owner of Vibrational Transcendance

https://www.instagram.com/vibrationaltranscendance/
https://www.vibrationaltranscendance.com/

As someone who has faced my own challenges and traumas, and now I'm here to support you on your healing journey. Life may throw curveballs, but you have the power to learn, grow, and rediscover joy. My mission is to help you find the healing path that suits you, reconnect with your true self, and embrace happiness. You are stronger than you realize, and you deserve a life full of bliss. While the past can't be changed, you can control how it impacts your future. Sometimes, we need to shift our mindset, from "this happened to me" to "this happened for me." I'm here to guide you in rediscovering how incredible and capable you truly are. Open your mind, heal your heart and free your soul. Your best life is waiting!

You Are Stronger Than You Give Yourself Credit For!

By Bec Koop

Looking back on my life, it's become easier to gain perspective on my experiences and how they have shaped me into the person that I am today. Every moment I've lived through has inspired growth and a passion to share my healing journey with others.

I now value all my experiences, including the hardships, as lessons. It took me a long time to realize that, for years, I had been living on the edge. During my younger years, I was addicted to adrenaline, the fast pace of life, and constantly pushing my limits. I often heard, "If you're not living on the edge, you're taking up too much room. These risky behaviors led to toxic relationships with men, alcohol, and more. When you reach your limits, you begin questioning if you're truly living the life you want. It becomes clear that change often requires making difficult choices.

Some of my earliest memories were filled with distress, turmoil, and uncertainty. I grew up near Washington, D.C., in northern Virginia. My parents divorced when I was four, and finances were always a point of contention, as they were on opposite ends of the financial spectrum. Though my mother had primary custody of my sibling and me, she didn't receive the financial support she deserved from my father. We spent the majority of our time with her and only every other weekend with my father and stepmother. When we were with our father, we enjoyed expensive vacations, shopping, and dining out—creating some positive memories. Our daily life with my mother, however, was often less luxurious. Despite her working multiple jobs, we frequently visited the food bank, and most of our clothing was secondhand. My mother did her best to raise my brother and me while also trying to balance her own struggles and needs. However, I found myself growing up quickly and taking on the responsibilities of a parent.

As a child, I was often bullied for my clothing, my last name, and, most frequently, my weight. Kids were mean, to say the least, and were often incredibly cruel. Many of the jokes were about how skinny I was, with some calling me bulimic or anorexic. I endured frequent jabs to my ribs from pointy fingers, leaving bruises, or being pushed around physically. The name-calling and harassment escalated, and I was even nicknamed "Koop Poop," with one bully even throwing dog poop at me more than once. These behaviors reached a peak near the end of 6th grade when I ended up in the ER with a broken wrist after my biggest bully tackled me during a game of no-tackle capture the flag. After that, I learned to defend myself better, gathered a larger group of allies, and thankfully, the bully was suspended, with a restraining order warning issued.

As I got older, I focused on doing well in school, staying out of trouble, and helping raise my younger brother. Sadly the harassment didn't stay on the school grounds, as there was increasing tension between my stepmother and me. Not only was I bullied at school, but it was happening at home, too. We never saw eye to eye because she wanted me to call her my mom when I was fully aware she was one of the reasons for my parents' divorce. Her words would cut like a dagger, often crushing my young and fragile self-esteem and always belittling me. The most common threat was being told I would be slapped so hard my eyeballs would splatter on the wall. I never felt safe speaking to my father about her verbal abuse and threats, fearing he would abandon me. A few years earlier, he had disowned his sister and parents due to similar conflicts with my stepmother and how she treated them and us. Before I had the opportunity to have a real heart-to-heart conversation with him, a physical altercation between me and my stepmother at 13 made her threats a reality. After the incident, my father and stepmother called me a failure and a waste of space, saying I would never amount to anything. The altercation led to a court hearing where my father legally disowned me, deciding I was disposable and that it was not worth repairing our relationship. The impact of their words and actions from my former caregivers forever changed me.

Beyond family dynamics, I often felt unsafe in my hometown. My mother lived in a poor, gang-violent neighborhood, and I frequently heard gunshots. I saw my first dead body outside our home when I was eight, after returning from a school field trip. My schools often received bomb threats, keeping me on high alert. During my junior year of high school, the events escalated. We saw violence across the country, as 9/11 also directly affected our local community. Just days after the tragedy, one of my closest family members went missing from a military base and was later found murdered. The case remains unsolved to this day. Then, my senior year arrived, along with the DC Sniper incidents that led to the cancellation of our homecoming parade and many school activities—moments other teens looked forward to but that we couldn't take for granted. I continued to experience the loss of people who were extremely important and influential to me. The following month, my childhood best friend's mother passed away, someone who had been incredibly important in my life. It felt like one loss after another, and I was constantly in fight-or-flight mode, bracing for the next threat.

By the time I was graduating high school, I began to push my limits even further, believing it gave me control over my life. Although I excelled academically, I often engaged in risky behaviors and heavy drinking. One evening before high school graduation, I drank too much, and in my vulnerable state, I was sexually assaulted by two men and had to physically fight my way out of the situation. Some people might have sobered up after such an event, but I dove deeper into partying, trying to numb my pain. Drinking until I blacked out became normalized.

Despite my toxic relationship with alcohol, I managed to do well in college. The constant memory of my father's doubts drove me to exceed expectations. I felt it was important to prove both him and my stepmother wrong, so I made sure to stay on the Dean's List while balancing multiple jobs. After earning straight A's for the first time in my life, I was faced with another challenge. During my final semester, I was nearly expelled for possessing cannabis. Thankfully, I won the case and still managed to graduate with honors. Still, it was a stark reminder that, despite my gratitude, nothing ever seemed easy or enough to overcome my negative self-beliefs.

After college, I moved a few hours away to a ski resort and continued to live fast, carelessly, and pushed my limits. I was drinking almost daily and was acting recklessly, which led to me totaling several cars in a very short period of time. After one particularly bad car accident, an older, wiser friend sat me down and asked, "What do you want from this life?" I laughed and said, "I want to live as fast and free as possible." He told me I had already used up my nine lives and was amazed I was still alive. Then, he asked if I knew what my life's purpose was. I stared at him blankly, struggling to find the words. As we sat in silence, I felt the full weight of a reality check.

Soon after that enlightening conversation with my wise friend, I met someone and got married quickly. After relocating from Virginia to Colorado, I soon realized that I was in a toxic, unstable, and verbally abusive relationship. Once again, I found myself with someone who would make it their mission to put self-doubt in my mind. I did what I knew best: I turned to alcohol yet again. Additionally, the hyper-independence I learned as a child led to a work addiction. I became a workaholic during the day, only to black out at night. I drank and focused on monetary success to numb the pain and cope.

Every once in a while, the conversation with my friend would cross my mind, but I quickly pushed it aside—until one day at the snowmobile rental company I managed. Once again, I was pushing my limits, and that's when I experienced a life-altering snowmobile accident.

It was a typical day on the mountain, chasing adrenaline with a friend deep in the backcountry in Grand Lake, Colorado. I was cruising around 60 mph on one of the main trails when someone unexpectedly popped out of the woods off of a side trail and T-boned my machine. Immediately after I crashed, I remember wishing I had died—because that would have been easier to handle than the reality of my world crumbling again. Along with the mental and physical trauma from the wreck, I had recently asked my abusive husband for a divorce, and now one of my few joys was gone.

My machine was totaled as I flew over the handlebars and hit a tree with my spine. The impact left me with four dislocated ribs, five misaligned vertebrae, and a severely sprained shoulder. After seeing several spine specialists, I was told to give up my dreams of being an athlete. I was prescribed opiates to handle the pain, and the doctors stated I would likely need back surgery within a few years. This news was devastating. My healthy and extremely active lifestyle was the only constant I could rely on, and it was the perfect distraction from my harsh reality. I spiraled into a deeper depression, even though I was told I was "lucky to be alive." It did not feel that way, but I heard the words louder this time. My body was as broken as my mind and heart, but I knew I had to change everything about who I was and start over again.

I replayed the conversation I had with my friend a couple of years earlier, and it left me pondering about my life purpose and how I could make lasting changes in my life. I also knew I wanted to impact others' lives, even if it was just by showing them how I heal.

Two weeks later, I stopped taking pain medicine, determined to heal naturally and prove the doctor wrong. That's when I discovered yoga, which helped heal both my body and mind. I also turned to breathwork and meditation to ease my depression and anxiety.

I went from using extreme sports gear daily and being stuck in an unhealthy marriage to living an incredibly slow-paced life, something I had never experienced before. My practice transformed my life, shifting it from a fast-paced, adrenaline-fueled existence to one where I could find the simple joys. It also allowed me to avoid intensive surgeries, and my entire life began to change drastically. This included where I lived, who I was dating, my daily routines, coping mechanisms, and even my career path. I truly believe that because of this accident, I found inner peace, bliss, and harmony—something I had longed for my entire life.

Fourteen years later, I'm stronger mentally and physically than I ever imagined, despite all the challenges I've faced. I now count my blessings, realizing I'm stronger than I once believed. I've also learned to transform negativity into motivation, but more importantly, I've come to understand that I need to be my own biggest cheerleader. Having these experiences and the ability to rewrite my story has given me a greater purpose in life, and it fuels my desire to help others do the same. I have a passion for working with those who have experienced great loss and trauma, showing them that there truly is light at the end of the dark tunnel. I'm also there to push them to realize that, in order to heal, they must be willing to walk through and out of those dark places in life.

Along my journey, I have explored different forms of therapy and healing modalities, including talk therapy, psychic readings, sound healing, soul retrieval work with shamans, psychedelics, art therapy, ecstatic dance, cold plunges, sweat lodges, sensory deprivation chambers, and even hypnosis. The biggest lesson I have learned is that there is no one-size-fits-all approach to healing, and as you grow, your tools may change. Ultimately, I discovered that my most profound healing came through embodiment practices, somatic techniques, moving my body, breathwork, and meditation. I fully encourage you, the reader, to explore various modalities with different healers until you find the medicine that truly resonates with your soul in the moment.

Although I've worked through a lot of trauma, I fully accept that I am—and will likely always be—a work in progress. As difficult as it may feel, sometimes we have to walk away from people, places, or experiences. Sometimes, we must reinvent ourselves—and that's perfectly okay! A fresh start can often be the best medicine, even if it feels terrifying at first. Once you learn to love yourself and fully accept where you are on your journey, it will become easier to embrace the gift of being alive. You'll find it easier to be grateful for the lessons you've endured, and it will become easier to recognize just how precious life truly is.

As I continue my journey, I seek out new modalities and healers to connect with, while also working to find inner peace on my own. It has become incredibly important for me to incorporate meditation, movement, and practices that bring me joy into my daily routine. This doesn't mean I never have bad days anymore—it simply means that I now have more tools in my mental health toolkit to help me shift my perspective more quickly and take charge of my reactions to outside circumstances, maintaining my inner peace. I've learned that happiness is truly an inside job, and it's something that deserves my attention every day, especially on the tough days.

When struggles arise now, I begin my process with breathwork to soothe my nervous system, starting with a technique called 4-5-7 breathing. This is simple: inhale through your nose for 4 seconds, hold your breath for 5 seconds, and then slowly exhale through your mouth for 7 seconds. If you repeat this cycle at least 5 times, it will gently help ease anxiety and calm your nervous system. The key is to inhale through the nose, exhale through the mouth, and allow the exhales to be longer than the inhales. Ultimately, do whatever feels best for you.

During moments of frustration and discomfort, I often find it helpful to get outside, breathe in fresh air, and change my scenery. If the situation is particularly intense and I feel called to do so, I'll dedicate at least 15 minutes to a vigorous workout, a yoga flow, or even an inner child dance party—anything that allows me to focus solely on moving energy. Afterward, I often feel clearer and less reactive when faced with stressful moments. I've also let go of any discomfort, shame, or pride around asking for help from friends and family, or scheduling a session with a therapist or healer. I truly feel blessed by the support network I have around me, and that's because I've put in the effort to make those connections and build those relationships.

Another experience that helped shift my mindset was when I decided to see a hypnotherapist to help rewire my thinking. Before I even went under hypnosis, she asked me a simple question: "How many traumas have you been through in your life?" My heart and mind began to race. I didn't know how to answer as I started recalling a long list of incidents. I asked her to define what she meant by "traumas" and how much time we had beyond our one-hour session if we were going to dive into that topic.

During these moments of reflection, I began to look at my life in chronological order and created a list of every trauma I had experienced each year until that present moment. Once I finished this extensive list, I placed a hand on my heart and began reading each incident aloud. This process allowed me to sense, in my body and nervous system, which of these traumas were still leaving a lasting impression on my psyche and which I had truly moved past emotionally. Not only did this help me identify areas that still needed healing, but it also revealed just how strong I was for overcoming the many hurdles I had faced in my life. This mental practice allowed me to shift my internal narrative from feeling like a victim to feeling like a badass warrior. I could look at the list and know, with confidence, that I was fully capable of facing nearly any challenge moving forward, based on everything I had already overcome.

I encourage you to create a similar list, noting the lessons you've learned from each experience. Even though it may be difficult, try to make peace with each incident or, if possible, find gratitude for the lessons they've taught you. The goal is to learn from them so that they don't need to be repeated in the future. It can be incredibly empowering to look back and realize how much you've grown since those moments occurred, and to give yourself credit for now being able to navigate life's challenges better than before.

It felt essential to help others along their healing journey and pay it forward, just as so many beautiful souls assisted me along my path. Sometimes, we need to harness the stuck and uncomfortable energy from our traumas because it is in those moments that we have the opportunity to alchemize it into strength—or even a superpower. Remember, you are not alone on this journey. You are capable of turning your trials into your triumphs! You are loved, and you deserve to be supported. Help is out there and often just a phone call or text away.

Community is immensely important to me, and in 2022, I officially opened my healing business called Vibrational Transcendance. My goal is to help people open their minds, heal their hearts, and free their souls. As someone who has experienced significant losses, heartaches, and traumas, I have made it my mission to help others heal their inner child wounds, find their calm, restore balance to their nervous system, and bring more harmony to their lives. I believe that, having walked through the fire myself, I have now returned with water to help those in need. I intend to offer various ways to help heal souls, just as I continue healing my own.

I strive to help others find their inner peace through tea ceremonies, Reiki, healing touch sessions, and sound healing experiences. For those seeking a more active session, I offer sacred cacao ceremonies, somatic movement, inner child dance parties, and various art outlets. Each session is uniquely tailored to meet the specific needs of the moment. Many of my clients have found profound healing in my larger community gatherings, while others have benefited from one-on-one sessions, both in person and virtually. My hope is to share sacred plant medicines, ancient breathwork techniques, mantras, and other healing modalities with those who are ready to open their hearts and let their inner child play.

Even if you haven't heard it from the people you desperately wish to hear it from, I want you to know that I am proud of everything you have overcome. I see you, I respect you, and I honor your journey. You are valuable, worthy of love, and more than enough.

You are not meant to connect with everyone, nor are you meant to be everyone's cup of tea. But you are meant to learn lessons from others, connect with your higher self, bring your inner child out to play, and discover true love for yourself. I encourage you to let your haters be your motivators to grow, adapt, and thrive. May you find your bliss, chase your passions, take leaps of faith to catch your dreams, and, most importantly, be kind to yourself along the way.

One of my all-time favorite quotes from the incredible Carl Jung is: "I am not what happened to me; I am what I choose to become." You have the power to grow, expand, and rise above your former circumstances. Like a phoenix rising from the ashes, you can be reborn and bloom into something magnificent—if you give yourself the chance.

Shine brightly, my friend, and be that light in the darkness. You deserve to live a beautiful life, but first, you must believe that you do. I wish you nothing but the best on your journey.

I am deeply grateful to all who have supported me along my healing path—my mother, stepfather, brother, extended family, wise friends, and the healers and magical souls I've encountered. Each of you has played a vital role in shaping the person I am today along my personal journey, and for that, I will be forever thankful.

Charlotte Cheetham

CEO of Lifeinsights

https://www.linkedin.com/in/charlotte-cheetham-3b01391a/
https://www.facebook.com/charlotte.cheetham.92/
https://www.instagram.com/charlotte.cheetham
https://lifeinsights.co.uk/

As a dedicated Gut Health Coach specialising in menopausal women, my mission is to empower women to take control of their health and well-being during one of the most transformative phases of their lives. I'm Charlotte Cheetham, and I bring a wealth of knowledge and experience to help you navigate the unique challenges that menopause presents. Taking a holistic approach, integrating nutrition, lifestyle modifications, and stress management techniques to create sustainable health improvements. Whether you're dealing with bloating, food sensitivities, or hormonal imbalances, I'm here to guide you every step of the way.

A Journey of Resilience and Transformation

By Charlotte Cheetham

I am Charlotte Cheetham, an award-winning Gut Health Coach for menopausal women. I specialise in empowering women to reclaim their vitality by addressing common symptoms like bloating, brain fog, fatigue, and sugar cravings. My approach blends education, mindset shifts, and practical lifestyle changes to help women rediscover the freedom and joy they deserve.

But my path to becoming who I am today was not a straightforward one. It was filled with trials, tribulations, and moments when the future seemed uncertain. Growing up in a household where I was expected to be "seen and not heard," I faced an environment where expressing my thoughts invited harsh reprimands. Any attempt at sharing my opinions was met with scolding, smacks, and solitude in my room. The words "stupid," "useless," and "not clever enough for university" became the narrative imposed on me.

The constant belittling from my parents chipped away at my confidence. I became shy, introverted, and burdened with low self-worth. School was no reprieve—every report echoed the same sentiments: "could do better" or "needs to try harder." No one acknowledged the countless late nights I spent diligently completing homework.

Amidst this challenging environment, music became my sanctuary. Learning to play the piano and violin provided a rare outlet for joy. Playing in the school orchestra was one of the few freedoms my parents allowed. Sitting at the piano, I could lose myself in the melody, finding solace and strength in the emotions the music evoked.

After school, I ventured to Oxford to study nursing. Yet, the self-doubt instilled in me as a child followed me. I spent three arduous years feeling inadequate, culminating in a tutor telling me she was surprised I passed my finals and insinuating I didn't deserve to.

When I married a Royal Air Force pilot, I believed life might offer stability, but the next 16 years proved otherwise. Moving every 6 to 12 months to different bases, raising 3 children largely on my own, and adjusting to each new environment felt like climbing a never-ending mountain. The loneliness and isolation were compounded by the relentless demands of caregiving and the absence of a supportive partner.

Our first posting took us to North Scotland in the dead of winter. With a baby who never slept for more than an hour and a house barely warm enough to shield us from the biting cold, I found myself battling exhaustion, depression, and an overwhelming sense of isolation. When I finally passed my driving test and started working part-time, I felt a glimmer of hope. However, my husband faced backlash for having a wife who worked, a reality that baffled and frustrated me.

Amid the challenges, I discovered orienteering—a sport that combined running and navigation in the outdoors. It became a lifeline, allowing me to reconnect with nature, improve my mental health, and feel a sense of accomplishment. Those weekends in the forests of Scotland gave me a reason to smile.

The Trials of Family Life

Life didn't get easier. With every new posting came fresh challenges. After my second child was born, my husband was diagnosed with a benign brain tumour. The uncertainty surrounding his health and career was terrifying. Watching him undergo a 16-hour surgery and then caring for him during recovery while managing 2 young children was one of the hardest chapters of my life.

Shortly after, he was relocated to work as a ground flying instructor in North Wales, a region where we faced overt prejudice for being English.

Navigating this environment while managing family life was a test of resilience. Yet, I found solace in walks along the rugged coastline and forged bonds with other military families who shared similar struggles.

But life's challenges were far from over. Our daughter began exhibiting worrying signs of illness, culminating in daily seizures and a devastating diagnosis: a benign brain tumour near her brainstem. The emotional toll of watching her suffer through seizures, memory loss, and bullying at school was immense. After years of ineffective treatments, she underwent a life-threatening surgery. Those tense hours in the hospital were among the most harrowing of my life.

Miraculously, the surgery succeeded, and her seizures diminished. Seeing her regain her ability to form memories and enjoy life again was an indescribable relief. Despite these improvements, her journey wasn't without hurdles. Diagnosed with atypical autism, she faced challenges in socialising and securing employment. Yet, her determination and resilience inspired me daily.

From Struggle to Strength

Through all these experiences—relentless relocations, caregiving, professional challenges, and personal battles—I began to recognise my inner strength. My struggles taught me resilience and the power of adaptation. Slowly but surely, I transformed my pain into purpose.

I realised that the physical and emotional toll of my experiences was linked to something deeper: my gut health. Years of stress had manifested in stomach aches, fatigue, and IBS. Once I discovered how nutrition, mindset, and holistic approaches could heal the gut, my life changed.

I trained as a Coach, NLP Master Practitioner, Nutritionist, and Advanced Gut Health Advisor. These qualifications became the tools I needed to not only rebuild my life but also to help others.

Today, I use my expertise to guide menopausal women through their own transformations. These women, often dismissed or misunderstood, deserve to reclaim their energy, confidence, and joy. I am living proof that it's possible to rise from the depths of despair to build a fulfilling, meaningful life.

The Power of Purpose

Every challenge I faced—whether as a child dismissed as "useless," a young mother battling isolation, or a caregiver navigating medical crises—shaped the person I am today. These experiences taught me compassion, resilience, and the importance of holistic healing.

I have dedicated my life to empowering women because I understand what it means to feel powerless. I know how it feels to be trapped by circumstances beyond your control, to doubt your own worth, and to long for a brighter future. And I also know the transformative power of hope, knowledge, and self-belief.

Through my coaching, I have helped countless women rediscover their potential. I teach them that their symptoms are not permanent, that they can feel vibrant, and that they deserve to enjoy this chapter of their lives.

My journey is far from over. Each woman I help reminds me of the strength we all carry within us. We are capable of overcoming unimaginable challenges, of rewriting our stories, and of finding joy even in the face of adversity

Your Turn to Transform

To anyone reading this who feels overwhelmed by life's trials, know this: You are not alone. You are stronger than you think, and your story is still being written. Every challenge you face is an opportunity to grow, learn, and transform.

If I can rise from a childhood of low self-worth, navigate the complexities of military life, and endure the pain of watching loved ones suffer, so can you. Let my story serve as a beacon of hope, a reminder that no matter how dark the night is, the dawn always comes.

DK Hillard

Founder of DK Hillard Art, LLC
Artist, Designer & Author

https://www.linkedin.com/in/debra-hillard-93526913/
https://www.facebook.com/dkhillardart/
https://www.instagram.com/dkhillard/
https://www.dkhillard.com/
https://www.dkhillardart.com/

Debra is a creator. It is how she lives and what she does in her work. Her art has been a consistent thread throughout her life, whether it be painting, writing or working with others. It is based in her spiritual journey, her Shamanic practice and her connection to nature.

For 20 years she was a life coach and personal trainer, a career that evolved out of her experience transforming her life through bodybuilding. During that time she developed a 12 week program using the body as a vehicle for transforming your entire life.

She transforms her paintings into sensual, luxurious fabrics-clothing, blankets and pillows called "Wraptures", bringing the energy of her artwork into forms you can touch. They are filled with the love that she puts into everything she creates. She works with individuals and small groups using many of the interactive processes she developed while teaching her program.

My Journey Back to Myself: Self-Empowerment Knows No Limits

By DK Hillard

The blessing of being different, of not fitting anywhere, and of having to forge my own path, has not been lost on me. Had I found a place, I would not have created my own, and doing so has challenged me to expand beyond any limits I once believed I had.

I worked for others doing all sorts of jobs throughout my young adulthood, but with each one, I found myself stretching the boundaries of their rules. As an artist and visionary, seeing what could be was so much more interesting to me than operating within the confines of what already existed. My favorite jobs were those where I had some leeway in how I interacted with customers, but somehow, it always came back to frustration on my part. I wanted more—for myself and for them.

Growing up in a family where there was little discipline, but unspoken expectations of how I should behave, my rebellious nature served to keep me from totally disappearing into normalcy. I took every opportunity to challenge the norms, question authority, and make others around me uncomfortable. At the time, it was both a survival tactic and a sign of immaturity in dealing with who I was.

I felt invisible, unheard, and dismissed. That pain drove me to a combination of excellence and failure in an attempt to claim my space. I failed over and over again, perhaps proving that my family's opinion of me was true, but I excelled in maintaining the core of truth that they never acknowledged. That was the key. I kept my true self alive even if I had to bury it so deeply that it became hidden from myself for decades.

Strength was never the question for me. I had to be strong to survive my childhood and eventually my adulthood as well. The challenges I faced, the trauma and loss, and eventually the medical issues that followed, required a high degree of strength to endure. All along the way, I had multiple forks in the road and choices to make that would determine whether I continued to live or not.

I knew that no matter what, I would always choose life. That seed, the ember of truth that I had hidden away as a child, still burned, and there were times when it flared up enough to burn away the fog and let me know I was still in there. Somewhere.

In my twenties, I was diagnosed with Chronic Fatigue and Fibromyalgia. Those were not well-known or documented diseases back then, and for the most part, I was on my own in treating myself. It wasn't just the medical profession that brushed me aside—my friends and family never acknowledged how ill I was, still believing that I was a failure and making it all up. I didn't look sick on the outside, but inside, I felt like I was dying, and alone in all of it. For almost ten years, I was nonfunctional, sometimes bedridden, and at the same time, having to rally to keep a roof over my head. The years spent in isolation, both physically and emotionally, drove me deeper within. I had to find the strength to keep going, and the only way I knew was to remember who I was—not the sick person lying in bed, but the essence that still burned in my gut.

Nearing forty with no medical solution in sight, I made a decision and a declaration. I had a young son, a business to run, and a husband I could not depend on. If I was ever going to have a chance at living, I knew I needed my physical strength back. So, I said the words that set in motion the next turning point of my life: "I am not a sick person. I am a strong, healthy person with some physical issues to deal with, and I need my physical strength."

That was a declaration of BEING. It wasn't about what I was going to do, it was WHO I was that was determining my next actions.

I hired a strength coach from a local university and began a long journey back to life. On that first day in the gym, neither of us knowing anything about how to proceed, he asked me to get down and do a pushup. Dressed in baggy sweats to hide my out-of-shape body, I got down on the floor in position and couldn't get back up.

And so it began.

One set of leg extensions sent me home to bed for two weeks. Our agreement was that as soon as I could get out of bed, I would pick up the phone and call him. We'd go at it again. And we did. Months went by, and I was creeping along between the gym and my bedroom, until about eight months into our work, he turned to me and said that it was time to start cycling my workouts because I hadn't been sick for so long. I knew I had turned a major corner. In those next few months, as I gained in strength physically, I also felt a newfound resilience emotionally, which led me to make another life-altering decision.

One day sitting on a bench in the gym between sets of cable crossovers, I turned to him and said, "I know what I have to do with the rest of my life. I'm going to become a trainer. This has given me my life back, and I want to do that for others."

That decision set me on a course of action that eventually gave me the fortitude to close a failing business, start my own training business, and move across the country to a place I had dreamt of living, following the call of my soul. I had a young son and a husband who was fairly useless when it came to supporting either of us, and I had no idea what life was going to ask of me in a strange new place. But I was strong enough now to take a stand for myself, and what I knew in my heart was my destiny. We moved from a small New England college town where we knew everyone, to a large city 2500 miles away where we knew no one. Life was about to get very real.

It was the mid-90s, and I was in my early 40s. Still young enough to pick up roots and start again, but old enough to be aware that I was putting us all in a precarious position by doing so. That was not enough to stop me from following my heart and listening to what I knew I needed to do. We struggled financially and personally for a number of years. My husband refused to get it together in any way, leaving me with the sole responsibility of supporting us. I worked cleaning houses while I grew my training business. Both my son and I stuck out like sore thumbs, living in a community where we were even more of an oddity than we had been in our close-knit New England town with the other "odd" souls. He was bullied in school for his long hair. I was stared at as an outsider in a city where most women didn't have muscles and cared more about their social standing than their spiritual well-being. We had moved to an upscale community without having an income or mindset to match.

The challenges served to fuel my fire for creating a new life for us all. I knew how to fight hard for what I wanted because life had trained me well. Being an outsider was nothing new to me. The only difference now was that I couldn't blend in anymore. I looked different than just about everyone around me, whereas, in my artsy college town in the East, I could hide amongst those who appeared to be my colleagues. I'll admit, it was lonely for a long time, but then again, I was used to that too.

My strength was tested in 2000 by a severe car accident that threatened my ability to use the right side of my body. Three surgeries, rehab, and months of losing clients left me on the edge of survival once again. I knew I needed my strength back, but the road was long and uncertain and in the meantime, we had to eat. Years before, I had given up my art, believing the words that had been drummed into my head since childhood, that I wasn't a real artist. Instead, I focused on business, first with my husband and then with my training. Now I was left with neither, and it was time to recreate myself again. I looked at my situation and what I needed to get back on my feet and realized that whether I could physically train others or not was not the issue. I had something to offer far beyond the physical training, and I'd been doing it all along without realizing it.

For all my years working with clients, I was more of an artist/coach/mentor than anything. The spiritual work I had instinctively done with myself had been filtering out in all of my interactions. My clients looked to me for guidance and insight more than physical training. I knew what I needed for myself to regain my life after the accident, so I set about creating a life-altering program, using the body as a vehicle to transform your relationship with yourself and your entire way of living.

My clients watched me bring myself back to life, and that inspired them. And as I worked with them through the processes I created for my program, I found myself growing and expanding as well. Every bit of training I had received over the years in personal development and awareness, in expanding consciousness, plus my experience in physical training and life coaching, came together in a synthesis of art and science. I called my work PhysioCentrics, The Art and Science of Transformation.

I finally did regain my physical strength, but what I had lost in that accident paled in comparison to the power I found within myself to contribute to others on a far more meaningful level. In the process, I also picked up a paintbrush and found my way back to my art and writing. I had to fall apart physically to recreate myself as a truer version of who I knew myself to be. But that was not the end.

The accident and subsequent growth from the experience, brought to light the extent of abuse in my marriage and just how much of myself I had given up to survive in it. Nearing fifty, after almost 30 years together, I told him I wanted out. I wouldn't have had the ability to make that move had it not been for the strength I gained creating my program, reclaiming my art, and finding my voice again. It took nine months to leave, and another few years to get myself out of debt and create a new business out of the old, but I was finally free. Or so I thought. At the very least, I was in charge of my own life again.

There were years of financial struggle, family challenges, and health issues to follow. I had empowered myself to reclaim my life, but what kind of life was it? I was totally alone and was ready to receive the love I had felt undeserving of all my life. On New Year's Eve, I made another declaration that brought me my true love, but loving required another kind of strength, the courage to surrender my heart. I knew how to fight, but surrender was another story altogether and one that would take years of oftentimes painful work. My heart had been broken so many times since childhood that for the first time ever, I had to face that brokenness and come to terms with it all.

Strength comes in many forms, but for someone who prided herself on the fight, this was the most terrifying. It was love and desire that provided the impetus to use my strength for what I wanted most.

It is now decades later. I have lived through life-threatening health challenges, loss, and more heartbreak, but having surrendered to being loved has been the single thing I can point to as my source of power. First, it was being loved by someone else, but eventually, it became a love *for myself* that I never believed I would find. Each step of the way on my journey back to my true self, I have uncovered more and more to love, cherish, and celebrate about myself. My work has been all about remembering who I am and living a fully embodied life, but without love, I wouldn't have had the strength to uncover the power that lies beneath the surface of who I am.

I speak now as an artist, creative visionary, Priestess, and Shaman. I know who I am, who I have always been and the gifts I have to offer. I am no longer afraid of my own power because I know my heart. I have found a different kind of strength that isn't dependent upon my physical condition. I have seen the brilliance of my energy and what it has the capacity to do when used with awareness, love, and guided by spirit.

I no longer have to hide, but I don't have to be seen by anyone else, either. I see myself, and that is true empowerment, when it is not subject to threat by outside forces or opinions. Now, being seen is a way of sharing the love I feel and not a necessity for validation.

The message I leave you with is this.

Listen closely to the whispers of your soul. If you can't hear them, find someone who can help you find your way back.

Then, surround yourself with things that remind you of that truth.

You are your own home. Your truth is your North Star. Let it be your guide.

When you remember who you are, not what you do, not what others have labeled you as, but the essence of your soul, you are unstoppable.

Beneath all of the roles you play, all of the faces you so bravely wear, is the person you were born to be. That person is not lacking anything. That person only needs to love herself, stand strong for herself, and empower herself to go beyond mere survival. She was not born merely to survive. She was born to relish being alive, shining her brilliant light as a beacon for those who have the eyes to see.

This takes real strength.

This is true empowerment.

And it comes from fully living your truth.

Dr. Farah Jindani

Farah Jindani Consulting
Educator, Therapist, Researcher & Change-Maker

https://www.linkedin.com/in/farah-jindani-aa216a22/
https://www.facebook.com/fjindani
http://www.drfarahjindani.com/

Dr. Farah Jindani is an experienced educator, therapist, researcher, and change-maker with demonstrated expertise in mental health, addictions and trauma. She is skilled in innovative program/curriculum development, evidence-based research, leadership, and training of healthcare and social service providers. She offers inclusive and strengths-based therapy. Farah's life changed in 2010 when she found Kundalini Yoga to support her own healing from trauma and has been a daily meditation practitioner since. In 2013, she developed and implemented an 8-week evidence-based research program in collaboration with the University of Toronto and Harvard University to explore the efficacy of body-mind approaches to support trauma treatment. The results have been published in numerous scientific journals. She has also written two manuals for practitioners to utilize in their practice. She is continually inspired by those who strive to grow from challenge and adversity and uplift others. Farah provides training to organizations, professionals and anyone striving to live from wholeness.

Rooted in Strength: Cultivating Resilience Through Actionable Intentional Living

By Dr. Farah Jindani

Trauma Legacies: Embodying the Weight of Generations

Has there ever been a time in your life when you felt the burden of your own struggles while quietly carrying the collective weight of generations that came before you? While no one is immune to this, for women, this is a deep reality often woven into the fabric of our lives. The legacy of trauma for women is a complex phenomenon shaped by personal, intergenerational, and societal experiences. In this book chapter, I overview the shared experience of challenge and trauma, a new paradigm towards living an empowered life, and actionable steps towards creating a ripple effect from me to us, along with actionable steps towards creating a more accepting, empathic, and unified society.

Women often carry the burdens of their own struggles alongside inherited pain passed down through family histories, societal norms, socialization, and cultural narratives. This legacy stems from systemic oppression and patriarchy, gender-based violence, the intersectional identities of women, and the historical silencing of women's voices. These experiences result in emotional, somatic, and psychological imprints that transcend generations. Many women are raised and conditioned to first care for others, often living the entirety of their lives distanced from their authentic selves, striving to make meaning instead and find voice through caring for others. In other cases, women may have internalized these notions and strive for success and power based on societal notions of success. While our behaviours are often rooted in our early experiences, the purpose is not to guilt, shame, or blame those who came before us, but to bring insight into our own individual patterning and the inherited trauma of our ancestors, and what they may not have had the privilege to unpack: an understanding that our life challenges often repeat until we have the courage to work together to face it. When we face the challenges courageously, there lies the opportunity to create a new, healthier pattern.

Understanding Trauma: A Shared Experience

What if I told you that I am a living example of how the challenges and burdens that we carry can be shifted to empowered, authentic, and resilient living? While I share aspects of my personal story, I cannot emphasize enough that each one of us holds a personally profound individual life narrative. It is not a competition of whose life challenge is worse. We share stories because they have the power to inspire and connect, they bring people together and create community. However, I encourage one step beyond the story—and that is taking actionable steps towards purposeful and intentional living.

Trauma is not just the catastrophic events we hear about in headlines. It's any experience that overwhelms our capacity to cope. It lives quietly in our minds, bodies, and spirits, shaping how we see ourselves and the world around us. But trauma is not just personal—it's also collective. In today's world, systemic racism, economic inequality, environmental degradation, and societal disconnection amplify the shared pain we carry.

"Trauma" originates from the Greek word for "wound," and these wounds run deep, unseen but palpable. Approaches and treatment of trauma conventionally focus on symptom suppression and diagnosis, often neglecting the whole person. But trauma is not just a mental experience; it lives in our nervous systems, our muscles, our very cells. Healing, therefore, must integrate the body, mind, and spirit—a perspective long held by Indigenous cultures worldwide.

Trauma, both personal and ancestral, lingers like an invisible thread, binding us to histories of displacement, loss, and pain. Recognizing these layers is not about competing over whose pain is greater but about understanding the shared human experience of challenge and resilience. I share aspects of my life narrative simply to highlight that trauma and pain are real and can also be a shared human experience. I am also cognizant that everyone has their own individual life challenges, narratives, and stories. I encourage holding each person we meet with authentic compassion and the capacity for growth and resilience.

I was born into a legacy of survival. I did not always view it or understand it this way. My parents, refugees at just 16, fled East Africa to seek safety in England amidst political upheaval and systemic nationalism that uprooted entire communities. My grandparents, who were orphans at a young age and migrated alone to Africa, through hard work and commitment, built successful lives only to lose everything again. While I heard bite-sized stories of financial and identity loss, forced migration, and everything that comes along with continual forced displacement and loss of home, identity, and safety, what I witnessed through spoken word and through actions and behaviour, was not a focus on the past but instead, on striving forward. What I did not understand were the profound impacts. For instance, both of my parents were diagnosed with life-threatening illnesses when I was a young child. I now understand that the illnesses likely manifested due to the trauma and pain held through in their bodies and of the generations past. Layered on to this was the added personal and systemic discrimination and everyday life challenges that first-generation immigrants experience. As they were focused on physical survival and trying to financially survive and raise children in a new country, they dealt with the stresses, anxieties, and life challenges and hardships, in the best way they believed to be true, by trying to make the best of situations and demonstrate gratitude for all aspects of life.

As an adult, I now understand that my grandparents and parents made a conscious choice to focus on moving forward and doing their utmost to create better lives for their families. I would often hear statements like,

"We can make a home wherever we hang our coats." I now understand their deep conviction and desire to protect their children from the hardship, pain, and loss that they had faced. Their resilience astounds me, as does their unwavering compassion for humanity despite facing horrific racism, isolation, and economic hardship. These stories of survival were not just theirs to carry—they became mine, too.

When I became a professional supporting the mental health and wellbeing of others, I truly became acutely aware of how this inherited trauma shaped my perceptions, behaviours, and relationships. I started to unpack and unravel my life history, my behaviours, how I showed up in my relationships, and how I behaved in various aspects of my professional work. I became shamefully cognizant of the internalization of challenges and how I evolved to hold my own unconscious limitations and understandings of the world. All of this, coupled with systemic challenges that manifest in workplaces that promote wellness and care but actually do the opposite, caused enormous tolls on my physical, emotional, and mental wellbeing. The resilience my parents modeled was both an inspiration and a heavy inheritance, an unspoken reminder of the cost of survival. Yet, amid these struggles, I found strength in their stories of perseverance and humanity, learning that healing is possible when we acknowledge the past and choose to create a different future.

Through my professional work, I also learnt the impact that life's challenges can have on physical and mental health conditions across the lifespan, including heart disease, diabetes, depression, and other ailments. The reality is that epigenetics, how environmental factors influence our gene expression, provided insight and a missing link to my understanding of how various challenging life experiences impact long-term health. Stress from adverse life experiences can alter gene expression, activating pathways linked to inflammation, hormonal imbalances, and disease susceptibility. These changes can persist across generations, illustrating how trauma is passed down biologically and behaviourally. However, healing is possible. Protective factors like supportive relationships, awareness of our individual challenges and susceptibility, and perhaps most importantly, taking intentional steps to engage in resilience-building practices can help mitigate earlier life challenges and experiences and promote recovery, breaking the cycle of intergenerational, individual, interpersonal, and related traumas.

From Survival to Empowerment: A New Paradigm

What if healing from trauma doesn't just mean finding ways to survive but actually thriving through intentionally empowered living? I am a dedicated educator, clinician, change-maker, and researcher dedicated to supporting others to explore this question and make meaningful changes towards living an empowered life. I support leaders, professionals, organizations, and everyday people to develop ways to make change from the inside out; when we make an intentional choice and implement actions to support our own wellbeing, the effects have a ripple effect. In making a commitment to change and heal ourselves, we can empower ourselves and others, creating communities of positive change around us and beyond us. We become change agents for a more inclusive, compassionate, and resilient world—this is the new paradigm of leadership, of business, and of living an intentional and empowered life.

Life challenges and experiences are real. However, we must learn that life challenge keeps us stuck in survival mode, activating our sympathetic or arousal based nervous system. When we are in survival mode, we become trapped in self-protection and fear, which prevent us from experiencing joy, growth, and connection. I teach practical exercises on how to first reset our nervous systems to reclaim a sense of safety and control.

Actionable Strategies to Thrive

The journey from trauma to empowerment is not easy, but it is possible. Here are some simple strategies that I have found transformative in supporting others to become the best versions of themselves:

1. **Nervous System Reset**
   Trauma lives in the body, so we must address it there first. Practices like deep breathing, movement, and sound can help regulate the nervous system. For example, a simple breathing exercise—inhale through your nose, then exhale through your nose for twice as long—can shift you from a reactive state to a restorative one.

2. **Create Rituals for Healing**
   Whether it's journaling, singing, crying, being with pets, art, or spending time in nature, find rituals that allow you to process emotions and reconnect with yourself. These practices can remind you of our place within the larger web of life.

3. **Reconnect with Your Body**
   Movement practices like walking, stretching, dance, and meditation can release accumulated trauma in our bodies and create a sense of safety in our own bodies.

4. **Rewrite Your Story**
   Our minds often get stuck in loops of negativity, replaying the same painful narratives. By consciously reframing these stories, we can create new neural pathways that empower rather than limit us.

5. **Cultivate Community**
   Healing is not a solitary journey. Surround yourself with people who support your growth and hold space for your struggles. The ripple effect of healing is powerful—when we heal, we inspire others to do the same.

The Ripple Effect: Stories of Resilience

The main lesson learnt from two decades of personal and professional experience in the trauma, mental health, and addiction field is that when one begins to heal and make intentional changes in their own life, a ripple effect is felt by others. In some cases, we open space for others to cultivate healing in their own lives, at other times, we or the people we have long-standing emotional patterns with may leave our lives. With these changes, come opportunities for grieving, loss, reflection, and consideration of authentic living. The process is not unicorns and fairies as it can sometimes feel as if everything we know to be true is shattering apart, but amidst the cracks and falling apart, shines the light for coming recreation. There is one guarantee: the internal and authentic voice from within that may have been silenced or struggling to be heard, can speak, and we begin to live from a place of connection, purpose, and joy—and from that place, we are reminded that this journey of healing is not just for ourselves.

Each step we take towards empowerment contributes to a healthier, more compassionate world. When we heal, we don't just break the cycles of trauma for ourselves—we create a new legacy for future generations.

Self-Nurturance as an Act of Resistance

The times in which we live are tenuous and stressful in several ways. Social disparities are increasing and access to the basic needs of life are challenging for many. We often hear about the various ways to 'self-care.' These approaches are fraught with connotations of social privilege and are challenged by many, simply because life does not afford the time, resources, or acceptance of these strategies.

I encourage readers to consider self-care as an act of self-nurturance, reclaiming one's internal locus of control. As we would care and give to others, if we hold true to the cultivation of inner confidence to embrace small micro-changes towards embracing your own power and make them short, micro-practices and actional strategies in our lives, we can develop the internalized understanding that strengths aren't just about getting over the challenge; it's about embracing our own power, finding our voice, and unlocking our full potential. It is essential in our healing journey.

In a world that often demands we prioritize others at the expense of ourselves, self-nurturance is a revolutionary act of self-preservation. It's about creating a relationship with yourself that nurtures your body, mind, and spirit, allowing you to show up fully for yourself and the people and causes you care about.

Consider this: How do you nurture and come back to your internal centre in times of stress? Do you have practices that help you reset and restore? Whether it's a walk in nature, a few minutes of listening to music, deep breathing, or simply holding space for your emotions, self-nurturance is the foundation of thriving.

A Shared Journey

The journey from trauma to empowerment is deeply personal, yet it's also profoundly communal. As we heal ourselves, we create space for others to heal, fostering a culture of compassion and resilience. I invite you to consider your own life, the ups and downs, the burdens and gifts. Together, we can move from surviving to thriving, creating ripples of change that transform not only our lives but the lives of those with whom we connect and those who come after us. Let us reclaim our inner strength, honour our stories, and step boldly into a future of actionable empowerment, love, and community.

Kerrie D. Stone

Founder of SheThatExists
Minister, Metaphysician, Mystical Life Coach,
Visionary & Creative Director

https://www.linkedin.com/in/rev-kerrie-d-stone-a19964299/
https://www.facebook.com/shethatexists
https://www.instagram.com/shethatexiststheuniteroftribes/
https://shethatexists.com/
https://kerriedstone.com/

Kerrie D. Stone, Founder of SheThatExists, is a former child performer in dance/theater performance arts at Story Book Theater Playhouse in Texas. She is a former gymnast and has performed in parades. A former select corporate softball athlete, she has played several team sports. She is a musician trained in clarinet, piano, and the xylophone, having performed in concert and jazz bands. She is an awarded esthetician. A former showwoman, she produced her own community show as a single mom. Born a spiritual child, she professed her faith in Creator at age 15. A champion in supporting others in their greatness, she has 36 years of team/leadership experience. Today she is an Ordained Minister in service of life as sacred, a mystical life coach, metaphysician, visionary, wisdom teacher, polymath, Creative Director, and Comedian. Her favorite passion is being momma. She is earning her Masters degree and is a PhD candidate.

Tragedies Can Open the Door to Our Higher Calling

By Kerrie D. Stone

Life is truly a heroine's journey. Some of us are born with great support systems, called parents, siblings, aunts, uncles, cousins, and family. Some of us are not born with great family support systems. There are also moments in our lives where we may have had great support systems in the past that were not completely functional and whole; however, they did provide a safe landing place for us to come back home to so that we would not be left to the harshness of the streets, trafficking, or total loss of being placed in a homeless concentration camp. These are real realities that we face today.

Trafficking inside the United States is at an all-time high, and protective mothers are being targeted for protecting their children and put in positions of homelessness and trafficking every day. Families are being targeted and left traumatized, and generations are facing generational trauma and not even really conscious and aware of what is going on and happening to them and don't understand why they can't connect anymore, repair the damage that has gone on in the family tree, and that we have intergenerational trauma and confusion. These are things that I have experienced in my own life as well as what I have witnessed and observed as an Ordained Minister. Mothers come to me with all kinds of horror stories, and I have experienced my own horrors as well. We live in a world of trauma, where people are afraid to support each other and do what they know is right in their hearts and in their Creator-gifted conscience. We live in a world where folks are afraid to show up for others and to do good. We live in a world where folks are too afraid to help a "stranger," even though religion and spirituality tell us to love each other as our Selves and to give to those in need and hunger. The

United States turns a blind eye to the evils of homelessness and trafficking, thinking that the government is the savior and is going to "help everyone" when in all reality, we are the ones who are called to help people directly.

One might ask what this has to do with growing stronger. For me, as a single momma and divorced Ordained Minister who has overcome a very unhealthy male patriarchy that has caused much harm to my daughter and me and our family tree, knowing the truths of what is currently an ongoing epidemic inside of the United States and having hundreds of survivors come to me and share their stories with me helped me to realize that life is a continued journey of growing stronger. My parents did not and do not support me or my purpose/calling as an Ordained Minister. My former husband, my daughter's father does not, either. After my divorce from a mentally, emotionally, and spiritually unhealthy male, I realized that I had to grow stronger for myself and my daughter. I began to see my parents for their imperfections and realized that one day they would die and that I had to stand strong for my daughter and me. I could not always rely on my parents and began to see their dysfunction more clearly. I remember that I began a practice of spiritual fasting when I was a teenager, and so after my divorce, I started a practice of spiritual fasting. My intention was that I was going too fast so that I could become stronger mentally, emotionally, and spiritually as a single mom. I wanted to become stronger for my daughter so that I could be both mother and father to my daughter. Her dad was distant in another state, yet he was still involved in visitations; he just did not contact our child daily, and no matter how much I begged him, he would not be a daily part of our daughter's life, even through phone calls or video conferences. I did not want to have to divorce my daughter's dad; however, he was so unhealthy mentally, emotionally, and spiritually that I felt guided by the Creator within that I needed to divorce him for my own safety and well-being because he kept promising me that he would get better but he never did. Fasting was a spiritual practice that helped me begin to grow stronger mentally, emotionally, and spiritually. It helped me connect to my Self in a deeper way. I had spent so many years devoting my Self as a momma, wife, and daughter that I had lost touch with my Self. Fasting helped me reconnect to my Self as a soul and with my true essence again and to feel more alive again.

The early years after my divorce were the beginning of when I started to realize that I was going to have to do what it took to continue to grow stronger—mentally, emotionally, and spiritually not just for me, but for my daughter and my possible future grandchildren. I realized consciously that I needed to take an even deeper dive within and focus on mental, emotional, and spiritual strength for my entire lineage and my entire family tree. Many folks teach that being strong means not crying, or that it means being "tough" and sticking things out that we really should not have to endure. To some people, "be strong" means to be tough and to become more masculine or to stay in situations that are not healthy and even downright abusive just because that is what society or religion expects of us. Depending on who you talk to, you will get a different definition of strength. Strength is physical; however, strength is also mental, emotional, and spiritual.

After my divorce, I waited until my daughter started kindergarten, and then I went back to school to continue my education. I was invited to a school of metaphysics where I was learning Self-Development, learning how to learn, how thinking occurs, the universal language of the mind, concentration, and the principles of will and willpower. I was also learning about different daily mental and spiritual disciplines. I was learning about consciousness and the divisions of the mind. I started learning about the true meaning of positive thinking. This was a new concept for me because my parents were always so negative. I was nothing like them in that regard; however, I started seeing things about my parents through my new learnings and realizing that they harmed my concept of life in a real way. I started to see why I was having some lack of confidence, and even why I attracted a man into my life whom I married, who was not a healthy individual for my daughter and me. In my Mastery in Consciousness I also started learning about meditation and how to practice proper concentration skills. I learned about why friendship is important to soul growth. I learned about healing practices, energy, and the power of visualization. I learned how physical disorders are simply symptoms of thoughts and attitude patterns that need to be changed and transformed. I learned about the importance, value, and power of communication—communication that heals. I started seeing this whole new world and way of being that was so different than how I was raised, and it made me realize that I had been aware of so much in my life and in my soul and knew that I was on the right path, knowing that the ways of my family and my former husband were not the path that was meant for me. I knew that I was always made for more. During my time in this higher education program, I learned that everything I pondered as a child, youth, and pre-teen about the purpose of life, the meaning of life, and my place in the world was natural and a normal part of the process of life and being alive. I started learning more about emotions and feelings—a whole new world was opening up to me because of this non-secular higher educational degree in metaphysics and a focus on mastering consciousness. I started to learn about the importance of connecting to my breath and how that is connected to consciousness. I started learning how to still my mind and how to be conscious of my thoughts, live deeper in my heart, and live an awakened life.

I started to grow!!!! I started to grow mentally, emotionally, and spiritually at a fast rate. I had always been more advanced than many of my peers and classmates as a spiritual being: I was always on a deeper level than most that I knew and always seeking the things of the deep and studying everything I could about the Creator, God, and all the world religions when I was 14. I bought Self-Help books written by

PhDs with my first paychecks from my first jobs in public after getting my driver's permit. My parents started to notice that I was growing mentally, emotionally, and spiritually and becoming more aware and more connected to consciousness. They started realizing that the brainwashing and programming that they normalized to me growing up, where they taught me not to love my Self and that there was something innately wrong with me, was starting to dissolve. My parents would watch my daughter for me when I would go to school and work. I noticed that when they started realizing how fast I was growing by attending the school of metaphysics that I was attending, they did not like it at all. They noticed that I started thinking for my Self. I think my dad started realizing that all of the grooming and conditioning that I was raised with was slowly dissolving. They did not like it at all. My parents started telling everyone in their circles that I was in a cult. They got others to play along with it, hurt me with my daughter, and used my daughter as a form of control to punish me. It was during this time that I was fasting and growing stronger mentally, emotionally, and spiritually by focusing diligently on my studies in my new school program—and I had also directed, created, produced, and organized my own live community variety show in the area. I also hosted and produced small events with my own funds as a single mom. I thought my parents would be proud of me. The exact opposite happened.

Things got bad after I graduated from this school. I thought my parents and family would be so happy for me and my accomplishments; however, the opposite happened. The abuse that I endured from them in childhood and in my teen years became worse, this time, they were using my daughter as a tool to punish me, and I didn't know it, but they were planting seeds in my daughter's precious innocent mind to turn her against me. When my daughter's dad got word that I was doing so many great things and accomplishing so much and doing so many great things as a single mom, he didn't like that at all and he made sure to put a stop to it.

Things got really bad after that.

During those times, life's challenges got even more surreal. I was navigating through things that I would not wish on anyone. Everyone in my family turned completely against me and used my daughter as a pawn in their war on me simply because I had a spiritual awakening, came into consciousness, and decided that I was not going to live under mind control and toxic, unnatural, and unhealthy patriarchal grooming. I had graduated with a Mastery in Consciousness and decided to walk away from mental, emotional, and spiritual abuse and programming that made me small, made me think that there was something wrong with me, and family programming that made me out to be the ritual scapegoat every time. I decided to use my heart and courage to move away to a different state.

Life completely fell apart during this time. I did not know literally if I was going to live or die or make it out alive during this time. I faced challenges and adversity that I would not wish on anyone, including being homeless and being without a vehicle due to hate crimes on my vehicle. It was during this time that my daughter's dad (my former husband) and my dad went full-on war with me, using my daughter as a pawn in their war. I could not see their mental, emotional, and spiritual illness at the time as I was right in the middle of their war on life and their own seedline and their own family tree.

Through this series of events during this time, I learned that there is a group of males who hate protective and loving mothers and women who think for them Selves, connect to consciousness, and truly listen to their Creator-gifted conscience, and live their life as a true soul, instead of allowing themselves to be groomed and staying programmed and uneducated. I later learned that there is an epidemic of moms who were/are targeted as a parent for being protective of their children and for refusing to live a life of toxic, unhealthy, and unnatural patriarchal grooming. My higher education saved my life; however, I also lost everything in the process of coming back into consciousness and saving my own life.

It was shortly after this time that I was being targeted left and right and doing everything I could to recover from the war on my life from my own dad and my own former husband, I even escaped being entrapped and set up for being traded to the Mexican cartels and that was when my car was destroyed, and I somehow miraculously escaped that with some help from Heaven. It was during this time that I really started to see things for how they are. Women/Mothers started coming to me with their truths of abuse—some of the most horrible things that were even traumatizing for me to hear. Truths of their own husbands molesting their own children and them having to stay silent in fear of being put in a mental institution. Mothers came to me about how their own fathers sexually abused them. Mothers told me how they were punished for being loving and caring mothers and almost put into trafficking situations by their own husbands, just for having a consciousness and standing for what they knew was right. Mothers came to me and told me their survivor stories and started opening up to me from all over the world. Folks started coming to me with their survival stories. It was too much for me at first. It even traumatized me. I thought, "Why me? Why are folks coming to me with this?" I had even spoken with a woman who uncovered all sorts of evil things done to children and her own child, and not long after that, she disappeared. I had deep survivor's guilt during this time.

It was not long after that the door opened for me to earn my bachelor's degree and to become an Ordained Minister. The door for higher/conscious education completely opened, and a stranger came in to support me, making sure that I would not be on the streets and that I had money for food. This stranger became a friend while I was earning my bachelor's degree to become Ordained as a Minister. This stranger honored me as a prophet. This stranger spoke with me as a friend and helped me to process more of what I had endured and what my parents and my former husband put me through. I did not know what was going on. I was always a spiritual child, and as a teenager, I started to go to church on my own. As a teenager at 15, I gave my life to God publically. I was baptized at 16 on my own. My family had come to church with me a few times during this time and became baptized as well, even my grandpa and my second cousin who was living with us for a while. I had always known I had a calling on my life because random people, grown-ups, would come to me when I was a teenager and tell me messages that God had told them for my life and my future. I had known that the Creator had plans for my life and a calling/purpose for my life, but I did not think that it was to become an Ordained Minister after all. One, my parents had always made me believe that I was less, and my family always used me as their ritual scapegoat. Two, my husband never supported me in my calling and purpose, either. Three, I was a GIRL: a female, a daughter, a mother, and a woman. Surely this thing called "God" and "Life" was making a mistake.

During my time of being "homeless" while earning my bachelor's degree, I learned even more about what being strong and resilient meant. It was during this time that I learned I could survive on my own without my "family" or my "husband." I learned that true strength is going within. I learned for my Self that the Creator is within. I started spending more time within, and today, I call it my "body temple practices." By going within, I found my indestructible essence again. I reconnected to my Self as soul. I realized that going within is the Source of renewing my Self, no matter what challenges I face.

Today, as a Single Ordained Minister, I still face many challenges; they haven't gone away. The weight I feel at times because of my oath to serve Life/God sometimes feels too heavy.

I share part and parcel of my life truths on growing in strength to say that we truly can overcome anything. Heaven will send strangers for our aid and safety; at least, that's how it worked for me. Strangers that were not even religious or spiritual have come to my aid. I want to share that tears are very powerful. For me, the most powerful strength I have is to allow my Self to cry. Feeling every emotion on the spectrum is the best actionable step I can give to be able to walk through this life as sacred. Life is not for the faint of heart. Our tears cleanse our souls, renew and restore us, and help see us through. They also connect us deeper to our own divinity. Embracing life's changes and challenges with trust and believing in our Selves is one of the most empowering things we can do.

I hope sharing part of my life truths can be of inspiration and encouragement to you. If you feel guided to connect with me and to learn more, please do.

In Honor of All of Life As Sacred,
Reverend Kerrie D. Stone

Lynsey Mahoskey

Founder of Curated Utah

https://www.linkedin.com/in/lynsey-mahoskey/
https://www.facebook.com/curatedutah
https://www.instagram.com/curatedutah/
https://www.curatedutah.com/

Meet Lynsey, your go-to Fractional CMO. As the CEO of Curated Utah, Lynsey helps parent-preneurs navigate the world of marketing while keeping their family front and center. She's a mom of two boys who knows how to juggle life's curveballs—whether that's helping clients hit their business goals or cheering from the sidelines.

Lynsey is all about creating simple marketing strategies that drive results without the overwhelm and time-suck of having to spend hours and hours marketing.

She believes in marketing that's real and authentic, making sure businesses don't have to choose between scaling their business and living their best lives. Lynsey is here to help entrepreneurs WIN without sacrificing who they are or what they stand for. When she's not hosting events or helping her clients, you'll find her at the ball field with her boys or sneaking in some binge-worthy TV.

My Journey to Purpose: Finding Strength in Truth and Transformation

By Lynsey Mahoskey

We often hear about people's "rock bottom" moment as the one defining moment that changed everything. For me, it felt like a series of them—moments where the weight of despair threatened to pull me under. Each one left its mark, shaping the woman I've become, but none of them truly defined me. Instead, they became stepping stones, forcing me to confront truths I'd hidden from and find strength in places that I never thought to look. My journey to purpose wasn't a straight path; it was a messy, winding road paved with heartbreak, resilience, and the unrelenting desire to live authentically.

The first time I truly felt the weight of hopelessness, I was just a teenager. I often sat alone in my room, suffocated by the belief that the world would be better off without me. I formulated plan after plan to leave it all behind until one day, I came so close to completing one of those plans that I can still feel the heaviness of that moment to this day—slowly blacking out, the sounds around me deafening as I slipped out of consciousness. The silence that consumed me was only shattered by the sound of my best friend sobbing over me. She shook me until I slowly opened my eyes, confused and clammy. I'd like to say that it was at that moment that I realized I wasn't just fighting for my life, but for the people who cared about me. But I was the broody teenager with the world against her and no one she could trust. Though that moment didn't erase the pain, it planted the seed of something new: a determination to rebuild, to start fresh, and to find my place in the world.

Looking back, the years after my darkest moment during my sophomore year were a whirlwind of reinvention and rebellion. I pulled back from the circle of friends I once leaned on for support, and I was determined to carve out a new path for myself. I immersed myself in school and learned a new trade, and while I was not academically stellar, I managed to earn enough credentials and a certification. I managed to leave school an entire semester early and work my way into freedom. But the distance I created wasn't just physical—it was emotional. I became colder, sharper, and less willing to let anyone in. I was a selfish bitch. I still hung out with some of the same crowd and even made new friends, but my walls were up, and I wasn't afraid to let the world feel it.

On my 18th birthday, I marked my newfound freedom with a tattoo and moved out just a few months later. I was working 60-plus hours a week, smoking, and living on the fumes of independence. The only time I came home was to walk across the stage for my diploma and occasionally bowl in my parents' bowling league. By late summer, though, the weight of it all started to settle in. I moved back into my parents' house, took a step back from the grind of my overbearing job, and started a seasonal position that led me almost two hours away. It was during this shuffle, at the end of October, that I met my now-husband in that bowling league I was in with my parents. He was older, like a lot older, hot as hell, and he was just as much of a closed-off asshole as me. He was perfect, and it freaked out my family, so that was a bonus.

Our connection was unexpected but immediate. While our relationship caused its fallouts and had its challenges, after just a few months, in January 2012, I moved in with him, back closer to my hometown. By this time, my parents had warmed to him, and clearly, so did I. Oh hell, I was straight up in love with the dude. Head over heels, I met my match. And by the end of that year, we found out I was pregnant—just one year into our relationship. It wasn't the storybook timeline, but it was the start of a new chapter I never saw coming.

Motherhood and Finding Connection

Becoming a mother at twenty wasn't in my plans, but life has a way of surprising you when you least expect it. My "oops" baby was a beautiful, squirming bundle of joy, but underneath the love I felt for him, a shadow grew. Postpartum depression hit me like a storm I wasn't prepared for. Despite having a supportive system around me, I felt lonelier than I ever had, trapped in a cycle of exhaustion, guilt, and the nagging thought that I wasn't enough.

Money was tight—so tight that even the idea of finding professional help felt like a luxury we couldn't afford. So I turned to the only place I could: the internet. Late nights were spent scrolling through Pinterest and reading blogs from other moms who seemed to understand exactly what I was feeling. Their words gave me a lifeline, a small sense of connection in a world that felt increasingly isolating.

It wasn't just about consuming content, though. I started sharing my story, writing out my thoughts and experiences, hoping that someone, somewhere, might feel less alone. In those moments, my first real taste of community began to take shape. The internet became more than just a distraction—it became a source of hope and healing. Slowly, I started to find myself again, piecing together the person I was before the fog of depression set in.

Separation and Rediscovery

In 2019, everything fell apart—AGAIN. After raising our son for a few years, my husband and I finally got married in August 2016. While I was over the moon about our marriage, and we had a lot of great years, my husband and I decided to separate. Well, I decided. He was completely blindsided by my decision. Yes, we had been fighting, but my husband is not the guy who gives up, so when I said I wanted a divorce and that I was moving out, I rocked his entire world and turned it upside down. For the first time since I was 19, I was on my own again.

Moving out of our shared home was one of the hardest things I've ever done. I bounced between my mom's house and my brother's, trying to figure out how to make ends meet without the dual income we'd relied on for so long. Financially, I was stretched thin. Emotionally, I was drained. So when my husband suggested marriage counseling, the guilt of leaving and the idea of going back to safe grounds convinced me to give it a try.

By then, I'd built a small following online as an "influencer," but most of the work I was doing was unpaid or in exchange for free products. I hustled hard, trying to turn that budding platform into something that could actually be something. It wasn't glamorous, but it gave me a sense of purpose. Slowly, I started to see the power of my voice and my ability to connect with others through my content.

When my husband and I chose to rekindle our relationship, it wasn't an easy decision. We both had to unlearn old patterns, face hard truths, and choose to rebuild together. We chose to reforge our family and even add to it with a new bundle of joy. Yes, seven years after our first. Our relationship grew and was stronger than ever, but so was I! By the time we welcomed our second child, I felt like a different person—stronger, more self-aware, and ready to face whatever came next.

But motherhood comes with its own challenges. I had braced myself for postpartum depression again, but what I didn't expect was postpartum rage. The intensity of my emotions scared me at times, but this time, I was better equipped. I had access to resources, a stellar support system, and the courage to seek professional help without hesitation. Those moments weren't easy, but they taught me an important lesson: Asking for help doesn't make you weak—it makes you resilient.

Each step of this journey, from the heartbreak of separation to the joy and chaos of reconciliation, pushed me closer to understanding my purpose. It wasn't just about surviving anymore—it was about thriving, about finding strength in the cracks and growing into the woman I was meant to be.

Struggling in the Shadows

From the outside, I looked like someone on the rise. I was still getting brand deals as an influencer and I had joined a brand new network marketing company as a brand ambassador. I was sharing wins, showing up consistently, and trying to build something meaningful. But the truth was, I felt like a fraud. My feed wasn't perfectly polished like other influencers, my achievements weren't groundbreaking, and every success felt dwarfed by the people around me who seemed to have it all together. Everyone else around me was growing faster, earning more, and shining brighter. No matter how hard I worked, it felt like I would never measure up.

By February 2022, the weight of it all became unbearable. I wasn't just tired—I was drained, defeated, and drowning in comparison. My business, which I had poured everything into, wasn't bringing in what I needed. Every dollar I earned went right back into it, and still, I couldn't keep up. The pressure to succeed collided with the belief that I wasn't good enough, and for the first time since 2011, the darkness crept back in. The freight train of self-doubt hit me full force, dragging along thoughts I thought I had left behind: *You're failing. You'll never be enough. Maybe it's time to give up.*

Desperate to find a way forward, I reached out to a life coach. I wasn't even sure what I was looking for—direction, clarity, maybe just someone to help me breathe again. I went in hoping for a guide but wasn't prepared for what she suggested. "Why don't you help others the way I'm helping you?" she asked. I laughed out loud. *Help others? Me?* I could barely keep myself afloat. The idea seemed absurd.

But the seed was planted, and as I worked through my own breakthroughs and began piecing myself back together, I couldn't ignore the pull. Maybe I didn't need to have it all figured out to help someone else take their first steps. Slowly, I started to believe that my story—the mess, the lessons, the resilience—could be enough. I became a confidence and clarity coach, focusing on helping moms prioritize themselves and build lives that felt meaningful. I encouraged them to embrace self-care and put their needs first, something I was still learning to do myself.

Becoming a certified breakthrough coach felt like a milestone, but the real breakthroughs came in the work. I noticed that my clients weren't just looking for personal clarity; they wanted to step into their power online. They wanted to share their stories, build their presence, and connect authentically with their audiences through social media. The more I guided them, the more I saw where my true calling might be.

Quietly, I dreamed about pivoting into business coaching. But the voice in my head—the one that constantly whispered *you're not good enough*—was deafening. How could I coach others to grow their businesses when mine felt so fragile? The doubt loomed large, but the spark had been lit. For the first time, I could see the possibility of a future where I wasn't just surviving—I was helping others thrive.

The Weight of Loss and the Wake-Up Call

November 2022 was a month I will never forget, a month that changed me in ways I never could have anticipated. I was two hours away from home at a retreat, trying to refocus and recharge. My mom was supposed to be with my kids while my husband was off at a bowling tournament. My sister was unavailable due to work, and my other closest sibling was also out of town with his family. I thought I was safe, removed, and just focused on myself and my business when I got the call. I had no idea that my world was about to shatter. My dad had taken his life.

The grief was unbearable, but so was the guilt. My dad knew we weren't close enough to intervene. He knew that none of us would be able to reach him in time, and in his mind, he was alone. Those thoughts—the ones that still haunted me from my struggles with depression years ago—came rushing back. I had thought I'd buried them, but now I could see clearly just how deeply they had influenced my life, how much I had tried to forget that moment in my own history when I had almost given in to the same feelings of hopelessness.

I knew the feelings my dad must have carried—the overwhelming weight of depression, the hopelessness that convinced him the world would be better off without him. And I hated that those lies won. I hated the stigmas that kept him—and so many others—from seeking the help they needed. The shame, the fear, the belief that reaching out would make him weak, unworthy of love, or worse—judged by those closest to him. It wasn't just my dad who had suffered in silence. It was a whole generation—many others too afraid to reach out for help. And I felt that grief and rage in every inch of my being.

It wasn't enough to mourn his loss and feel sorrow. I had a burning rage inside me, a fire to break the silence, to be a voice for people who felt just like he did, who felt just like I had once felt. This was a wake-up call like no other. His death wasn't just the loss of a father, a man I had loved; it was a catalyst for a new purpose—one that fueled me to live fully and unapologetically.

I couldn't let my dad's story be one of just sadness and regret. I couldn't let his death be in vain. In his passing, I found my purpose: to live. Not just to exist, but to thrive, to make a difference, and to be a voice that would never let someone feel like they were alone in the darkness. I knew I had to honor his memory by fighting against the stigmas that nearly cost us both our lives, and I would do it with everything I had.

This loss propelled me forward in ways I never imagined. It ignited a drive in me to chase my dreams, to pursue my purpose, and to live fully, with no regrets. I would no longer let fear hold me back. I would no longer let doubt and shame take root. What happened next—how I took that anger and grief and turned it into action—is the story of how I found my true calling, and it began with making the decision to live for myself, for my family, and for everyone who struggles in silence.

From Doubt to Defying the Odds

Fueled by grief and an emerging sense of purpose, I knew I had to make a change. My dad's passing ignited a fire within me—one that demanded I stop holding back. I knew deep down that he would have wanted me to follow my passions, so I took a leap of faith. I began the transition from Confidence Coach to becoming a Social Media Coach. With my background and personal experiences, I felt uniquely positioned to help women show up confidently online and teach them how to leverage the tools available to them.

I loved it. Every fiber of my being knew this was the right direction. But imposter syndrome hit hard, feeding me doubts: I didn't have enough followers, I didn't have formal training in marketing, and I hadn't "proven" myself yet. My coach even warned me against jumping in too soon, suggesting I focus on smaller goals or stick to coaching. But I couldn't shake the feeling that I was meant for more. In September 2023, I ignored her advice, trusted my instincts, and launched my social media agency anyway.

The challenges came fast and furious. Financial stress, long hours, and moments of doubt hit me hard. There were days I questioned everything, wondering if I'd made a huge mistake. But with every small win, with every new client success story, I felt more validated. I was seeing results, my network grew, and I continually felt like I was exactly where I needed to be. However, things took a personal turn. My once-trusted business coach, who had guided me for so long, started to undermine me. Her words grew colder, her actions more distant. It felt like I was outgrowing her, and the relationship turned toxic. After working with her for over a year and enduring her narcissism, we had a falling out in December 2023, and I had to make the painful decision to cut her out of my life and my business.

Despite the backlash and anger that followed, I refused to let it deter me. I chose to focus on myself, my passion, and the community I was building. By September 2024, it became clear that my agency had outgrown its original vision, and I once again rebranded my agency, but this time into a full-service digital marketing agency, offering more than just social media coaching and management.

A Story Still Unfolding

While I have every intention to continue growing my marketing agency—after all, it's my baby and my passion—I'm not stopping there. I want to do more, to help more, and to reach beyond just business success. The core purpose of my agency has always been to create connections, and now I feel called to take everything I've endured—every peak, every valley—and pour it into something even greater: helping others live, thrive, and, most importantly, stay alive.

Through it all, one truth has remained constant: My story is my greatest strength. Whether I'm helping a business owner find their voice online, a family become financially secure, or advocating for mental health awareness, I've come to understand that vulnerability is the bridge that connects us all. Sharing my journey—from the struggles of motherhood to the heartbreak of loss—has created a ripple effect of hope and encouragement. Today, my work isn't just about social media strategies or business growth. It's about empowering people to embrace their stories, to live authentically, and to know they're not alone. It's about breaking down the stigmas surrounding mental health and reminding others—especially fellow moms and entrepreneurs—that it's okay to ask for help, to pivot, and to start over when necessary.

My journey to purpose hasn't been linear or easy, but it's been worth every twist and turn. If you take one thing from my story, let it be this: You are capable of transforming pain into purpose. You are worthy of living a life that lights you up. And no matter where you are right now, the best chapters of your story are still waiting to be written.

Maureen Byers, GRI, MRE

Real Estate Broker, Investor, Consultant & Visionary

https://www.linkedin.com/in/maureen-b-63938997
https://www.facebook.com/share/1AxVaGqnER/
https://www.instagram.com/byersmaureen
https://wa.me/+18584137887
https://maureenbyers.com/
https://www.tiktok.com/@renalandangel?_t=ZP-8tfoqlZ6BeY&_r=1

Maureen Byers is a pioneering force in Colorado, Arizona, and California real estate. Starting as a single mother relying on assistance, she transformed her life into that of a successful broker, investor, and entrepreneur. With an advanced education and extensive experience facilitating high-value real estate transactions, Maureen specializes in commercial investment, creative financing, and property development. As a 1031 tax-deferred exchanger and seller financing expert, she skillfully navigates complex transactions for a global clientele. Her entrepreneurial spirit led her to establish a brokerage where she has represented and supported aspiring real estate professionals. Maureen's approach combines hard work with innovative strategies she learned along her journey, allowing her to embrace her uniqueness and authenticity. She believes true achievement is not just measured by financial milestones but by the ability to inspire others and help them reach their goals. Today, Maureen leads a vibrant real estate investment network dedicated to empowering individuals in their pursuit of financial independence.

Women Grow Stronger: Building a Legacy Through Real Estate

By Maureen Byers, GRI, MRE

*"Real estate is more than just transactions;
it's about building relationships and transforming lives."*
—Maureen Byers, GRI, MRE

My only son was in school as a minority, practicing martial arts and taking guitar lessons, and I was attending dance lessons, running, and had a couple of girlfriends, partying and clubbing while going to college. It was the first freedom and independent living I had in my entire life, and the freedom felt amazing. I was modeling, always working, and studying. The boyfriend that I had, who was puppy love, came back into my life. He was in real estate and had made $30,000 in one summer. His dad and his dad's friend had a brokerage and were licensed. They were going down to Mexico to get opals and sell them, and their office was in the historical May D&F huge warehouse in downtown Denver, which is now LoDo, full of very expensive condos, apartments, and retail.

I thought, "Why am I doing this in college and working so hard while struggling financially?" I had to get assistance, and I was tired of it—tired of hustling and not making ends meet, while also having to order medicine from the back of magazines and selling it at the salon up the street for weight loss. It was really hard. So, I decided that in talking to my older brother, who had always been there for me and helped me, even though he teased me, I felt like he could change my energy and get me out of this sadness caused by my mother being mean to me.

His teasing, which I didn't appreciate growing up, made me laugh and helped me realize that I could bounce back. This was part of understanding how the way someone else makes you feel—especially if they are a mother figure or someone you love—can influence your life. I went back and forth between the comfort of my brother and the challenges posed by my mother.

That break and space they created for me changed my energy. I learned how to start over, whether it was going out to eat, shopping, or taking a trip. I cherished moments like riding on the back of my brother's motorcycle or going for a bike ride. Those breaks from pain and suffering reignited my self-love and taught me the importance of self-care.

Years later, I flipped a coin after my brother asked what I wanted to do: gemology or real estate. Real estate won. He paid for my courses, and instead of working for two years to become a broker, there was an option to obtain a degree in real estate through a two-year program at the University of Colorado at Boulder. I took that path, and my brother split the costs with my current boyfriend, who also wanted to marry me.

While I appreciated the relationship, I desired the satisfaction of making money and being successful for myself and my son. As I focused on studying and passing exams to get my license, I became one of the youngest licensed brokers in Colorado.

When I graduated, I was disappointed to find that my family wasn't particularly interested in my accomplishments. They had their own commitments, and only my brother celebrated my achievement as he started his own commercial electric company. I helped him by becoming his real estate broker, and he became my first client. He always had faith in me, and I realized that sometimes we need just one person to believe in us.

I transitioned to work for a commercial investment brokerage after successfully selling land that summer. I got off assistance and became a commercial investment real estate broker. There was only one other woman in my department, and I quickly established myself among a team of men. I loved the competition and worked hard, often putting in 80-hour weeks.

During this time, I faced personal challenges. I had to entrust my son to his father temporarily, but when I realized he wasn't taking good care of him, I acted quickly to retrieve him. I focused on my career but was determined to balance my responsibilities as a young mother.

I began to explore motivational speaking events and mentorship, which became pivotal in my growth. Learning from renowned coaches and investing in my personal development changed my life. I encountered challenges negotiating transactions and learned the importance of standing firm in my worth.

As I immersed myself in real estate, I used my earnings to purchase a vehicle and, eventually, my first home, where my son and I could build our lives together. I loved decorating my space and finally felt a sense of stability.

After months of searching, I found a property in Englewood, Colorado, advertised as an estate sale. I negotiated with the executrix and had an opportunity to implement my knowledge of how to leverage financing options, such as seller financing, and present a rezoning proposal through the city effectively. My late brother and I collaborated on several projects, sharing resources and navigating the complexities of real estate together.

Unfortunately, in the business world, trust can sometimes be misplaced. We had shared a bookkeeper who embezzled $100,000 from us, a painful lesson that taught me the importance of overseeing my own finances. However, I continued to broker, invest, and finance development projects in remote areas which may be isolating, with limited amenities nearby. I embraced the challenges and continued my original marketing plan having clients often traveling great distances to connect with me and secure properties of their dreams.

Among my favorite experiences was taking my mother and sister along the Million Dollar Highway to Telluride—a seasonal breathtaking drive filled with stunning fall views that served as a reminder of my family's roots. I discovered that my great-uncle had played a significant role in the development of the area, which instilled a sense of pride and connection to my family's legacy in real estate.

The development I worked on spanned 2,200 acres, surrounded by 3.5 million acres of public land. As a female broker in a male-dominated industry, I took pride in my accomplishments, showing clients the beauty of the Colorado mountains and navigating the challenges of working in a small town filled with wildlife.

If I had to do it all over again, I would prioritize delegating tasks. Learning to let go of control has been a journey, but it's essential as we grow older and take on more responsibilities. In my community, I sought to give back, launching initiatives like a beauty pageant and a college fund for our respective clientele. My brother and I financed individuals with poor credit or those who had faced bankruptcy, empowering them to build homes and create stability in their lives.

Real estate is more than just transactions; it's about building relationships and transforming lives. I found joy in matching clients with properties that resonated with them, understanding that the emotional connection is just as crucial as the financial aspect. My love for this field has only deepened over the years, and I've remained committed to empowering all people with an emphasis on women investors with my energy, experience, education, and expertise, whether as a partner or investor in defaults nationally, including broker representation in Arizona, California, and Colorado in almost all types of the real estate serving a global clientele for a half-century in real estate.

I host weekly meetings with investors, mostly women, offering collaboration and presentations, and attend a monthly local coastal women real estate investors meeting up in Southern California, offering free consulting and sharing valuable insights. The sense of community among these women is uplifting, and I take pride in witnessing their growth as they transition from corporate jobs to becoming entrepreneurs and investors. Each success story fills my heart with joy, reaffirming that real estate can be a vehicle for change and opportunity.

Through my experiences, I have learned that education alone is not enough; it's about taking action and having a vision. The journey of investing in real estate is filled with ups and downs, but the rewards of helping others find their homes, businesses, and investment properties and create legacies for their families are immeasurable. I trust in the power of movement—growing a family, embracing new opportunities, and adapting to life's changes.

I have always been passionate about flipping and buying and holding, whether they are unfurnished or furnished long-term, mid-term, or short-term co-living rentals, multigenerational, or assisted living. My heart lies in industrial real estate, where I enjoy working with business-minded tenants. I love the thrill of flipping land, which offers endless possibilities and flexibility.

Throughout my career, I have built lasting friendships with clients and witnessed their transformational journeys evolve over generations. The referrals I receive are a testament to the trust and connection we've established.

In every aspect of my work, I emphasize the importance of empowering women. I have guided countless men, women, entries, groups, and companies through the process of leasing, financing, entrepreneurship, and property ownership and investments. Many have come to me feeling overwhelmed, but I help them navigate the complexities of financing and investing by providing inventory and consultation.

As I continue to lead my women's real estate investment network, I remain dedicated to fostering a supportive environment where everyone can thrive. I believe that by sharing our experiences and knowledge, we can uplift each other and create a brighter future for ourselves and our families.

In conclusion, my journey through real estate has been transformative and, filled with challenges and triumphs. I have learned to embrace the lessons that come with each experience and to cherish the connections I've made along the way. Real estate is not just a profession; it is a passion that allows me to impact lives, create opportunities, and foster a sense of community. I encourage everyone to pursue their dreams, take risks, and empower others along the way.

As we embark on this journey of growth and empowerment with She Rises, I warmly invite you to connect with me. If you are a woman investor, whether novice or experienced, looking to cultivate meaningful partnerships or explore opportunities in real estate ownership, small business ventures, or entrepreneurial pursuits, this is your opportunity. With almost half a century of experience serving a global clientele, along with my advanced education and professional licenses, I specialize in creating small, strategically leveraged investments across various types of real estate. Together, we can build connections rooted in trust and collaboration. If this resonates with you, please reach out at oceansidemaureen@gmail.com or visit sherisesstudios.com. Let's cultivate a future filled with success and opportunities in the realm of real estate and beyond.

Meghan Skrepenski

Balanced 4 Life
Health Coach & Wellness Specialist

https://www.linkedin.com/in/meghanskrepenski/
https://www.facebook.com/MeghanSkrepenski
https://www.instagram.com/fitmama_balanced4life/
https://www.balanced4life.org/

Meghan Skrepenski is a health and wellness professional focused on health coaching, personal training and behavior change; she also incorporates leadership training and organizational development with specialized business and personalized wellness plans. She has a background in physical and health education and worked as a licensed Physical Therapist Assistant. She is currently certified as a personal trainer, health coach and behavior change coach, as well as a yoga teacher. Meghan excels in promoting physical, mental, and spiritual wellness through dynamic and engaging training sessions. All of her training focuses on enhancing physical strength, mental clarity, and incorporating mindfulness and relaxation techniques like breathwork, while performing physical or mental exercises that create an inclusive environment, fostering personal growth and development. Meghan believes finding balance in life is vital, and enjoys healthy habits like paddleboarding, swimming and biking, she is a firm believer in savoring time daily with family, friends and fun.

Be Still and Know

By Meghan Skrepenski

"Be still and know…" The phrase played over and over in my head as I struggled to be still and just breathe. My chest was tight, my head pounding. I slowly came to the realization that I hadn't breathed deeply and just hadn't been still and present in my brain and body for months. Throughout my time in a foreign country that wasn't always welcoming to females, to the military, or to those in powerful positions, I had pushed everything to the back of my mind and gone on autopilot. And mindfulness and breathwork (although I was aware of these nuances) were not programmed into my psyche as a part of being on autopilot. So, I held my breath and just hoped to come out on the other side ok.

To say my nervous system was rattled was an understatement; I was constantly on high alert, having to be conscious of my environment and yet still caring for others— at all times, ready to run for cover, as the buzz of planes and drones overhead was also a constant in life. A constant noise but not always a threat, just a protective measure; however, someone needed to tell that to my already frayed mental state, as I couldn't dare relax. As I averaged roughly four hours of sleep each night, the lack of sleep also became a constant during this phase of life. My body was at its wit's end: combining the stress plus the lack of sleep, with walking 10 miles a day or more, and then instead of resting, I decided to beat my body up even more with a daily workout, constantly moving with High-Intensity Interval Training (HIIT) or running workouts. I couldn't bring myself to slow down, breathe, and just be still, as I knew was required in mindfulness, meditation, and yoga, which I had practiced frequently, prior to leaving the life I had known behind.

A war zone was not the place for any of that! Nor was there really a good place to do yoga, as nearly every surface had a solid coating of silty sand covering it, including the floors and even the equipment in the gyms.

Damn, did I hate the dust and dirt; if I never saw another desert, I would die happy. I dreamed of green grass, quiet mountainsides, shady forests, and still open water, and I yearned for the sounds of nature instead of the constant rumbling of generators and motors. I wanted nothing more than the dark and quiet in the comfort of my own space again.

I dreamt of the light, as I actually lived and slept in constant quiet and darkness in my tent, which was designed for those who worked both day and night shifts, so it was designated a 24-7 dark/quiet zone. I never saw it with the lights on inside, nor had a conversation inside that tent until the day that we all left. I worked the night shift, effectively staying away from the light. That darkness was a lonely existence. Still to this day, I am thankful for the people in my life who checked in on me daily, who knew the hardships I was facing, who would allow me to vent without judgment, because damn was it dark and lonely there, especially in the role that I played.

I went days without real, meaningful conversations, without anyone asking if I was doing okay, and wanting to really hear the answer…and the threads that were barely holding my life back home together continued to unravel. I finally realized that I could no longer live in a space where the person who was supposed to love me and care for me the most made me feel so terribly alone. The tears running down my face then, as they are now, made me feel desolate, and it was clear that a change had to happen, as the sense of knowing became steady and true.

"Be still and know" is most often quoted as a verse of the Bible, but I was finally able to apply it to myself, just being able to still the world that was tumbling out of control all around me. I leaned into the knowing and confided in my therapist and friends and journaled my truth. I knew finally what I needed, and I stepped into my power as I demanded changes made upon my return, knowing that this would possibly be the hardest and possibly the bravest thing that I ever had to do in all of my life.

I finally returned home months later, broken and battered in both my body and mind. My mind was constantly at war, my gaze sweeping the horizon, no longer able to enjoy large crowds and noisy environments, yet being still in the peaceful quiet was also a foreign concept to me. I couldn't calm my fight-or-flight response and the physical and mental response that my body constantly faced because of this. All of this manifested into migraine headaches, which I incessantly fought to find the cause of.

I tried it all: acupuncture, chiropractic care, physical therapy, traditional over-the-counter prescription medications, yet nothing made my head stop pounding. I read the book, *The Body Keeps the Score: Brain, Mind and Body in the Healing of Trauma* by Bessel van der Kolk, and realized now that I had been fighting my body for too long, and I needed to embrace the quiet and the slowness and really address the traumas that I had faced. Yet, in the midst of all of this, there was still so little support, but then as the pain became off-putting, it was seen as an excuse to not be in the family environment. The aches were seen as a cover-up for the true feelings brewing under the surface. And finally, at this point, I realized I had to change or continue to feel the pain.

The constant alert state had to be turned off… I returned to my yoga mat wholeheartedly, showing up for me, finally. Once on my mat, the saying continued in my head, "Be still and know," and as this ran through my mind, I lay there, tears streaming down my face, breathing deep and knowing that I could do big, scary, hard things. I had the power in me to make a change. I had always had the power, and I just had to step into that power and take that first step to move towards the unknown and finally find balance. With this knowledge and understanding, I finally stood tall and breathed a sigh of relief.

"She believed she could, so she did," then became a daily quote running through my mind over the next year. I tattooed this phrase onto my foot (along with the phoenix rising) the day after my divorce was finalized. A symbol of walking away from what no longer serves me, and a symbol of rising from the ashes to soar; I use this temporary pain of the tattoo to remind me that I can do anything I believe I can do. Finally, I now sit in quiet and meditate frequently; the peace I find in the stillness is a feeling I love to embrace, that all is just as it should be because I learned how to "be still and know."

I ask that you would also slow down and listen to that little voice that says to take big, scary action so that you can truly find peace, love, and happiness in the life that you choose to live wholeheartedly. I invite you in this moment to be still and know, you will find your way if you believe and take action.

3 Action Steps for You to Be Still and Know How to Step Into Your Power!

1. Your power lies in self-love and acceptance, in the understanding that deep down and in the stillness, YOU really do know what you need. Your desires are not silly or stupid but big, bold, and beautiful, and when you bring them to the light, you will know and speak your truth, to voice the dreams that you have, to voice experiences that you have had, and to finally understand you're not alone in the hardships that you have faced. I promise there are understanding and empathetic listeners out there who want to hear you and support your journey to healing.

2. Bring your needs and desires to the light by focusing on you— do the things that allow you to live and thrive in your truth. Do the things that light your soul on fire. Dance, sing, create, get out in nature, or spend time with friends... Getting to a place where you are also OK to just be by yourself and to truly be yourself will allow you to feel so much lighter and freer in who you are.

3. Finally, live in the light: This is a sacred space where your peace, joy, and love are of utmost importance, and you do the things

that make you feel in alignment with those goals to feel loved and supported as much as possible, in all aspects of your life. Surround yourself with people, places or things that bring you joy, and at the very least, do one thing daily that cultivates peace, love, and joy in your life.

Coming from a place of utter chaos in my life, to the peace that I chose for myself when I stepped into my truth. I began to breathe deeply again, and I was finally able to be still and to know that I would be okay again, as long as I could love myself, no matter my past, and then I learned to share that love and acceptance with others. I can promise you that finding your peace and calm in the midst of a storm will also help you find your mantra and live your truth.

My wish for you is that you will find peace, love, and joy in your life. I hope that you will live a long, healthy, and happy life and that you'll find a peaceful place to feel grounded and free to just let go, to breathe and be still, and to know that you are loved so that true joy may be yours abundantly. Finally, step into your power; there is no one else in this world who can offer what you can, so embrace that strength and move forward in big ways. I believe you got this, and deep down, you know it too, so be still and know, breathe deep, and embrace the journey all along the way.

In Love and Light,
~Meghan

Michelle Gill

Founder of Change Hypnosis

Michelle Gill is an Advanced Clinical Hypnotherapist, Coach, Neuro Change Practitioner and Beauty Coach, specializing in empowering women through transformative healing and personal growth. With a profound commitment to helping women heal from relationship trauma and rebuild their lives. Michelle has dedicated her career to the art of nurturing inner strength and fostering resilience. She is also a passionate women's empowerment coach, utilizing innovative techniques in hypnosis and neuro change to guide women toward reclaiming their inherent worth and embracing their full potential. Her work is driven by a deep belief in the transformative power of education, encouragement, and personal awareness knowledge. She aims to inspire women to thrive in love and life without losing their true selves. Her approach is not just about healing—it's about thriving, reflecting her holistic view of wellness and empowerment.

Dear New Victim: The Survivor of Your Narcissist

By Michelle Gill

It's strange how clarity comes in waves, each one crashing over you with a new, painful truth. For six and a half years, I was entangled in what I now recognize as a toxic dance. But for those final ten weeks, the veil lifted, and I saw my partner—the covert narcissist—for what he truly was. This chapter is not just about those last weeks of our relationship. It's about the emotional labyrinth I navigated while grappling with betrayal, deceit, and the slow realization of the man I thought I knew. And it is for you, dear new victim, who stands where I once stood, unaware of what lies ahead.

The Charm That Binds

When I first met him, he seemed like the answer to every silent prayer. His charm was constant (love bombing stage). His adoration was genuine (idealization). I was placed on a pedestal so high even I couldn't see it. He noticed things about me that no one else did and made me feel safe in a way I hadn't experienced before. He mirrored my dreams, my fears, and my joys so perfectly that I thought I had found my soulmate. But now, looking back, I realize it wasn't a connection; it was a calculation.

He made me feel special, unique, irreplaceable. That's their hook, isn't it? The covert narcissist is no roaring lion; they're the quiet predator, wrapping you in a web of admiration and devotion until you're too entangled to escape.

The Cracks Begin to Show

The first cracks in the facade were subtle. The fact that he had bipolar disorder certainly didn't help the matter; in fact, it made everything all the more confusing for me because I attributed much of his toxic behavior and mood swings to it. The way he spoke about women made it clear he didn't respect them, which he put down to past exes who had betrayed him.

There was the way he always had to be right, the way he'd spend hours in his office yet achieve very little. He wouldn't let me go near his bank account statements and always seemed to need to stop on the way home, sitting in his car to make phone calls to clients—calls he could have made in ten minutes at home. His nightly 40-minute bathroom visits with his phone. A dismissive comment here, a defensive comment there.

When I voiced my concerns, he'd immediately become defensive, gaslight me, and say, "That's not what I said," turning my intuition into insecurity.

I learned to bury my needs, convinced he was turning into something that wasn't coming back. The love bombing I'd once basked in became intermittent, replaced by bouts of manic chatter or sullen mood swings and control disguised as care. He was a master of ambiguity, keeping me off-balance with gaslighting, justifications, and conversations that would go on for hours until I got to the point of agreeing with him just to shut him up. His need to control the narrative, be right all the time, and be the center of attention, requiring constant validation, was becoming an irritation, and I was losing respect. And still, I stayed.

The Last Ten Weeks of Revelation

The lengthy discard was both shattering and illuminating.

I found his spare phone charging under two strategically placed socks—further proof of his unending betrayal. His lies, meticulously crafted over the years, unraveled in an instant. I confronted him, expecting remorse or at least an explanation. What I got instead was gaslighting: "You're imagining things." "You're crazy." "If you weren't so paranoid, this wouldn't be an issue." He claimed, "I'm just using it to take work videos." So why did he feel the need to hide this phone? More denial. Apparently, when you kick off your socks, they magically fly through the air and land perfectly flat, side by side, on top of your phone under the bed—yeah, right.

Insulting my intelligence wasn't winning him any favors. I realized that the pattern of cheating I had uncovered the year before had not ceased, despite his promises. I came to the painful understanding that the person I loved had a problem that had nothing to do with me. In fact, it existed long before me and would persist long after me.

It was the beginning of the end. The lack of accountability, the gaslighting, and the utter deceit—without any remorse or regret for his behavior—was mind-boggling and deeply concerning to me. Just 12 months earlier, I had discovered all his passwords for the numerous dating sites he was on. These profiles featured my face cropped out and used the same bio he had written on the Bumble dating app to land a date with me six years ago. "Stick with what works," he must have been thinking.

I had to leave the family home that we had moved into only 1.5 years earlier after uprooting nine of us from one island to the other to start a new life. We separated temporarily, intending to work on our personal and couples therapy and aim for reconciliation in the new year. By week seven, I abandoned our couples therapy sessions and the relationship. He was using our sessions to punish me for leaving (to deflect from his cheating disorder), typically monopolizing the entire hour with his childish antics and rages.

Apparently, the worst thing you can say to a covert narcissist is, "I see you now," and then leaving them creates a narcissistic injury from which they don't recover well without a healthy amount of rage and hatred toward you. This is when the smear campaign started. How dare I leave him, all he did was cheat multiple times, and I deserved it because I drank too much 5 years ago during the COVID lockdown! Yes, he had been holding a grudge, or was he just picking something, anything to magnify and fixate on? I was receiving my rewards, and the final discard was imminent. He just had to breadcrumb me along with some healthy mental abuse until he'd lured in his next victim.

I didn't have to wait long. By week two of our official separation, he was already madly in love with someone new. I discovered this by walking in on them in the family home, where he had brought her for "coffee."

I had suspected that he had little interest in reconciliation. He knew that I had seen his true face, and for someone like him, that meant he had to discard me. But I never imagined it could get worse—much worse.

One night, before my departure, there was a physical altercation. He was intimidating me, getting in my face. I pressed my forehead against his and said, "So, you want to hit me? Go on, then—hit me!" I didnt back down, far from it. He said if I'd been a man, I'd be dead! Where did my strength come from, I don't know, but I've never backed down in a fight, and I wasn't about to start even if it meant I'd die that night. The way he spun me around and violently shoved me out the door, and told me to f*** off out of *his* house was an eye-opener for both of us, though likely not for the same reasons. Neither of us was at our best, but it was shocking to see how low we could sink in just a matter of weeks. It had never escalated to anything close to that point before. It was as if he no longer cared. Even the way he spoke to me had changed; it was like he hated me.

He later said something broke in him that night. I wonder if he realized that he would never be able to control me, he'd lost control, and the game was up. He could never return to the mask for comfort and deceit; the demon had been revealed.

And in his mind, I deserved all of this... because I had left him. Now it was time to set up his smear campaign so that no one would believe me when I told my story.

She Grows Stronger | 123

At least three weeks before I had confirmation in my face, I already sensed it was happening. I already knew before I caught him out that I was never going back. And... I was right. When you know, you know!

I knew immediately that the Lord didn't bring me here to *not* see what I saw. He knew without my seeing it, I was at risk of being gaslit. I needed to see with my own eyes the level of deceit I was dealing with. And now? I cannot unsee how I see him. He is the weed that keeps growing no matter what crack it's in. Looking for distraction and comfort from his shame, guilt, and childhood trauma.

In those last ten weeks, I witnessed the full arsenal of his manipulation techniques: blame-shifting, stonewalling, more cheating, lies, future faking, breadcrumbing, triangulation, smear campaigns, and coercion disguised as love. He'd love-bomb me, then sprinkle it with judgment and criticism, only to ghost me for a couple of days and do it all again. And this was all before we officially split—week eight of separation, for those of you doing the calculations. I was so confused. I had no idea what was happening; he was saying one thing but acting the opposite. This was the trauma bonding stage. He had mastered taking no accountability for any of his betrayals, painting me as the unstable one with an alcohol problem so that he could play the victim. His charm, once my solace, became a weapon wielded against me.

He refused to engage in any meaningful conversation, leaving me adrift in a sea of unanswered questions and unresolved pain. Every interaction felt like a chess game, with him always a few moves ahead.

I felt discarded, replaced, and betrayed on every level. The longer he left me alone to think, the more I discovered what I was dealing with. Research, reel after reel, day after day, teaching myself what I'd gotten into. And you know what, I discovered quite a lot about why he is the way he is, what I could and couldn't expect relationship-wise, and I came to have a lot of compassion for his plight. However, I also learned that my life for the last 6.5 years had been a fabrication that suited his needs and that he'd been spending that time also looking for something better. God Himself severed our soul contract for the acts He could see him doing in secret. For that, karma is coming for him, and it's not going to be pleasant. He was removed from my path, and for that, I am grateful. But I also felt something else—a growing determination to reclaim my life.

Dear New Victim: A Letter I Will Never Send

Dear New Victim,

You don't know me, but I know you. I was you. Bright-eyed, hopeful, and captivated by the man who now holds your attention. He probably seems like everything you've ever wanted—charming, attentive, and utterly devoted to making you feel special. But please, look closer.

He will make you feel like you're the only one, that he's never felt love like this before, and that all his exes were crazy. But soon, you will feel drained financially, physically, and emotionally, invisible and sexually used. He will subtly erode your own opinion, making you question your worth, your sanity, and even your reality. You will give and give, pouring your love into a vessel that can never be filled. And he will take, always take, without giving back.

His love is not unconditional. It is a transaction, a means to control and validate his fragile ego. He doesn't see you; he sees what you can do for him. And when you begin to falter under the weight of his expectations, he will punish you—not with fists, but with infidelity, indifference, and expertly placed barbs that pierce deeper than any blade. And when you are no longer of use, watch his demeanor abruptly change… the discard is in the post.

I hope you see through the facade before it's too late. You deserve real love, not manipulation and lies. Love that uplifts, nurtures, and celebrates you for who you are. Please, take care of yourself. Listen to your instincts, even when he tries to silence them.

With all the hope in the world, The Survivor of Your Narcissist

The Road to Healing

Walking away wasn't easy. The emotional hooks were deep, and the scars he left were raw and tender. But I learned to lean into my pain, to let it guide me toward healing. Therapy through every platform available and in person became my anchor, and self-compassion and forgiveness my lifeline.

I began to understand the patterns—not just his but mine. Why I stayed as long as I did; why I ignored the red flags. It wasn't weakness; it was hope, a belief in the goodness of people, in the love we shared, at least for me, even when they repeatedly proved me wrong.

Now, I'm learning to trust myself again, to rebuild the vitality he so methodically dismantled. And while the wounds he inflicted may never fully disappear, they no longer define me. They made me stronger, wiser, and more determined in my purpose of healing other women who suffer under the rule of these vile predators. He did not succeed in breaking me; he made me remember who I am. I am closer to my god than ever before. I have been awakened, and it is not for the meek at heart. Hiding in plain sight are many wolves in sheep's clothing. Become self aware, heal childhood wounds, and learn to be detached and in love with your man by loving yourself first, by doing right by you, whether he likes it or not. If he's right for you, he won't just say sorry, but he will change his behavior, so he doesn't have to say sorry again. That's called respect.

Trust and listen to your instincts. My instincts told me not this one, but I allowed the love bombing to bedazzle me because I craved love from difficult men (because of my upbringing, but that's another story). What it actually taught me is that I needed to find that love within myself, and then I wouldn't *need* it from anyone else again. I'm a healing mess in progress, but damn, I'm one strong lady, and I've got this: watch me rise and embrace the power of my magnetism. I am a woman, bloody hear me roar! No one will dim my light or voice. I have been awakened and my energy is returned to me.

For Anyone Reading This

If you see yourself in my story, please know you're not alone. The pain you feel is real, but so is the strength within you to break free and heal. No one knows they are with a narcissist until the discard happens, and you are left in a world of pain trying to make sense of it all! The fact that you have no idea you are with someone who is not who they are pretending to be defies all logic! That a person could wear a mask for years is incomprehensible! The confusion is real! Healing is not linear, and it's not easy, but it's possible. Surround yourself with people who truly care for you, seek professional support if you can, and remember: You are worthy of love that is loyal, honest, and kind that starts inside you for you first! Above all, seek out knowledge and get the healing you need to expand your light far and wide.

The covert narcissist may have hidden in plain sight, but now so can your resilience. Let it shine. Let it guide you to the life and the love you deserve within you and for you.

I am Michelle Gill, owner and founder of Change Hypnosis. I specialize in women's recovery from toxic relational abuse. I use the power of hypnosis to effect fast and lasting changes in your subconscious. Let me guide you to release the trauma and empower you to find peace within FAST. You can contact me at www.changehypnosis.co.nz. Taking women from trauma to triumph fast!

Molly Hurd

Learning is Fun Every Day
Teen Life Coach

https://www.linkedin.com/in/molly-hurd-b02133128/
https://www.facebook.com/molly.hurd
https://www.instagram.com/mollyhurd9/
https://mollyhurd.com/

Molly grew up on the Oregon coast, where a love for nature—especially marine biology—was fostered. She earned her BS in Biology and secondary teaching certification at Seattle Pacific University and later completed a Master's in Curriculum and Instruction. After 13 years of teaching in public schools, she transitioned to homeschool co-ops, designing science classes for all ages. She also founded summer science camps, which she has successfully run for 14 years.

Recognizing the challenges teens face today, Molly became a Wholistic Neuro Growth Learning Success Coach and Life Coach, focusing on equipping teens with tools to thrive. Married for 29 years with two adult children, she balances her passion for teaching and coaching with hobbies like running, traveling, and scrapbooking. A two-time Boston Marathon finisher, she estimates she's on her second lap around the Earth through running. Her goal is to help teens become happy, confident individuals.

Coming Out of the Grey

By Molly Hurd

Grey. It's not black. It's not white. There is a sliding scale between black and white. When I think of grey, I think of fog. It's not dry, and it's not raining, but it's damp. It's the in-between. The fog wraps around my body and my brain. Sometimes, I think grey is a safe zone; other times, it's hiding the truth or maybe stretching the truth. It reminds me of the speed limit. If the speed limit is 60, 65 is OK, 70 is over the speed limit. The grey area is between 60-65. That was my life – somewhere in a nebula zone of nothingness.

I was a middle child – 3rd of 4, and my parents divorced when I was 11. My mom remarried shortly after to a man 20 years older, and she became a different person. What I would call a nonperson. My older siblings left to go live with my dad, and my younger sister and I were with my mom. For 8 years, I was the youngest, then became a middle and now became the oldest sibling in the house. Neither my mom or step dad worked. They mostly stayed at the house, and I was never sure what they did all day while I was at school. My room was my sanctuary, although I knew they could come in any time. At least I could hear them coming up the stairs.

I was never beaten, rarely yelled at, and we lived in a nice home in a nice neighborhood. Once my mom remarried, going to church became important, and we went Sunday morning and evening and Wednesday night as well. As an outsider, everything looked fine. People would even tell me how nice my mom and stepdad were, which just added to my angst, guilt, and shame. Why was I so miserable on the inside?

The Grey of Sexual Abuse

I lay in my bed, almost holding my breath as I could hear him coming up the stairs. He had a prosthetic leg, so I could hear him grab onto the rail, and it would creak, lift the leg, and thunk on the stair.. Repeat. Creak, lift, thunk. I can still hear that sound in my mind 50 years later.

The room door was pushed open, and he walked in and stood beside my bed. He would start to rub my back and then tell me to flip over.

I would lay so still, pretending I wasn't in the room. Massage breasts. Reach into panties and massage.

Lie motionless, and he would leave the room.

I don't know how many times it happened, but it went on during middle school and high school.

I look back now and wonder why I didn't yell or scream or push him away, but I know why. I felt powerless. Voiceless. Frozen.

I didn't even understand what was happening. I didn't understand what an orgasm was or the feelings around it. I just knew to lie still and pretend nothing was happening. I felt guilty, powerless, and fearful. That was what I always felt inside.

It took years for me to admit what happened. It took even more years to accept this was sexual abuse. Sexual abuse. That sounds so bad. I wasn't beaten, it wasn't forced intercourse, and it really "wasn't that bad." It's grey. It's not black or white. I often asked myself what my problem was. It really wasn't bad, was it? The problem when we try to scale it is we try to minimize it and tell ourselves it was really nothing. Many abuse victims will be the first to tell you that it wasn't that bad and that it was really their fault for something they did or didn't do. For me, it was my fault because I didn't know any better and didn't know how to say no.

"Sexual abuse refers to **any sexual activity that occurs without consent**[1,2]. It is also referred to as sexual assault or sexual violence[1]. Sexual abuse can include **unwanted sexual touching, forced oral sex, and rape**, among other sexual acts[1]. It is often perpetrated using force or by taking advantage of another[3]. Sexual abuse can happen to anyone and can occur online or in person."

There are three responses to fear: flight, fight, or freeze. As much as I wanted to fly away or fight, my option was to freeze. That was my way of survival. I often thought of running away and living in a forest. We would sometimes drive 30 minutes to a smaller town, and I would longingly look at the forest and wonder how long I could survive in the woods.

I was always taught that sex was something saved for marriage and anything else was bad. I felt like I was bad. I felt so guilty that I liked the feeling of an orgasm even though I didn't understand it. I just knew to lie still, frozen in time.

Into adulthood, sex is something I've never felt comfortable with. I still have a hard time talking about it with anyone, including my OB, doctor, or counselor. I feel embarrassed to enjoy it even in the sanctity of marriage. It's taken years to shake off the tendrils of shame and guilt. There are times I wish it had been more black – like the abuse was worse and then maybe I could understand more of my shame or actually acknowledge why I was feeling the way I was, but therein lies the shame and guilt. Maybe I was the one seeking it out, maybe it was all my fault. If I had just known better. If I could just get over it.

It's crazy how something affects the rest of your life without you really knowing it or understanding it. It seemed so small and insignificant. Grey.

Guilt, shame, and, oh, unworthiness.

My stepdad was a talker. I called him a lecturer. He could talk anyone to death. My mom just sat and nodded her head and listened. Was she listening? Sometimes, she would sew or cook. Looking back, I think she was glad of the form of attention it was. One time, I remember him saying to her in front of me that he had touched me in certain places, and she just nodded in agreement, busy with whatever she was working on.

Betrayal is a strong word, but that is what I felt from my mother. No conversation was sacred between us, and I learned quickly to say nothing of consequence, or it would come back with a lecture of some kind. I went through my teenage years alone.

It's easy to feel resentful. I resented my mom who didn't protect me. I resented being so constricted with what I could and couldn't do or wear or who I could see or not see. I resented my younger sister who later was able to go to dances, date, and so many things I was never allowed to do. I realized later that it was all about control.

It's easy to have resentment when we don't feel accepted for who we are. Resentment is actually a form of scarcity. I didn't feel loved for who I was and felt that love was very conditional. How can you talk about unconditional love at church and not feel it at home? I must be unworthy.

Allowing myself to let go of resentment is a beautiful thing. I was taught to forgive and forget. It took me years to realize I could forgive but not forget the lessons I learned. It's the same with resentment. I can write these things in peace as this is my story.

I can be mad/angry at my mother for not doing more, but she was incapable. I can be angry for that (and I have been) but what good will come of that? It would only breed bitterness. It's a choice.

I really hated those images about turning into a butterfly. To me, it meant that someday I would FINALLY arrive. I would try a program thinking this would be it, this would be the answer! A new business…this would be it, this is how I'm going to make money! Someday, I will get my wings. All that did was make me feel like I was never going to be worthy. I was never going to fly.

I settled on being a cockroach. You see, there are actually different types of metamorphosis. Complete metamorphosis is egg, larva, pupa, adult-like the butterfly. Gradual metamorphosis is when the young look similar to an adult and molt periodically to become an adult. Grow, molt, grow, molt. Looking at it this way, I realized I would always be growing and molting. I didn't have to someday arrive!

However, Jaime Kern Lima, shares in her book *Worthy* that becoming a butterfly doesn't mean that life is perfect, and you get to just flit around and be happy as a butterfly. It's more about defying the odds and coming through seasons of difficulty. It's about the journey of using your gifts and talents.

My mom stayed a caterpillar her entire life. She stayed safe. She was the boat in the harbor. There was a time when my older siblings remember her actually living her life and being a butterfly, but for some reason, she retreated and went back to being a caterpillar and lived out the rest of her days. Fear gripped her very being, and she lived in her safe little bubble.

I look back through my journals and see days of moving forward and days of retreating and doubt. My mom was comfy…why work so hard? Who am I to be a coach for teens, to run my own camps, break free from childhood traumas? God tells me who am I not?

The Grey of Food Issues

Those deep feelings of unworthiness, shame, and guilt carried over into my eating and body shaming. I teetered on the brink of bulimia, what is now called Binge Eating Disorder. That area of grey where I could hide what I was doing and be on the edge of the slippery slope without admitting my shame.

In college, there is a joke about gaining the freshman 10. I gained the freshman 20. Peanut butter and honey were such a lovely thing to eat in the cafeteria when there weren't a lot of other great choices. This was back in the day when it was cafeteria-style, and food was plopped on your plate. A Monte Cristo sandwich was leftover French toast from breakfast with a piece of lunch meat and American cheese. It was pretty easy to gain weight on peanut butter and honey. I have to admit, I also loved having hot food, as my stepdad was known for lengthy prayers.

In my freshman year, I was diagnosed with an ulcer. In the book *Heal Your Body* by Louise Hay, ulcers are a sign of fear and a strong belief of unworthiness. That certainly fit, but I was not in a place where I could recognize or diagnose my underlying causes. Food became my way to feed it, especially on a bland diet of peanut butter and honey.

At one point, reaching my maximum weight, I vowed to go on a diet. I went on a yo-yo pattern of skipping breakfast and lunch, surviving on diet soda, and binging in the evenings. There was a scale at a place where I often studied, and I would weigh myself after each visit to the bathroom to see if I had lost weight. I never threw up so I told myself I wasn't bulimic. I thought about food constantly. It makes my brain hurt thinking about all the years when I constantly thought about food. What I would eat, what I wouldn't eat, and when I would eat. There were times I used laxatives just to make things clear out, but since I didn't use them regularly and I wasn't throwing up, I wasn't bulimic. I just lived in the grey – the in-between spaces where no one would notice except me.

This pattern continued for years. I would plan out what I was going to eat that day and vow to "be good," only to binge in the evenings and go to bed in tears and promise myself that tomorrow I would be better. It was such a vicious cycle. The crazy thing is how the brain gets ADDICTED to this cycle. This is the rut our brains have carved out, just like the Colorado River going through the Grand Canyon. Day after day, year after year. I could try all the diets in the world, but until I fixed my unworthiness, shame, and guilt, nothing would change.

I would like to tell you that I conquered it in my 20s or 30s or 40s, but it wasn't until my 50s that the years of digging my Grand Canyon had gone to a trickle and reversed. Today, I no longer spend hours thinking about what I'm going to eat or not eat. I can't even begin to tell you what a relief that is. I no longer eat the box of chocolate or the bag of potato chips. Or eat handfuls of each bag so no one notices that some is missing from each. The scale doesn't dictate my happiness or how I feel about myself. I will still overeat sometimes, like on holidays or vacations, but it is a meal and not a regular occurrence. Nor do I berate myself for overeating. The more I heal emotionally, the less I overate.

No one noticed I had an eating issue. I could go up and down 5 pounds, and no one would notice except me. That's how I hid. I think if I had $1 for every time I gained and lost 5 pounds, I could probably buy a plane ticket somewhere.

Outside, I was happy. I could exude happiness and cheerfulness to others. I was always happy, always busy. Being happy is truly part of my personality, but I used it to hide from the scared child on the inside. The one suffering from guilt and shame.

Learning to truly love yourself is the best gift you can give to yourself and others. Look in the mirror and love every part of your body. Look in your eyes and tell the person in the mirror how much you love and appreciate them. Do this daily. Make it a habit. Just as it takes years to program the brain, it can take time to lay new neural pathways and develop new patterns. It takes consistent effort. There isn't a day that goes by that I don't say my mantras and list things I am grateful for.

The more you love yourself, the healthier you will become.

The Grey of Alcohol

When my parents divorced, my mom became much more conservative, and alcohol was not allowed in the house. Granted, I was underage but was also told how sinful it was. My dad, on the other hand, was not of the same mindset. He wasn't an alcoholic, but I believe he had a healthy approach. Having a drink wasn't a big deal. I was able to see him once a week, even though we lived 10 minutes away in the same town. We would often play cards or go bowling – both things my mother and stepfather didn't like. The bowling alley attracted people who smoked and drank, which was bad. Cards led to gambling, and the list went on. Even my older brother and sister were considered sinful and not good to be around. My dad would sometimes fix me hot chocolate with rum in it. Oh, that was so delightful! If it was close to the time to go back to my mother's, he would give me a breath mint before I walked into the house and headed up to my room. Living in the grey. I would sneak to see him after school periodically as I would walk home and stop by to visit and sometimes, he would take me out to lunch at school. I had to sneak time to see my father but pretended to leave the innocent child at my mother's. I felt like I was living a lie. Somewhere in the grey.

I married right out of college, and my fiancé had the stance of no alcohol. I grudgingly agreed out of fear of not finding anyone else who would love me, and 3 years later ended up in divorce, with alcohol being one of the issues. I was tired of pretending to be something I wasn't. For many years after, I would feel guilty having a drink. Like the feeling when you are a little kid and sneaking something you aren't supposed to. It took me years to finally let that go. I felt guilty for not agreeing and not living up to his standards. I was not black and white, and he didn't like grey. I had to learn to be OK with that.

Guilt. A friend of mine who is Catholic said that Catholics have the edge on guilt. I beg to disagree as a Protestant. I learned that God loves us, but it seemed like anytime God could change His mind, we could be punished. Can we let go of the guilt and shame, please? Guilt and shame weigh us down and lurk around every corner if we allow them to. The hardest person to forgive is yourself. I had so much shame from my past.

Shame keeps us feeling so unworthy of joy and peace. Our brains get stuck in the loop of hopelessness. It's a vicious cycle. I'm not worthy, therefore, I will overeat and show how unworthy I am. Then, I can berate myself more. One of my mentors even used the word addiction for this kind of thinking because we literally get addicted to our feelings of shame and unworthiness. Mentorship and counseling are a form of rehab along with tools.

Did you know you can retrain your brain? It doesn't happen overnight, and it has literally taken years of reading and mentorship, but I can tell you it is totally worth it. I think of how much energy I've spent worrying about food and my weight and can't tell you what a relief it is to NOT wake up thinking about what I can and can't eat in a day.

Think of a time that you made a mistake. Picture that in your mind. Now, turn that picture black and white. All the color is drained out of it. Shrink the image to the size of a postage stamp and then flick it away with your fingers and send it off to Neverland. This takes practice but is so rewarding and therapeutic. It's time to let go.

Focus on positive mantras and repeat them every day. Write them on your bathroom mirror, paste them in your car, wake up with them, and go to sleep with them. Mine is simple. I chose 3–4 words that I want to have more of in my life. I am capable, confident, calm, and consistent. These are words that empower me and help me navigate rough situations.

One of the dysfunctional traits of golden retrievers is not having a voice because they are so busy pleasing others. My stepdad was a lion, and I was a golden retriever. I wasn't allowed to have a voice. I wasn't even allowed to be angry or mad at something. I remember one of my counselors teaching me that it was OK to be angry. I got a big blow-up kid's toy punching bag and set it in my living room. When I allowed myself to be angry, I would kick it, hit it, and pick it up and whack it on the floor back and forth.

Anger is a God-given emotion. It's the opposite of calm, cheerfulness, and joy. I firmly believe unless we connect and learn all emotions, that we will never be who we are fully meant to be.

"Never be a prisoner of your past. It was a lesson, not a life sentence."
Dannette May

Emerging from the Grey?

I always felt like I was a step behind in my tweens and teens. I wasn't as smart or didn't catch on as quickly as my friends seemed to. Maybe you can relate to that. Where were the answers I needed? Somewhere in the fog. I did poorly on my SATs, and a high school counselor told me she didn't think I would be accepted or make it through college. I cried with sheer joy when I got my acceptance letter from the school I wanted to go to. I struggled with the confidence of learning but finally figured out a system that seemed to work for me by rewriting my lecture notes along with things from the textbook. Rewriting was a key and later learned how important that is for my learning style. In one of my education classes, I was introduced to learning styles and took several different inventories. Light bulbs went off, and I realized I wasn't dumb or stupid. These inventories also gave me insight into my personality. My favorite inventory is one I modified from a couple of different ones, and it labels you as a lion, otter, golden retriever, or beaver. I was definitely a golden retriever – the people pleaser.

I understood why I operated in the grey. I was (and am) a people pleaser. Look at me wrong and I could wither. I can be gullible (oh, the embarrassing stories I could tell) and hate confrontation. This explained why I often felt a step behind, why I had a hard time making decisions, and why I could be what I call a chameleon with others. I'll be whoever you need me to be. This was my survival technique. Not flight, not fight, but freeze.

When I started teaching public school, I started giving a series of inventories to my classes. It gave me such great insight into my students! I knew how to motivate students differently, and how to put them in groups. It helped tremendously with classroom management. I still give these inventories to my older students today and my camp counselors in the summer. One of the best things for me is seeing how I have grown from a dysfunctional golden retriever to being more balanced between the 4 quadrants. I have learned to play again, I can be in charge, I can take constructive criticism, and I do appreciate details! Learning style inventories are steps into understanding who you are. One of my passions now is to give them to students and their families and then spend time on the analysis so that the entire family has insight into how to better communicate.

Otters are the playful ones. They often like to tell jokes and can be the life of the party. Lions love to be in charge and be in leadership roles. Beavers tend to love facts and information. I have a story that if someone asked the 4 different personalities to go on a trip to a tropical beach with them, all their responses would be different. The otter would instantly say yes and grab their swimsuit and bright print shirt. The golden retriever would be so enamored that they were asked to go. The lion would immediately take charge and start planning the itinerary. The beaver would want to know more details, including what time of plane they would be traveling on before they could commit.

There are many types of learning styles or personality style inventories. Right-brained – left-brained; visual, auditory, or kinesthetic; DISC; and Enneagram are just a few. Many can be found online and are free. Please remember that these are tools to use to understand yourself and those around you. One inventory gives one piece of the puzzle and may not reflect your total self.

Another favorite is by Gallup.com. These identified traits that I didn't know were attributes such as positivity. I was in a small group that studied the traits over a couple of months and highly recommend this inventory.

I've been in education now for about 30 years, and the more I have molted layers of my past and grown my future, the more I have resolved to help teens. My inspiration is to give them tools that I never had so that they can go into adulthood with a toolbox to help them navigate all that life will throw at them. I continue learning new tools and have incorporated several into my classes from resetting the vagus nerve, class mantra, tapping, and music therapy for the first few minutes of my classes.

As the years have gone by, I can say I'm proud of my journey. Now in my early 60s, I continue the journey and want to give hope to those who, like me, live in the grey and need to find their voice. Writing this chapter gave me trepidation – what do I have to offer? Hope. Joy. Peace. Forgiving your past and looking to the future with anticipation of who you can become. Letting go of the guilt and shame. Be any color you like. You don't have to live in the grey. You have a voice and a story to tell. You have a victory lap to run over guilt and shame. I'm rooting for you.

Phuoc Anne Nguyen, PharmD, MS, BCPS, FTSHP

Franbyte Business Consulting-Southwest
Franchise Business Broker

Anne@franbyte.com
https://www.linkedin.com/in/phuocannenguyen/
https://www.facebook.com/profile.php?id=61556265279662
https://www.instagram.com/dranneleads/
https://www.youtube.com/@DrAnneleads
https://linktr.eeDrAnneLeads

Dr. Phuoc Anne Nguyen is a pharmacist by training, an entrepreneur by nature, and a coach by choice. While enjoying her fulfilling pharmacy career, she discovers her true passion lies in empowering individuals—particularly high-achieving women and aspiring entrepreneurs—to chart their paths. With over a decade of leadership and business experience, she specializes in guiding aspiring entrepreneurs toward ideal franchise opportunities that reflect their values, lifestyle, financial goals, and personal passions.

From healthcare to hospitality and everything in between, she knows the GOOD franchises and can help you select a model that leverages your strengths while accommodating your working style. Best of all, her services are completely free, allowing you to invest your time, energy, and resources where they count the most.

Ready to break free from limitations and create a meaningful future? Let's connect and start exploring your franchise business possibilities.

In her free time, she enjoys hiking, traveling, and meditation. Her goal is to visit 50 national parks by age 50.

Rising Stronger with Purpose: Owning Your Future in Life and Business

By Phuoc Anne Nguyen, PharmD, MS, BCPS, FTSHP

I used to believe my life was as close to perfect as one could get. I had checked all the boxes—an amazing family with two beautiful children and a thriving career. To the outside world, I was the image of success, the woman who had it all. But sometimes, life has a way of stripping us down to our core, showing us who we are beneath all the roles and titles. My story, like so many others, is one of learning, unlearning, and finally understanding what it means to be truly strong.

My life seemed to change overnight. *I made a choice that would change everything.* I chose to step into the hardest journey of my life—single parenthood. It wasn't something that happened *to* me; it was something I *chose* to face head-on. I knew the road ahead would be grueling and filled with obstacles, but I also knew that if I wanted to build the future my children deserved, I had to embrace it fully.

Still, knowing didn't make it easier. The weight of everything—the responsibilities, the uncertainty, the overwhelming silence in my home—pressed down on me with relentless force. The life I had built, the family I had envisioned, had shifted in an instant, leaving me standing alone. I felt as though I had been thrust into a dark tunnel with no end in sight. *I had chosen this path, but that didn't mean I wasn't afraid of what lay ahead.*

At times, the doubts consumed me. *Was I strong enough for this? Would my children be okay? Had I just made a mistake that would haunt me forever?* The questions were endless, and the weight of them left me breathless.

The simplest tasks—getting up, brushing my teeth, eating a meal—felt impossible. Friends and family, the ones who had always seen me as the strong, unwavering pillar, now spoke in soft, worried tones, urging me to hold on, to keep going. They reminded me that I had always been resilient, that I had always found a way. But what if this time, I couldn't?

The victim mindset threatened to take over. *It would have been easier to surrender to the pain, to believe that I was powerless, to ask "Why me?" over and over again.*

I had made a choice—a choice to have a new life for myself and my children. And even in my darkest moments, a quiet but persistent voice within me whispered: *This is happening for you, not to you. This is here to grow you, not to defeat you.*

Little by little, I began to listen. I stopped seeing my pain as a punishment and started seeing it as a teacher. Instead of letting my struggles define me, I let them shape me. I let them make me stronger.

I had chosen the hard path, and because of that, I would own it. And that changed everything.

Step 1: Embracing the Pain as Part of the Journey

One of the hardest lessons I learned was to embrace my pain instead of resisting it. We live in a culture that glorifies strength, yet often equates vulnerability with weakness. But here's what I found to be true: vulnerability is where real strength begins. *It's in our raw, unguarded moments that we discover the depths of who we are.*

As I started my journey, I remembered something Oprah Winfrey once said: "Turn your wounds into wisdom." Those words resonated deeply within me. I began to look at my pain as a teacher, guiding me toward a new way of seeing myself and the world. *Each tear, each moment of despair, shaped the woman I was becoming—one who could truly own her future.*

This understanding didn't come easily—or quickly. The pain felt all-consuming, hitting me at the most unexpected times. I remember crying while driving, my hands gripping the steering wheel as tears blurred my vision. The silence of the car amplified my grief. Some days, I couldn't even reach my destination without pulling over. At night, after putting my children to bed, I'd linger in their room, holding them close as they drifted off to sleep. Their little arms around my neck brought comfort, but also heartbreak. I'd sit in the dark, tears streaming silently, praying they wouldn't wake up and see me like this. *How could I possibly be their rock when I felt so broken?*

During one of these moments, when the ache felt too heavy to carry, I reached out to a mentor I had worked with indirectly. She was someone I deeply admired, whose wisdom had always left a mark. I felt an urgency to meet her, not as a professional contact, but as someone who could help me make sense of my chaos.

When I reached out, she responded with warmth and grace, agreeing to meet me for dinner. That evening, as rain tapped gently against the restaurant windows, I sat across from her, nervous and unsure where to begin. She had a calm, steady presence—like the eye of a storm. Her eyes carried a softness that invited me to speak.

"Tell me, what's going on?" she asked, her voice carrying the kind of understanding that only comes from having weathered storms of her own.

Her question opened the floodgates. I poured out everything—the sudden shift in my life, the suffocating weight of responsibilities, and the way the grief seemed to seep into every moment, from the drive to work to the quiet of bedtime. I told her about the nights when I held my children close, willing myself to be strong for them, even as my heart broke into a thousand pieces.

I told her about the tears that seemed to come endlessly, as though they would never stop.

"Let your tears fall," she said softly. "Your tears have their expiration dates."

I looked up, startled by the unexpected wisdom in her words. "Expiration dates?" I repeated.

She nodded. "There will come a day when you'll think about this chapter of your life, and the tears won't come. One day, you'll look back and see how far you've come. And when the tears stop, you'll know you've healed."

Her words settled over me like a balm, soothing the rawness I carried inside. I hadn't considered that my grief might have an end date, that the endless nights of crying in my children's room or the tears shed on solitary drives would eventually give way to something else. *She wasn't telling me to rush through the pain but to trust the process. The storm wouldn't last forever.*

"Pain," she said, "is like a storm. It feels endless when you're in the middle of it, but no storm lasts forever. And when it clears, you'll see how much stronger you've become."

Her wisdom deeply resonated. "The world will tell you to move on quickly," she said. "But healing isn't about rushing forward. It's about letting yourself feel everything, knowing that every tear waters the seeds of the person you're becoming."

At one point, I asked her, "How do you keep going when it feels like the pain will never end?"

She paused, her gaze softening. "By remembering that pain is temporary and purpose is forever. Find the purpose in your pain. Use it to shape your future and help others. That's how you turn your wounds into wisdom."

Her words reminded me of Oprah's quote and brought it to life in a way I hadn't fully understood until now. Pain wasn't just something to endure—it was something to learn from, something that could guide me toward becoming the person I was meant to be. In that moment, I realized that my tears weren't a sign of weakness. They were part of the process, the bridge between who I was and who I was becoming. *The tears weren't weakness; they were part of my transformation.*

Before we parted, she offered one final piece of advice. "Every tear you cry has meaning. One day, the tears will stop. Until then, let yourself grieve. Don't rush. When the tears are gone, use what you've learned to create something beautiful. That's what it means to own your future."

That dinner became a turning point. Her words carried me through the darkest days. Whenever the tears came—during quiet drives or nights holding my children—I'd remind myself: *These tears have an expiration date.* Slowly, they did. The despair grew less frequent, and the weight of grief began to lift.

She wasn't just a guide—she was a mirror, reflecting back the strength I had but couldn't see. Her wisdom transformed how I approached my pain, showing me that each tear was part of becoming the woman I was meant to be.

Now, when I look back on that evening, I don't feel sadness. I feel gratitude. Gratitude for her words, her kindness, and her willingness to share her own story to help me see the path ahead. It was her belief in my ability to rise that reminded me of my own strength. Pain, I realized, wasn't the end of my story. It was the beginning of a new chapter. *One where I could own my future.*

Exercise for Reflection: Take a moment to sit with a difficult experience you've faced recently. Write it down in detail, then reflect on what it has taught you. Ask yourself:

- What has this experience revealed about my strengths?
- What lessons am I learning from this?
- How can I use this experience to grow?

Doing this exercise regularly has the power to transform your mindset, helping you see every challenge as an opportunity for growth and a chance to take ownership of your own future.

Step 2: Reframing "Why Me?" to "What For?"

I remember the moment that changed everything. We had just downsized to a smaller house, and as I was packing boxes, my five-year-old looked up at me, his eyes wide with confusion and vulnerability. "Why, Mom? Why are we moving to another house?" he asked. My heart ached; I wanted to shield him from the uncertainty and, from the fear. But I knew I couldn't pretend everything was the same.

I knelt down, took his small hands in mine, and whispered, "Yes, sweetheart, everything is going to be great. This is our new adventure."

At that moment, I made a promise—to him and to myself—that I would be strong. Not just for them, but for *me*. I realized that strength was not about pretending nothing was wrong; it was about facing the truth with courage. As Buddha once said, "Pain is certain, suffering is optional." I chose to let go of suffering and embrace the journey ahead, however difficult it might be. This was the beginning of learning to *own my future,* no matter what had come before.

Exercise for Perspective Shift:

When you find yourself asking, "Why is this happening to me?" try reframing it by asking, "What can I learn from this? What purpose could this challenge serve in my life?" Rewriting the narrative gives you the power to shift from a victim mindset to a growth mindset, opening up possibilities and empowering you to *own your future* and your response to it.

Step 3: Balancing Strength and Vulnerability with My Children

Throughout this journey, my children have been my biggest motivation. They have seen me at my best and my worst, and they have taught me that strength and vulnerability are not opposites but companions. I am their rock, yes, but I am also human, and they deserve to see that. Some days, I have it all together; other days, I am learning right alongside them. And that's okay.

Gandhi said, "The best way to find yourself is to lose yourself in the service of others." In serving my children, I found strength I didn't know I had. I learned that being their mother didn't mean I had to have all the answers—it meant showing up, imperfect but present, and modeling the courage to *own my future* even in times of uncertainty.

Exercise for Embracing Vulnerability:

Reflect on a moment when you showed vulnerability in front of your children or loved ones. How did it feel? What did it teach you about strength? Write about this experience, and explore ways you can continue to model authenticity in your relationships.

Step 4: Redefining Self-Worth with Daily Affirmations

In the days that followed, I realized how essential it was to rebuild my sense of self. My worth wasn't tied to being a wife, a mother, or a successful professional. *It was inherent, something no life event could take away.*

Every morning, I would sit in the quiet and repeat to myself: "I am enough. I am worthy. I am abundant." These words, inspired by Jamie Kern Lima, became my lifeline, a mantra that reminded me of my inner strength even when I felt weakest. Jamie once said, "You are worthy simply because you are you." That idea, so simple yet so profound, became the cornerstone of my journey toward self-worth and the foundation for owning my future.

At first, these words felt strange, almost hollow. But the more I repeated them, the more they began to feel true. Gradually, they took root, forming a foundation upon which I could rebuild my life, grounded in self-belief.

Meditation had been a part of my life for over a decade, offering me calm and balance amidst life's stresses. But during this time, as the weight of my pain felt unbearable, I knew I needed more. My practice, though grounding, wasn't enough to guide me through the storm. *I needed deeper wisdom—a guide to help me find the stillness I had lost.*

One day while hiking in the forest, I found myself tuning into the rhythm of my breath and the sound of the wind brushing through the trees. A surge of energy coursed through me—a deep sense of connection and clarity I hadn't felt in a long time. *It was as if the forest itself was whispering to me, urging me to revisit something I'd left behind.*

That's when I remembered my visit, years ago, to Zen Master Thich Dieu Thien's Universal Door meditation center. I had visited only once, but her calm presence and profound words surfaced in my memory. The following Sunday, I returned for her Dharma talk. As she spoke, it felt as though she was addressing me directly. Her voice, steady and compassionate, carried a wisdom that cut through my pain.

I learned that suffering is a mirror—it reflects the attachments and beliefs I hold onto, but it also holds the key to setting me free.

I had been clinging to my grief, trying to control it, when what I needed was to let go. "What you seek," she said, "is already within you. Awaken the truth already living in your heart."

During a meditation session, she guided us to sit quietly with our thoughts, letting them come and go without judgment.

At first, the practice was challenging. My mind raced with thoughts of everything I had lost, but gradually, I noticed something remarkable: the thoughts would come, but they would also go. I didn't have to hold onto them. I could observe them, like clouds drifting across the sky.

Her teachings gave my meditation a renewed sense of purpose, reminding me that stillness wasn't about escaping emotions but creating space to see them clearly.

Zen Master Thich Dieu Thien often spoke of living as a "Living Buddha," someone awake to their truth. This resonated deeply. *It wasn't about perfection but about trusting the wisdom within.*

Through meditation, affirmations, and her teachings, I saw my situation not as a setback but as an opportunity to grow and create a future aligned with my true self. *Pain wasn't the end of my story—it was the beginning of my awakening.*

Meditation & Affirmation Practice:

- Sit in a quiet space, focus on your breath, and let thoughts come and go without judgment.

- When your mind wanders, return to your breath. Repeat silently: "Be still, and see."

  After meditating, repeat:

  1. "I am worthy."
  2. "I am awake."
  3. "I am abundant."

Write these affirmations on sticky notes and place them where you'll see them often—your mirror, desk, or phone wallpaper.

Step 5: Finding Purpose in Empowering Others

As I began to rebuild my life, I found a new sense of purpose—one that allowed me to empower others while honoring the lessons from my own journey. While continuing to thrive as a pharmacy leader, where I helped develop new businesses to close care gaps, I felt a pull to expand my impact. *Pharmacy had taught me how to identify needs, create solutions, and build trust, but I saw an opportunity to empower others on a broader scale.*

For years, I dedicated myself to career and leadership coaching, guiding others to unlock their potential. But as I navigated my own transformation, I saw an opportunity to empower aspiring business owners to take control of their future, build stability, and create lasting impact for their families. *This realization led me to being a franchise broker.*

The Seeds of a New Vision

My decision to pursue franchise brokerage wasn't random; it was deeply rooted in my upbringing. I come from a family of small business owners, and from a young age, I saw the grit and determination it takes to build something from the ground up. My father, siblings, and extended family worked tirelessly to create businesses that not only provided for their households but also built legacy income.

While I admired their work ethic, I also witnessed the sacrifices they made. Starting a business from scratch often meant long hours, financial uncertainty, and strain on family life. These experiences planted a seed of understanding: business ownership is empowering but can be grueling without a solid foundation. *Later, as I faced my own challenges, I saw how franchise ownership offered a proven model for success—a bridge between entrepreneurship and stability.*

Pharmacy to Franchise Brokerage: A Natural Evolution

My pharmacy career played a significant role in shaping this journey. I sought to close care gaps and help hospital practice grow into thriving, patient-centered businesses. I loved identifying opportunities and creating solutions—skills that seamlessly translated to guiding aspiring business owners as a franchise broker.

Franchise brokerage became about more than matching people with opportunities. *It was about understanding their needs, addressing their fears, and guiding them toward a business model aligned with their vision.* My pharmacy background gave me the empathy, strategy, and commitment to serve others effectively.

Empowering Others Through Ownership

Franchise ownership has empowered countless individuals to achieve financial independence and build lives filled with purpose. For women and healthcare professionals especially, it offers a path to entrepreneurship with support systems in place. *This mission resonated deeply with me.*

Helping others find their footing in business ownership became my way of turning pain into power. *When I guide someone through the franchise process, helping them see the possibilities and make informed decisions, I'm not just building a business—I'm building a legacy.*

As Tony Robbins said, "The secret to living is giving." By helping others achieve their dreams, I discovered a renewed sense of meaning in my life. Franchise brokerage became not just a profession but a purpose: an opportunity to help others own their future, create generational wealth, and align their lives with their values.

An Invitation to Reflect

If you've ever felt the pull to take control of your future, I encourage you to explore your path to empowerment. *Reflect on what lights you up and how your experiences can shape a meaningful journey.* Often, purpose arises when we use our challenges to uplift others.

Exercise for Finding Purpose:

Take a moment to reflect on these questions:

- What lights you up?
- What experiences in your life have shaped who you are?
- How can you use your skills and experiences to make a difference in someone else's life?

Write down your answers and consider how they connect to your current goals. Often, purpose arises when we use our journey to uplift others, empowering them to own their future.

Step 6: Investing in Growth: The Power of Community and Continuous Learning

One of the most transformative decisions I made on this journey was to *invest in myself*. I knew that if I wanted to create a better future—not just for my children, but for myself—I needed to elevate my mindset, develop new skills, and surround myself with people who had already walked the path I was embarking on.

At first, the idea of spending money on personal development felt uncomfortable. I had already experienced so much change, so much uncertainty. But I also knew that staying stagnant wasn't an option. I had to *become* the person capable of building the life I envisioned. That meant learning from those who had already mastered the principles of resilience, business, and leadership.

So, I took a leap. I invested *thousands of dollars* into coaching programs and courses with some of the most brilliant minds in business and personal growth—*Dean Graziosi, Tony Robbins, Christina Fontana, Evelyn Weiss, Codie Sanchez, Brendon Burchard, and many more*. Each program pushed me beyond my limitations, helping me reframe my challenges into opportunities. I didn't just absorb their teachings—I applied them. But personal growth isn't just about courses and coaching; it's about the people you choose to surround yourself with. I knew I needed a strong community, so I sought out environments that would uplift and challenge me.

I completed the *Stimulating Urban Renewal Through Entrepreneurship (SURE) Program at the University of Houston*, which provided hands-on business development training and connected me with experienced mentors who helped refine my vision. I also worked with *SCORE mentors*, whose wisdom and guidance allowed me to navigate business ownership with clarity and confidence. These mentorships reinforced a simple truth: *success is not a solo journey—it is built through relationships, learning, and resilience.*

I also joined powerful business communities like the *Franchise Brokers Association* and *Franbyte*, where I surrounded myself with like-minded entrepreneurs who understood the journey I was on. These weren't just networking opportunities—they were lifelines. *Being in rooms with people who thought bigger, pushed harder, and supported each other changed everything.*

Through these experiences, I learned that *growth isn't a luxury—it's a necessity.* If we want to rise, we must invest in ourselves. Whether it's through education, mentorship, or surrounding ourselves with the right people, our future is shaped by what we are willing to invest in today.

And so, I continue to invest—not just in business, but in becoming the best version of myself. Because when we grow, we don't just change our own lives—we create a ripple effect that impacts everyone around us.

Practical Tips for Investing in Yourself

1. **Find the Right Mentors** – Seek guidance from those who have walked the path you want to take. Organizations like *SCORE* offer free mentorship, while business networks like *SURE* provide structured programs to help you refine your strategy.

2. **Join Growth-Oriented Communities** – Surround yourself with people who push you to think bigger. Whether it's joining a mastermind, a business association, or a professional network, being in the right rooms can change everything.

3. **Commit to Lifelong Learning** – Invest in books, coaching, and courses that align with your goals. Learning from experts like *Tony Robbins and Dean Graziosi* can provide insights that accelerate your growth and keep you ahead of challenges.

If you're not investing in your growth, you're staying in the same place. *So, how are you investing in yourself today?*

Final Reflection: Rising from the Ashes

As I reflect on this journey, I realize that strength isn't about never falling down. It's about rising each time you do, stronger and more aligned with who you truly are. My path has been marked by tears, setbacks, and challenges, but each of these experiences has forged me into the woman I am today.

Remember, as you walk your own path, that *you are worthy simply because you are you.* Every experience, every hardship, is shaping you into someone powerful, someone with the courage to rise. You are not alone, and your story, like mine, has the potential to light the way for others. *Own your future,* because it is yours to shape.

A Personal Invitation: Take the Next Step Toward Empowerment

If you're reading this and feel the desire to take control of your own destiny, to build something meaningful for yourself and your family, I invite you to connect with me. Franchise ownership has empowered many individuals to achieve financial independence and create lives filled with purpose and control. Whether you're looking to pivot, build a legacy, or simply explore new opportunities, I'm here to guide you through every step. *Own your future, own your franchise.*

Let's explore how franchise ownership can be your path to a brighter future. This journey is about more than business—it's about building a life that aligns with who you truly are.

Reach out, ask questions, and take the leap. *Your future is waiting. Own it.*

- **LinkedIn:** https://www.linkedin.com/in/phuocannenguyen/
- **YouTube:** https://www.youtube.com/@DrAnneleads
- **Facebook:** https://www.facebook.com/profile.php?id=61556265279662

- **Website:** https://linktr.eeDrAnneLeads
- **Instagram:** https://www.instagram.com/dranneleads/

In the words of Jamie and so many others, know that your worth is not defined by what happens to you, but by how you choose to rise from it. Hold these words close, let them fuel your journey, and remember: *Everything is going to be great.*

Resources for Continued Growth and Empowerment

As you walk your own journey of resilience and empowerment, here are some resources that have supported me along the way:

- **Books on Leadership and Empowerment:**
    - *Becoming* by Michelle Obama
    - *The Moment of Lift: How Empowering Women Changes the World* by Melinda Gates
    - *You Are Worthy* by Jamie Kern Lima, whose story of resilience inspired my journey
- **Practical Resources for Business Ownership:**
    - **SCORE (Service Corps of Retired Executives):** Free mentorship and tools for aspiring entrepreneurs.
        - **Website:** www.score.org
    - **Small Business Administration (SBA):** Resources, loans, and training for small business owners.
        - **Website:** www.sba.gov
    - **Small Business Development Centers (SBDC):** Expert advice and support for entrepreneurs.
        - **Website:** www.sba.gov/local-assistance/find
- **Podcasts and Talks:**
    - *SuperSoul Conversations* by Oprah Winfrey – Episodes on purpose, resilience, and self-worth.
    - *How I Built This* by Guy Raz – Interviews with successful business owners on overcoming adversity.

Roxanne Dinel

SocialFreedom4u
Small Business Owner

https://www.linkedin.com/in/roxanne-dinel/
https://www.facebook.com/roxanne.d.14
https://www.instagram.com/socialfreedom4u/

As a single mother of four, healing from a 14-year relationship with a narcissist, I've found strength and resilience I never knew I had. My journey hasn't been easy, but it's taught me the value of self-love, perseverance, and unwavering dedication to my children. While raising them, I've also been building my business, balancing the demands of motherhood and entrepreneurship. Every day is a new challenge, but it's also an opportunity to grow, both for myself and my family. I want to inspire other women—especially moms—to embrace their journey, heal from their past, and chase their dreams unapologetically. I'm proof that it's possible to rise above, rebuild, and thrive.

Rising Above

By Roxanne Dinel

The morning sun streamed through the kitchen window, casting a warm glow on the cluttered table. Amidst the chaos of cereal boxes, milk cartons, and homework sheets, I stood with a heart heavy with the weight of my past and present. Four children were around me, their energy a stark contrast to the exhaustion I felt. It was just another day in the life I had come to accept, but one I was determined to change.

For fourteen years, I had been with a man who, on the surface, seemed charming and successful. But beneath that facade lay a narcissist whose manipulations and emotional abuse had slowly eroded my self-worth. The promises of love and support had long been replaced by criticism, control, and a constant need for admiration that left me feeling invisible.

Nine pregnancies had also marked a turbulent marriage, with four beautiful children to show for it. Each pregnancy had been a rollercoaster of emotions, punctuated by the heartbreak of five miscarriages. Yet, through it all, my love for the children never wavered. They were my anchors, the reason I found the strength to face each day.

Balancing motherhood and the demands of a toxic relationship was challenging enough, but I had a dream that refused to be silenced. I wanted to build a business, to create something that was mine and mine alone. It was a vision born out of a need for independence, for a sense of self that had been lost in the shadows of the dominance, led in the relationship.

My journey began with small steps. Late at night, when the children were finally asleep, and the house was quiet, I would sit with my laptop open, researching, planning, and dreaming. It was during these stolen hours that I felt a spark of hope, a glimpse of the life I wanted to create for myself and my children.

Of course, my partner was less than supportive at the time. He belittled my efforts, dismissed all ideas, and made it clear that he believed my place was at home, catering to his needs. Towards the last year, I learned to tune out his negativity and become adept at compartmentalizing my pain, focusing instead on the future I was determined to build.

The turning point came on a night when his temper flared over something trivial. As he yelled and criticized, I felt a surge of anger and resolve. I had endured enough. It was time to reclaim my life. I couldn't let the children grow up thinking this was what love looked like. I finally made a decision to leave. It wasn't an easy choice—fear of the unknown and financial instability loomed large—but the prospect of a future free from his control was too powerful to ignore.

With the support of friends and family, I made it through. It was a humble beginning, but it was finally mine. The relief of being free from toxic presence was immediate, but the challenges were far from over. Juggling single motherhood, the emotional scars of my past, and the demands of my business were overwhelming.

But I was resilient and poured my heart into my business, a small online social media management company. Each client that I was able to help was a symbol of my journey—a testament to my strength and creativity. The business kept growing and clients appreciated the personal touch in my work and designs, and word continued to spread.

As the months passed, I found myself surrounded by a community of supportive women. They shared stories, advice, and encouragement, lifting each other up in a way that was both empowering and healing. I realized I wasn't alone—there were countless women like me, fighting their own battles and seeking their own paths to freedom.

The children were finally thriving in their environment. The absence of an oppressive presence brought a lightness to their lives. They laughed more, played more, and now saw their mother as the strong, independent woman she truly was. My heart swelled with pride as I watched them grow, knowing I was finally setting an example of resilience and determination.

The journey has been anything but easy, but each challenge has only strengthened me.

One sunny afternoon, I was at home working while the children were at school. I received a message that brought tears to my eyes. It was from a woman, a mother of two, who was trapped in an abusive relationship and stated how my story had given her the courage to leave her own toxic situation and start anew. She thanked me for being a beacon of hope, for showing her that it was possible to rise above.

I realized my journey was about more than just personal success. It was about creating a ripple effect, empowering others to break free from their own chains and pursue their dreams. I knew the road ahead would still have its challenges, but I faced it with a heart full of gratitude and a spirit that refused to be broken.

My life started to transform in ways I had once only dreamed of. I was starting to rebuild a life of independence and joy, surrounded by love and support. Through my story, I became a guiding light for countless women who needed a reminder that they, too, could rise above.

Finally, feeling a deep sense of peace, I had found a way out of the darkness. My journey was a testament to the power of resilience, determination, and the unwavering belief that every woman deserves to shine.

Sarah Carswell

Sarah Louisa
Coach

https://www.linkedin.com/in/sarah-louisa-carswell-18602a49/
https://www.facebook.com/SarahLouisaOnlineUK
https://www.instagram.com/sarahlouisauk
https://www.sarahlouisa.co.uk/

Sarah Carswell is a self-care and empowerment coach who turned her experience with energy burnout into a journey of transformation. Her chapter in She Rises, "The Power of the Energy Burnout," delves into her path to self-discovery, highlighting the significance of self-care, self-esteem, and authentic living. Sarah created the "Love You, Be You" coaching program to help others reconnect with themselves, build confidence, and harness their inner strength to lead more empowered lives. Through her coaching, Sarah guides individuals toward personal empowerment and fulfillment. Her mission is to inspire others to recognize their worth and potential, crafting lives filled with purpose and joy. When she's not coaching or writing, Sarah enjoys her dogs, nature walks, growing vegetables & fine dinning as well as pursuing growth and self development. Connect with Sarah to embark on your journey towards empowerment and renewal.

The Power of an Energy Burnout

By Sarah Carswell

I built a successful beauty salon business. My clients came to me in Birmingham (UK) from all over England, Scotland and even as far as Ireland. I specialised in waxing and grew my business through word of mouth. My business was built on the foundation of my low self-esteem to desperately build security for myself and my young son Brandon. My survival mode had kicked in through having to experience being a first-time mom when he was 6 months old, living in a hostel. I did not want him to grow up and feel like I did at the time. My only choice was to work for myself as I had no child care to support a typical 9-5 job. I had my Beauty therapy qualification but had no home, no money, no experience and no clients.

My world was crushed beyond belief, and I was only 21 years old. If you are struggling right now, no matter how big or small, in time things will inevitably change. Everything will progress forward, no matter how fast or slow you will reach your goal in the end. This is a story of what happens when you pour your life into everyone and everything else except for yourself.

Patience is certainly a virtue. It grows your experience and will, without a doubt, grow you to become stronger and more confident. Thanks to The Prince's Trust, a charity helped me with a small amount of funding and business accountant training that helped me start up my first beauty business in 2002. I rented a room in a hair salon, and the rest was a journey of bumpy roads, roadblocks, and then smooth, wonderful sailing. This is my story, and I hope it helps to inspire others on their unique journey.

I didn't have any experience with waxing clients when I started at Beauty College. All I had done was a few classes in waxing and probably only worked on a couple of models while training. That was when I was 16 years old. I was now 23 years old, and my life was not just about me; I had Brandon to protect and grow.

I bought a second-hand beauty couch and furniture and will never forget the day on the bus traveling with a big black bag of towels, thinking I have to make this work. The Prince's Trust gave me a step up in support. I experienced those around me laughing at me and constantly telling me how I had ruined my life. Everyone had me doomed going forward, with limited thinking and reminders that there are lots of beauty businesses out there. How could I possibly compete? I had no other choice but to move forward and make it work. I felt awful inside and so hurt by the world around me. I didn't expect my young life to start like this. I was literally dragging myself through each day.

I just could not give up. I set up my beauty business in a hair salon, where I rented a room upstairs. Clients started to come to me. I just knew I had to give them immaculate results for them to come back. I looked and searched for how my business could be different from the others. This worked, and as I became regularly busy, I started to create my own skills and techniques, as my clients' needs were not what we had learnt in college. I experienced a lot of clients who were embarrassed of their bodies, and who suffered with ingrown hairs. Then there were those who had hairs in places we were not taught how to remove. Even though I had not experienced these problems myself, we had one thing in common: low self-esteem.

I naturally empathised and made it my mission to solve these problems. I created my own unique skills and developed new treatments like the Paris Arch & Paris Curve Eyebrow Shape. I trademarked my very popular treatment called the Perfect Bikini Wax. I also welcomed my clients' male family members for body waxing and body hair trimming, eyebrow tidying, facial waxing and facials. Back then, in the UK, there was a stigma attached to men and beauty salons; it just wasn't heard of, and men were made to feel unwelcomed by many beauty salons as they didn't want or didn't know how to do male treatments. This was one of the reasons my furthest client Johnathan travelled to me from Scotland, as he wasn't welcome anywhere else. Men were having my treatments to feel more confident about themselves; they felt more hygienically clean after a back wax or chest trim. The same pattern with the ladies: my treatments encouraged building clients' confidence and self-worth and made them feel good. One male client would come every year when going on holiday as his kids and wife would make fun of his hairy feet. So, I would wax them so that he did not feel embarrassed.

Within the first year of removing 100s of ingrown hairs for my clients, something happened that was almost magical. As I was dropping my pointy standard ingrown hair tweezers into my sterilising dish, a tiny hook formed perfectly on one end of one of the pointy ends. This was a complete breakthrough that helped me remove ingrown hairs, easily and faster without damaging the skin. The results were amazing. Soon, I was fully booked and making extremely good money.

I had other salons sending me clients as they didn't do the treatments I was doing. Naturally, I had tapped into a growing trend of people who wanted to experience first-class service, immaculate results and new treatments that were unique to their individual preference, like my Perfect Bikini Wax. My clients were traveling from all over, so I expanded my business in 2004 to a bigger salon in a new area. The business kept on growing. I was back-to-back with clients working 6 days a week. Then, going home and working around the family and home, until one day, my whole life changed.

I was sitting at the reception desk, and suddenly my arms went limp, pins and needles were climbing up my spine and the back of my scalp, and tears started streaming down my face, but I didn't have any feeling of emotion; I wasn't crying, in fact, I felt numb. All my energy drained from me. I couldn't walk without support, and talking was a huge effort.

It felt like my soul was trying to lift out of my body. I had no vitality left. My nervous system had crashed, and I had suffered a huge energy burnout. The roadblock had hit me without me even realising it was there. I just went head-on straight into it without a thought to even stop, and my body completely crashed and burned.

The turning point in my life was here. I was 30 years old with two kids now. I was pouring everything I had into everyone and everything except for myself. It sounds so silly now, but I didn't even consider myself, my own time, my own body, my own health, my own emotions. My life was being lived for everyone else's needs except for mine. The outgoings of my salon were over £1,000 a week, and I was on autopilot to keep these payments up. Everyone wanted me to do their treatments, and I had no experience running the business without me in it, as I was the business.

I had a lot of learning from this experience, in business and personally. The main one I want to share with you is Be True To You. As women, we always put everyone first; some of us are brought up this way. If you are one of these ladies. STOP, self-care is important!

Yes, book yourself in for a massage and a facial. Why not treat yourself? This is a form of self-care. It runs a lot deeper than getting your hair done. There is a whole course of self-care that I can teach, but here is the simplest for you to become aware of in your life and not take for granted. Take note of what self-care you do for yourself and start looking after yourself like never before.

Six important areas that you need to apply self-care to yourself constantly:

Your body – Listen to what it is telling you
Your Mind – Take control of your thinking
Your Heart – Tune in and nurture with positive actions
Your Energy – It is your beauty

Your Time – It is so so precious
Others – We all have free choice

Focus on all the areas above that will grow your experience so you can rise up and grow stronger in an area of your life where your self-care needs your attention.

Nothing is perfect in life, so don't try to be perfect or try to fit in to please another, you will never please them. This life is yours for you to please yourself. That is when everything in your life experience will fall into alignment. Once you learn to ride the wave of life with your self-care skills in place, it is honestly a really cool adventure.

Life is a progression that has revealed to me that my dreams and wishes really do come true. The journey of how I got there has been full of surprises and lots of learning experiences that bring home my truth. Truth to stand in my own light and love. Now finally, I have the power not to allow others to change the rhythm of my energy.

This is my energy and happiness, and my life experience is all down to me. Listening to myself is the most important part of my life. I choose to be my unique self and have my own unique experience. What do you choose? My passion is for growth, and I love to help others. My life experience taught me that if I continue to learn, I will grow stronger and rise up higher. I once walked a path in my life that was so dark and lonely for many, many years. The value I have from understanding life on the other side gives me so much gratitude and compassion. I have my wings spread, and I am flying now. I am enjoying the bumpy rides that come and go, and if I need to stop and take note of when I'm sad, I do, and I give myself time. I never push myself like I used to; I give myself permission to rest and restore.

I could not have achieved all my dreams coming true back when I was 21 years old. I didn't have any dreams or wishes. I was just reacting to life with no knowing or understanding of myself. I needed to learn about self-love. I wasn't born with confidence and my life experience brought that. So when you are uncomfortable in life, remember that's a peak time of your life. It is actually a unique time that is for learning and finding out what it is you do actually want. This is when you can create your dreams, write down in a journal what it is you truly want. This can inspire you to move out of your uncomfortable space and shift into a direction that takes you where you really desire. Be kind to yourself and also recognise where you are. Ask yourself: Do I have people's opinions pressed upon me? Or am I trying to influence a part of my life to go a certain way? This will feel like you're hitting your head against a brick wall. No flowing energy anywhere around you. These times are when it's good to surrender and let go and know inside you that it is okay, problems always work themselves out in the end.

We push for things to go a certain way, and we pull at things to go our way, but just like other people, we can't control everything in life. What we most certainly can control is our inner self and our actions and reactions to situations. Clean up your self-care in whichever area is bringing you unhappiness, and get back to flowing in your beauty and in your energy. We all come across good times in life, these moments we need to relish and keep in our memory banks to recall on days that aren't so good. I once had a sign in my house that said, "Life is about the journey, not the destination," and it took me a while to truly realise what this actually meant. I spent a lot of time just wanting the outcome (destination). I thought that would bring me the happiness I seeked. Forgetting completely about enjoying the now time to rest, to create, to do things that make my heart sing while I'm waiting for my outcome. The NOW moment is really important to take note of; it is all the goodness of your amazing experiences, and it is respecting your life and the precious time in your life. This is how you set yourself up for great confidence building that leads to dreams coming true.

After my energy burnout, I had to learn self-care on many deep levels. I went very deep on many issues I had with areas of life I struggled with. I think when I look back, if I could advise my younger self, it would be to start learning and exploring around you. Who are you, what are your likes and dislikes, and what are your values in life and your life expectations? What do you want to experience more of?

Even though I was a victim of abusive behaviours and toxic relationships, I had to change my mindset as I did feel like a victim for many years of my life. I simply felt sorry for myself constantly. It wasn't good for me and my energy to keep myself feeling like this. I also had to find my identity, and that I was not a victim. I didn't actually know who I was.

My biggest takeaway advice to myself would be to look after myself first and foremost, as this is the most important part of life. This enabled my love and passion to help others even further. If I didn't hit my roadblock, I would have never changed. I needed to change as my life and businesses weren't working for me. I was working for my business and everyone else's happiness. I made mega-life changes and decisions. I cut down my responsibilities at home and in business. I delegated jobs out and only spent time on what was most precious to me. I studied health and life coaching, business coaching, energy field healing, endless personal development and spiritual courses. I discovered my love for good quality food, homemade recipes, growing vegetables, walking in nature and dogs.

I cut down my working hours drastically to only two days a week. I moved my business twice to my two different home addresses, and because I was tuned in to my heart, everything went the way I wished it to go. This gave me the luxury to work from home and cut down on my travel, so my time was spent on other things dear to me. All the time, I was making decisions that made my life easier and happier, and the power was simply making the goal, understanding what I wanted the most from my life and taking the steps towards it.

I became more confident over the years in all areas of my life. When I made more time in my life for myself, my dreams started to come true. I put a stop to abusive relationships. I met my dream husband when I was 38 years old, bought my dream home and created my IngrownOut Tweezer for the public to buy. I published the world's first Ingrown hair course for wax therapists. I dreamed about living in America, and this happened in 2023 out of the blue. My next goals are to live in a detached home surrounded by nature, grow my own food and become more environmentally self-sufficient. I am also planning to grow out my hair dye and embrace my natural hair colour, even if I have grey and silver hair coming through. My message to you is Love you, Be you and everything will fall into place for your dreams and wishes. Trust me, everything is possible. If you would like to follow me on Instagram @sarahlouisauk or drop me a line at info@sarahlouisa.co.uk www.sarahlouisa.co.uk

Shannon Addison

Founder of My Crumby World, LLC

https://www.linkedin.com/in/shannon-addison/
https://www.facebook.com/sgaddison
https://www.instagram.com/mycrumbyworld/
https://mycrumbyworld.com/

Shannon is a dedicated mom, entrepreneur, and professional speaker passionate about connection and empowerment. She created My Crumby World, a unique children's brand designed especially for girls, featuring an engaging collection of books, interactive products, and problem-solving packets. These resources equip young girls with the tools needed to navigate friendships, manage emotions, resolve conflicts, and embrace failure as a steppingstone to growth. Through relatable characters and inspiring stories, Shannon helps girls celebrate their individuality while discovering their inner strength, kindness, and generosity.

As a speaker, Shannon focuses on the transformative power of connection. She emphasizes the importance of building strong bonds with children to better understand and address the challenges they face at school and with peers. Shannon also advocates for connected workplaces, explaining how trust-driven environments enhance relationships, foster knowledge-sharing, and boost collaboration. She believes that the stronger the connections we cultivate—the more empowered and effective we become.

Forced Paths, Found Strength: Lessons from the Road We Didn't Choose

By Shannon Addison

The Journey Begins, Looking for Answers

Huddled in the fetal position on the floor of my office, tears streamed down my face as I stared out the window at the clear blue sky. My voice broke through the silence, a desperate cry for the one person who always knew how to soothe my fears.

"WHERE ARE YOU?" I yelled. "CAN YOU HELP ME?"

My mother had always been my rock, the voice of reason who could pull me back from the edge and spark creativity when I hit a block. Whenever our kids felt under the weather, she was on the internet, researching symptoms even before I thought to call the doctor.

But now, she was gone.

My mother has always been my anchor, the one who steadied me amidst life's storms. She was not just a confidant but also an active partner in every challenge I faced, always ready with advice or quick to calm my nerves during moments of high stress. Now, as my daughter faced an inexplicable health scare during middle school, the absence of my mother's wisdom was palpable. The situation was far more serious than I had anticipated, and my husband and I were desperately searching for answers, feeling the strain of our relentless quest for a diagnosis. We were going from doctor to doctor—but getting nowhere. We had become overwhelmed, trying to piece together what was afflicting our daughter during her tumultuous seventh-grade year. She had complained of feeling "a little off" just days before Christmas. I had dismissed it as typical end-of-semester exhaustion mixed with holiday stress, but the reality was far graver.

Dealing with a prolonged illness is never easy, and it feels even more overwhelming when it affects your child. We spent countless hours worried about each of her symptoms, hoping to obtain an accurate diagnosis so that a treatment plan could follow as soon as possible. It was challenging to balance the emotions surrounding our daughter's situation with the need to maintain realistic expectations. We had to concentrate on her immediate needs and determine what actions we could take each day to help her stay engaged in her life.

When faced with a major life change, such as an unexpected illness, the instinct is to return to normal as quickly as possible. However, if we don't allow ourselves the flexibility to evaluate a "new normal," we may miss potential solutions to our problems. I also realized the importance of being open about our experiences rather than keeping them private, as you never know where you will find valuable insights. This lesson was highlighted when our oldest daughter had friends over, and I overheard one of them ask her what was wrong with her sister. For a moment, I thought about brushing him off by saying it was "too complicated" to explain, as I was busy researching her symptoms for possible diagnoses. However, when I relented and shared her complaints with him, he nodded thoughtfully and said, "It sounds like she has P.O.T.S. I know someone else who has it and complains about similar issues."

Could it be possible that he just diagnosed her? I quickly Googled P.O.T.S. and discovered that it stands for Postural Orthostatic Tachycardia Syndrome. Within minutes, I was reading stories and examples that eerily resembled what we were experiencing with our daughter.

By discussing our experiences with others and welcoming their insights, we uncovered the answers we were seeking.

Armed with our new knowledge and unwavering persistence, we managed to get her seen by a specialist, receiving a diagnosis and treatment plan within four months. This was remarkably shorter than the 5–7-year average that most patients were facing at the time to obtain an accurate diagnosis for her condition.

Having to Change Course

Just before my daughter fell ill, I launched a business dedicated to teaching girls about friendship, connection, acceptance, and kindness. I was fully immersed, working closely with teachers, guidance counselors, and students across multiple schools. But as my daughter's symptoms intensified and she struggled to make it through a single school day, my focus shifted entirely. I still remember dropping her off in the mornings and parking in the visitor lot, anxiously waiting for the call telling me she couldn't stay. During those days, I was filled with dread, knowing that at any moment, I'd have to rush back inside to take her home. The knot in my stomach tightened every time she only managed to last an hour.

Eventually, a guidance counselor suggested hospital homebound status so she could keep up with her studies. I sat in her office and wept as I described our situation to her. She gently said, "You can't keep waiting in the parking lot every morning. This isn't sustainable for either of you." Though difficult to hear, her words were one of the few sources of real guidance I had in the darkness I was navigating. Most people around me simply stepped back, offering "space" to figure things out. But that space felt vast and isolating, filled with silence that echoed my own fears. I felt so alone.

My daughter, feeling that same isolation, turned to social media to fill the void and maintain connections with her peers. At the time, my husband and I thought her internet presence might help her stay integrated with her friend group; we had no idea what impact social media would have on her mental health. In retrospect, it is clear to me now that social media only compounded the alienation my daughter was experiencing. Instagram, Snapchat, and similar platforms proved to be inadequate replacements for real friendships. In fact, these platforms caused significant harm to her already fragile sense of identity. I now recognize that this issue affects many teenage girls and needs to be addressed on a larger scale.

Through all of this, I was wracked with guilt over the pain and isolation I felt, knowing that my daughter was the one enduring this unpredictable illness firsthand. I would have traded places with her if it meant she could have her life back. My business, which I'd been so passionate about, became a distant memory. I stepped away entirely, too consumed and distracted to think about speaking engagements or presentations. I had no idea at the time how much this experience would ultimately reshape my journey.

By the time she reached the end of middle school, I had watched her face the difficulties of a complex medical condition but also the scrutiny of her peers, who didn't understand what she was going through. It was excruciating to witness. Despite everything, what kept her going was the dream of returning to school. She missed her friends, the energy, and the sense of belonging that came with being part of her community. A few friends reached out with messages and visits, bringing cards and hugs.

She was thrilled to finally return, filled with hope for a fresh start. But the reality was harsher than either of us expected. Instead of the warmth she envisioned, she was met with whispers and skepticism.

"You don't look sick!" "What's wrong with you?"

Her classmates and her friends demanded answers she didn't have and couldn't explain. When she struggled to satisfy their curiosity, they began crafting their own narratives.

"She's faking it." "She just wants attention." "She even drank bleach."

It wasn't until I received a call from a concerned teacher that I realized how deeply these rumors had taken root. These were her peers, her friends—seventh-grade girls.

My daughter never fully disclosed how difficult things had become for her at school because she was concerned about us worrying about her. Later, she admitted that she perceived her illness as a kind of failure and wanted to prove to us that she was capable of handling school and everything that came with it. Although she continued to struggle with the effects of her illness and social fallout at school, you'd never know it just by looking at her.

I understood, during the most challenging times of this journey, that I couldn't serve two masters. The health of our daughter came first—there was no question about that. Even so, stepping away from my business to care for her felt like a personal failure. Giving up something into which I had invested so much time, energy, and passion was devastating for me. What I didn't initially realize when I took that step back was the capacity it gave me to evaluate my direction and refocus from a fresh perspective.

By embracing the unexpected shift that led me off my prior path, I uncovered a transformative direction for my business that has the potential to drive significant success.

My business is predicated on empowering girls by fostering acceptance and understanding through the values of kindness, compassion, empathy, and resilience. When I started my business, my daughter was still in elementary school, and at that time, I observed manipulation tactics and relational aggression through the nonverbal communication of fourth-grade girls. These observations were the initial inspiration for my business's mission, but witnessing my daughter experience interpersonal cruelty among her peers after falling ill opened my eyes to the full extent of this pervasive issue.

I felt compelled to create resources for parents and caregivers to help their daughters recognize feelings of inadequacy or lack of acceptance, which can lead to a tendency to tear others down rather than uplift them. At that time, my daughter had not yet faced the full scope of the bullying and cruelty that began in middle school and continued through high school.

Watching her endure such torment prompted me to engage with parents, teachers, guidance counselors, and others about the harmful behaviors that begin in early grades. My goal is to help correct these issues as they develop and provide girls with opportunities to make better choices about how they treat one another.

My mom instilled in me the importance of using my voice for good. This valuable lesson guided me to uncover the distinct qualities of my voice and inspired me to leverage it to drive meaningful change in the world.

Unexpected Potholes Along the Way and How to Address Them

After placing our daughter in a private school for her first year of high school, we ended up moving her to a public high school where she was able to resume some of her favorite activities. This allowed us to establish a routine, and life finally began to resemble something closer to normal. Seemingly, she was managing the challenges of school, volleyball, and her illness much better than she had during her last year of middle school. We, like everyone else at the time, were unaware that we were about to face another significant setback, one of far broader magnitude. One evening during spring break that year, while sitting down for dinner, we received a robocall from the school district informing us that students would not be returning to school for the rest of the school year due to COVID-19. At that time, no one had a comprehensive understanding of what exactly COVID-19 was; my husband and I agonized over the impact it may have on our daughter, given her medical condition, and we did whatever we could to prevent her potential exposure to the virus.

Like the rest of the world, my children and I were adjusting to life behind a screen. My husband and I were so focused on maintaining our youngest daughter's physical health due to a relentless fear of relapse, and our hypervigilance prevented us from seeing the impact this experience was having on her mental health. Isolation was once again taking its toll on her.

We had hoped that the brief time she spent in school would help my daughter adjust to the balance of school life, but it only provided a small glimpse of what it would be like to face COVID-19 alongside a chronic illness. As a precaution, we placed her in therapy, where the therapist proclaimed how remarkably well-adjusted and intelligent she was. However, we later discovered that she approached therapy the same way she approached other kinds of challenging environments—not as a means of help, but as a setting in which she had to prove she was not failing.

She was a people pleaser and knew exactly what to say to satisfy those evaluating her, which gave the perception that she was making continuous, uninterrupted progress. My husband and I were reassured by our daughter's perceived progress, eager for any growth our daughter might find under such unprecedented circumstances. After enduring a difficult year, followed by another challenging one, we were so desperate for good news that we readily trusted that our daughter's mental health was in a good place.

When the time came to resume in-person classes, she assured us that she was ready, but her enthusiasm was not as strong as it had been when she first received approval to return after her extended absence during middle school. She was going back to public high school with some of her middle school peers, with whom she had formed strong bonds. We were hopeful that we would return to a life and schedule that felt normal. However, things were different this time. She began forming friendships with girls who were very different from her previous friends;

these new friendships often led her into trouble. She started hanging out with agitators. Some of these girls we met, while others we did not. None of them, though, were friends she had known previously who had supported her during her most difficult times. This was the first warning sign that I failed to recognize.

Even though she was back in school full-time, she would retreat to her room for hours at a time when she was at home, not wanting to engage with us except for meals or going to and from school. This was a clear indication of trouble that we couldn't ignore. We began to set requirements for her to spend more time outside of her room. Although she complied grudgingly, she quickly became skilled at pretending everything was fine when she was around us.

When her grades began to slip, we knew something was wrong, even though she was doing her best to reassure us that it was just a hiccup, and everything was fine. After struggling so much alongside my daughter to define a new semblance of normal life, I wanted to see her doing better, more than anything. When she assured me that I had nothing to worry about, I needed to believe her. My perception of her mental state didn't last long, however: one night, when my daughter and I were home alone together, she ventured out of her room and plopped down next to me with a heaviness I could feel from the moment she sat.

"What is it?" I asked.

Rather than responding to me, she lifted the side of her shorts to show me an area where she had been cutting herself. It took me a couple of minutes to register what she was showing me and what it meant.

"I'm not okay, Mom." All at once she was speaking and sobbing and telling me how bad things were in school, with friends, with everything. And somewhere inside, I already knew this but didn't want to acknowledge it.

"It's okay. It's going to be okay. Thank you for telling me what is going on. We will get you help. It's all going to be okay." These words kept spilling from my mouth almost robotically; it was like I was following a manual. I kept thinking of all the things I was supposed to say, rather than what I wanted to say.

She hugged me for a minute, then wiped her tears and went back to her room. I went into my bathroom and sat down on the floor next to the toilet. I was desperately trying to figure out how I felt. I was sick to my stomach; I was profoundly sad; I was terribly angry at myself; I was so incredibly desperate to talk to my mom.

"Why does she have to go through this?" I cried out loud. "Why her and not me?"

I sat there on the floor in silence, completely bewildered for the longest time. I didn't know what I was supposed to do. There was no manual for this. My husband was away for work, and I did not want to share this with him until he got home.

After lying awake for most of the night, I woke up the next morning determined to handle the situation as best as I could on my own. I realized that I needed to explore crisis counseling for her due to the self-harming behavior she was exhibiting. Feeling overwhelmed, I began by calling our family physician for recommendations.

Finding the right counselor for her was not an easy task. We needed to have an honest conversation about what therapy is and what it isn't. We tried out half a dozen counselors before discovering one with whom she felt completely comfortable confiding.

The biggest challenge I faced was helping my daughter understand that, as her mother, my role was to protect her from anyone who could cause her harm. In this case, the person causing her harm was herself. I struggled with how to trust that she wouldn't pose a threat to herself in the future, and I was unsure how to proactively recognize when she might be struggling. I also worried that she might not feel she could trust me to help her when she really needed it. Ultimately, I decided to seek therapy for myself as well.

This hurdle taught me that even though I had done extensive research on her illness and the complications that accompanied it, I wasn't as prepared for the impact this illness would have on her mental health. Given her history as a perfectionist, I assumed she was approaching her social and mental health struggles with the same drive. This unexpected turn of events hit me like a pothole in the road—something that could damage your car without warning. I realized that to avoid such hazards, one must continuously pay attention to the journey and always be scanning ahead. I wasn't interpreting the warning signs quickly enough, and as a result, I faced the consequences. I was approaching her illness with tunnel vision, and it prevented me from paying attention to the other potential hazards around me.

Stay vigilant for potential hazards on your journey, allowing yourself to be ready to respond swiftly. By seeking a holistic understanding of the path forward, you can navigate smoothly and perhaps even steer clear of the potholes entirely.

When You Get Lost, Ask for Help

Recognizing that some situations are beyond your control can be challenging, but it's an important realization. At that moment, I knew I was completely out of my depth with my daughter. When faced with such obstacles in life, it's essential to seek help. If you're unsure where to turn, start with the most obvious resources: your doctor, your priest, your parent, or your best friend. As mothers and women, it can be especially difficult for us to admit when something is too overwhelming to handle alone. However, asking for help is crucial for overcoming unforeseen challenges, particularly those that exceed our abilities.

In times of crisis, my first response was always to turn to my mother. Without her, it felt like my support system had been disabled. However, I realized that it wasn't. I needed to be open to creating a new normal with a different group of supportive people. This wasn't easy, but it was achievable.

The key is to establish your support system before a crisis occurs and to communicate to your contacts the roles they will play. We live in a society that craves interdependence; we want to feel needed, yet we often hesitate to rely on others. This approach simply doesn't work—it is vital to become comfortable with asking our loved ones for help when we need it most.

Allow others to help you when you need it, and be ready to help when others are in need. It's really that simple.

Finding Your Way Home

I remember reaching a point where we finally felt like we were out of the woods with our daughter. We were managing her symptoms (for the most part), and she was dual enrolled for her senior year of high school. This meant she was taking classes at a local community college, earning credits for both her high school and some college requirements.

She had endured a lot of bullying from a couple of girls in her senior class. These girls had become friends with her during a low point in her mental state but had since fallen out of favor. While we were relieved that she no longer spent time around them, believing they were not contributing to her overall well-being, we were concerned that she still went out of her way to avoid them. It was sometimes unavoidable for her to encounter them, which led to setbacks in her happiness.

Home is not always what it used to be. One evening during the holidays, after enjoying a wonderful dinner with our daughter, we experienced this firsthand. She had been opening a fun advent calendar that revealed little surprises each day. After finishing her meal, she excitedly asked if she could open the door to see that day's gift. To her delight, she found a bath bomb hidden inside.

Thrilled, she cleared her place at the table and announced that she was going to take a nice bubble bath and get ready for bed.

After washing up and putting on our pajamas, I suddenly heard an alarming sound coming from the front room.

"BAM! BAM! BAM!"

I turned to my husband, feeling anxious as I couldn't imagine what was happening.

"BAM! BAM! BAM!" My heart started pounding as I quickly grabbed a robe. Together, we headed to the front door and turned on the light. When we opened the door, we stood in shock at the sight of two uniformed sheriff's officers, who looked very concerned.

"We received a call to conduct a welfare check at this address," one of them said emphatically. I struggled to understand what was going on.

"This must be a mistake," I started. "We were just getting ready for..."

"Is this 5111...?" I listened as they recited our address.

"Yes," I replied, and my husband looked at me, realizing what was happening.

The gravity of the situation hit me like an avalanche. I knew we were about to take a trip to the hospital. My daughter had just confided in someone that she didn't feel her life was worth living, just moments after telling us how excited she was about her new bath bomb.

After coaxing her out of the bathroom and helping her get dressed while she cried in fear and embarrassment, we loaded into the car and began our journey to the hospital. It felt as though I was observing the entire experience from above, creating a parallel universe in which I imagined my mother watching me witness life unravel in a silent mix of horror and sadness.

I thought we had safely returned to a state of normalcy, but it became clear that we hadn't. We were retracing our steps, re-evaluating our approach, to ensure that my daughter had the support she needed to heal. At the hospital, after our daughter was thoroughly evaluated to ensure that she was not an immediate threat to herself, we were allowed to take her home. This experience prompted us to take a different approach to her mental health counseling, which now includes group therapy, a change in medication, and intensive counseling.

I realized that we had not yet found our way home. While we reached a place that felt comfortable, comfort doesn't always equate to a true state of completion.

I also came to understand that, despite being a protective mother who tried to shield her children from all harm, I couldn't protect my daughter from this situation. I had to learn how to best support my daughter even when I could not outright protect her.

Are we home now? Yes and no. Ironically, we sold the house where everything happened and are now living in a rental. This feels fitting for our situation. We don't let ourselves get too comfortable, and we conduct regular inspections to ensure everything is in working order.

Our daughter is currently working but is not attending school. After completing two years at junior college, she requested some time to figure out her relationship with education. We are supporting her by giving her the space she needs to determine her own path. She is still in therapy, and she has an immense talent and passion for crochet and other forms of craft art.

We are all constantly learning how to be better stewards of our journey.

Reaching a comfortable place amidst conflict does not mean it is resolved.

Lessons From the Path

Our journey began on one path but took an unexpected turn. As parents, we must be prepared for our lives with children to take various directions and brace ourselves for the challenges we will face while navigating this journey. The same principle applies to our professional lives; we must pay attention to where our path leads when it suddenly shifts course. Instead of reacting hastily, we need to observe the new direction and remain open to the insights that accompany it. While I wouldn't want to relive the difficult experiences with my daughter, I am grateful for what they have taught me. They provide me with a unique perspective to share with other parents—one that comes from having faced challenges, navigated through tough situations, and ultimately emerged stronger.

Robin Roberts created the mantra, "Make your mess your message," which encourages us to serve others by sharing our personal experiences. Each of us can do this. For me, many messages of hope have emerged from moments of deep despair. I remember days spent curled up on the floor of my office, crying out for my mom, and the sleepless nights filled with anxiety about managing a chronic condition in one of our children. I never would have imagined that something good could come from something bad. But it had.

I have a deep passion for delivering speeches to parents, where I warn them about the dangers of peer pressure and social media. I also share effective ways to help protect our children. Having experienced this journey with my daughter, I am determined to change the cruel dynamics that often exist among girls. My goal is to spare other parents from this kind of pain. Together, we can empower our young girls by providing them with the tools they need to combat these negative behaviors and create a brighter future for everyone.

Shanon Opp

Therapist Assistant

https://www.linkedin.com/in/shanon-opp-a99601226/
https://www.facebook.com/profile.php?id=750509765
https://www.instagram.com/shanondulc/

I am a passionate 52 year old who works as a Therapy Assistant. At age 43 I went back to college to get my diploma and am driven to help others make an impact in their lives, by working with Physical and Occupational therapists. I motivate, encourage, and teach seniors to live a better functioning life or get back to the fulfilling life they once had prior to injury, surgery or other health issues. I am physically active, adventurous, curious and resilient with a heart filled with compassion. My inner beauty shines most when I am enjoying outdoor activities and nature.

I believe age is just a number that we seem to put our own limitations on. If we change the thoughts of what our limits are, anything is possible and age is no longer a factor and shouldn't define what we can do.

Change starts in the mind!

I Am Enough!

By Shanon Opp

I Never Saw It till It Was Too Late

It all started around July 24, 2021, when I had my first car accident that was unexplained but treated as a seizure. Then, it happened: The day that would end it all. The day when my heart was shattered, and I felt the world turn upside down. The day where I found the email that proved what I had been suspecting. He was having an affair, and I felt he was in love with her. I never want anyone to feel like I felt at that moment. I couldn't breathe, my heart hurt/shattered. I don't know how to explain the pain I felt. Why would he do this? What had I done to deserve this betrayal? When did this happen? I had so many questions and no answers. How could he live with himself constantly lying to me?

Suddenly it all became clear. I saw all the signs. I no longer trusted him.

With that shield of trust gone, I started seeing things, putting together things he said or neglected to say. I felt like I was going crazy with all the emotions and thoughts I was having. I wanted to deny it but yet I couldn't. I wouldn't. I held onto all that I had learned for two weeks, then confronted him on Aug 16, 2021. When I confronted him, he denied it 3 times until I stated I had hired an investigator. He drove us to a spot out in the country, and we talked only to figure out that he had more respect for his lover than he did for his wife of 26 years. He called her in private to tell her they were done and had her text me. Yes, text me that she was sorry their friendship had to end. Friendship? I saw naked pictures of her. What kind of friendship was she thinking she had with my husband? He treated me as a buddy, not his wife, when he divulged details about his affairs and experiences over the past few years. He bragged about the things he had been experiencing and learning on sites as if it was something I wanted to know about. It was a punch in the gut.

What sane person would think this was acceptable, respectful, or even normal?

How could the unbreakable life I thought I had, be so broken, and how could the man I chose to live the rest of my life with be so cold, calculating, manipulative, angry, unrelenting, demanding, and a compulsive liar? Only those who have felt this kind of betrayal could comprehend some of what I felt. I did things and said things that were out of character for me, not realizing I still loved him and was trying to gain control over the events that were erupting before me.

The day came when everything started spiraling, and things escalated to the point where the cops were called. Emotionally distraught. The officers were concerned about my welfare and asked me if I had plans of killing myself. I replied that I hadn't thought about it, but now, why not! I couldn't believe my life was at the lowest point I had ever been at. Thinking straight was impossible. My heart was officially shattered, and I did not believe it would ever be repaired. The person who swore to love me till death do us part was vastly helping to destroy my self-worth. Looking back at that time, I felt like I had multiple personalities to help me cope with all that I went through.

Driven to the hospital by an officer where victim services asked me several questions. I cried more than I care to admit. I was desolate. I felt so disrespected, lonely, so unloved and unworthy. No trust in anyone or anything. I was left in a room for many hours with a guard outside the door. While in there, I heard other women crying. One in particular sticks out in my head as being so destroyed that I will never forget it. I remember thinking that situations like what I was experiencing needed to stop. No more hurt, no more affairs, and men destroying women's self-worth through words, lack of words, or disrespect. No more women crying for hours. For days. For weeks, because they felt unworthy of how they had been treated emotionally, physically, mentally, or all of the above.

I spent about 10 days in the mental health unit collecting my soul, self-worth, my strength to move on and be the best I could be despite how my husband made me feel. During my time there, I ended up helping others to keep myself from overthinking and going down the dark hole that kept threatening to swallow me whole. I found comfort in helping others, and by focusing on others, I was able to start healing. Beginning to now believe, I had more self-worth and strength than what I kept telling myself those days. My thoughts were an issue, and I was learning how to take control of them. By listening to others and their issues, I was able to see that my life was not as bad as I thought. My husband was upset that the doctor would not disclose anything to him. He made many statements to make it seem like I had bipolar or another mental health issue. Perhaps to plead a case of insanity or whatever he had planned in his head to avoid paying me alimony. I believe he systematically planned to make less money than me for 3-4 years to avoid owing me alimony.

All the talk we had about others going through a divorce was about him trying to get a feel for how I would react when he broke the news that he wanted a divorce. What kind of guy does that to the mother of their children? No remorse and no regrets. It was clear on numerous occasions it would not bother him if I had killed myself, or died before the divorce was settled. He wanted his lover and his new life and no longer cared about who he hurt in the process.

The day I was released from the hospital, reality hit hard. It was time to tell my family and get their support. I was embarrassed and ashamed of my unfaithful husband. I felt like I failed at my marriage, which I soon validated by changing my thoughts. I never failed at my marriage cause I never gave up. I can't fix something if I am not aware that it is broken. I cannot control anyone but myself and it takes two to make things work in a marriage.

It was Christmas 2021, and I was now down 20 lbs and looked anorexic. I was living with my mom off and on and was dealing with an overload of advice from those who wanted to help. I was struggling to keep it all together at work while dealing with my health issues, sleepless nights, and weight loss. I tried everything. Journaling, counseling, drugs, alcohol, binge-watching TV, binge-shopping, staying insanely busy, meditating, reading positive motivational quotes, going to church, anything to keep me on the right path. I desperately was looking for a way out of this nightmare that kept threatening my day-to-day routine.

Who was I? I couldn't recognize myself. I was pretending, acting. Someone who was trying to figure out who they were and what they wanted to become. I was fighting the voices in my head daily, sometimes hourly, that said I wasn't good enough, wasn't perfect, not fun or interesting. I would never be loved the way I deserved, so I should give up on any relationship in the future. I started to read what other women had gone through, and they were so full of hate, bitterness, disgust, hurt, anger, and so much more. They were reliving what had happened to them and would not let it go. I was going down that same path, and it only made things worse. I hated how I felt and decided that I was NOT going to stay in that frame of mind. I did not want those feelings to keep occurring in my life. I wanted love, joy, happiness, and rainbows.

My children were also going through the divorce in their own way, and I had to set up boundaries with them. By doing this, I was able to keep the hurt from taking over my days or weeks. By setting boundaries, I was able to take control and live my life freely without feeling bad when they asked for money or told me things about their father, which was hurtful. I made myself a priority and decided I would help if I had the means and it didn't compromise my self-worth, beliefs, values, or the respect I deserved. I am now estranged from both of my children due to the illusion of truth. It has been a struggle and it led me to research how others deal with this issue. I was astonished to learn that there are thousands out there. In fact, one in four people are dealing with family members who are estranged in one way or another. I have respected my childrens space and have given them time to see what truly is the truth. Not, the illusion.

I had a second car accident at the end of May 2022. Again, not allowed to drive for 3 months. I had a concussion and was on modified work. Luckily, my work accommodated me for this as it happened during working hours. No driving meant I was back to taking the bus, walking, and using my bike when possible. I had to rely on friends and family for support, and I can't express how grateful I was for their help. Still trying to negotiate separation issues and move towards divorce. What would the future hold? No support from my kids and desperately trying to keep moving forward with the tools I had gained. My husband would not budge on giving me spousal support. Apparently, I did not deserve it for all the years and effort I put into my marriage and kids.

Being the conscientious person I was, I was not satisfied with my diagnosis that the car accidents were caused by seizures. I was persistent in my search and worked with doctors to figure out what was causing these episodes.

Finally, a New Diagnosis

Syncope was my diagnosis in March 2023. During a simple test called the tilt table test, my heart stopped for 15 seconds. This meant I needed a pacemaker and was not safe to drive again until I had surgery and recovered for 6 weeks. No driving again for the third time in two years. At this time, I was blessed. I had found someone who wanted to be with me and was willing to help me get back and forth to work until it was time to have surgery. A man that I had only been dating for less than a month stepped up and became my knight in shining armor. A man of integrity and honor. A man who gave me the respect I desperately required in a relationship after having been cheated on. A man who made me feel like I was enough. A man who continues day after day to remind me about what I have to offer the world. A man that I am now engaged to.

I tried many things to get where I am today. It wasn't easy, and I learned I needed to be patient with myself. I needed to be mindful every hour of every day until I felt I was battling the negative thoughts successfully and on a regular basis. I needed to take my thoughts and change them to think positively. I needed to be kind and gentle and remind myself how wonderful I was. I was/am ENOUGH for anyone, especially ME. I am worthy of the best life I can have.

I remind myself daily that I am enough for anyone to love. I wasn't perfect, but I did the best I could. I wasn't the one that ruined my marriage or the family I once had. I am attractive, smart, fun, and adventurous, so why would I deny myself an amazing, authentic life, just because my husband chose his ego over me? Why punish myself and deny myself love? I would rather love again than avoid it and never have the full life I deserved. I stopped with self-pity as it would not allow me to move forward. It only allowed me to punish myself over and over again and kept me living in the past.

Things I Did to Persevere, Heal, and Move Forward

Practice Gratitude:

For what you have and how strong you are becoming. Tell yourself 3–5 things you are grateful for that morning, and before bed each night this helps you to see and appreciate many things we take for granted. It helps to show you that what you thought you lost, is not as great as you once thought. You have the ability to have a greater life than what you ever had or dreamed possible.

Practice Faith:

I took a course called Freedom Session at my church, which helped me learn more about my relationship with Jesus. By growing in my faith and in the Word during this difficult time, I was able to grow and change, knowing that I was loved no matter what and that God is always with me to help if I ask for it. There were so many negative thoughts I battled, and I needed to change them to change how I felt, said, or did. I changed them so I could have peace of mind, move forward, and stop the endless loop of negativity, ruminating, and assumptions that threatened to consume me. Through the word, my faith taught me how and why I should forgive. Through God, anything is possible.

Practice Forgiveness:

Forgiveness for yourself for all the bad things you tell yourself you are, but are not true. Tell yourself three positive things about yourself or strengths you have, daily. Remove any negative thoughts and replace them with three positive things instead. Stop self-pity. It doesn't get you anywhere but going down a negative and self-destructive road.

Forgiveness for your ex. Extremely hard, and it will take time. The more you practice it, the better you feel. When you forgive, bitterness, anger, and hatred go away, leaving room for love, happiness, new experiences, and exciting things to enter your life.

Forgiveness for the people in your life that mean well but express too much or make you second guess what is best for you. Forgiveness is more for you than it is for them. Forgiving those who have hurt you helps you to heal. I know it's hard to believe, but like others before me, I can tell you: It REALLY does work.

Spend time alone: Time gathering your thoughts and what you want, not what others think you should do. This is your life, so be authentic and live it the way you want. Be true to yourself. Get to know and love yourself again. Figure out what your values, beliefs and attitude are towards people or events in your life. What does that look like, and do you need to make changes?

Be gentle with myself: Bad days, hours, or weeks may occur. Stop using negative terms when referring to yourself. Look at what you achieved, not what you haven't completed yet. Look at mistakes or failures as a chance to grow, not a reason to give up.

Set boundaries: People's reaction to what happened was out of my control, and I had to deal with how they perceived things even if it wasn't the truth. The things I could control, I set boundaries up to protect my heart. By setting boundaries, I was able to control who made me feel my best while avoiding or limiting those who tended to hurt me. I am learning to give those I can't control, space to grow and hopefully start a new relationship in the future.

I still have moments that throw me for a loop, but I remind myself that I don't want hatred, anger, judgment, bitterness, resentfulness, self-pity, or vengeful thoughts to have any kind of leverage in my new life. Changes were made, gratitude was expressed, boundaries were set, forgiveness practiced, and the persistence of happiness has helped me develop into a woman who now knows her self-worth. A woman who wants others to know that they are worthy and have the power to start over again and succeed in their quest. Believe in themselves and know they are worthy of anything and anyone, most importantly, themself. We need more positivity in the world. We need to start listening to each other's stories and ask them, "How can I support you?"

People are so quick to help, but we have the answers within us if we are listened to and asked the right questions.

Every day, I work on getting beyond my comfort zone and fears, by trying new things and challenging myself to do what I once believed impossible or daunting. I am contemplating a couple of ideas for online businesses. Taking singing lessons to feel more confident performing in front of people. I procrastinate and am working on getting past this issue, as this is something new for me. I once got things done as soon as possible, and now I have many days of anxiety before I get them done. I know I will get past this too. I AM my own WORST ENEMY.

If I continue to practice my faith and believe in myself, I CAN DO ANYTHING because I AM ENOUGH! So are YOU!

I wrote this poem in this trying time of my life. I just found it and wanted to share it with you all. I hope you enjoy it.

I AM ENOUGH

I gave you the key to my heart
I trusted you to open, not break apart

I was ensured my heart could be mended by
Family, friends and faith
So that I may show many, it could not be replaced

I shared my scars for all to see
So pride and grace would set me free

We can all be healed when we share what has been done
For others to know the fight we have won

The spirit within me keeps me going strong
My scars will not define me as I move along

The feelings of grief wash me in waves
Until calmness floods me and time throws then away

My key is now hidden for me to control
By believing in my power, I will achieve my goals

With Peace, love and acceptance, doubt will no longer exist
I hold my head high, as life is worth the risk

Mistakes make us persevere and able to foresee
It's not about perfection, but reality

So when I feel unworthy or feel all alone
I look myself in the Mirror and shout,
"I AM ENOUGH"

By: Shanon Opp

Sheena L. Smith

Life Simply Put
Brave Thinking Life Coach, CMWC, CNC, CYW

https://www.linkedin.com/in/sheena-smith-life-coach/
https://www.facebook.com/sheenazzy2/
https://www.instagram.com/sheenazzy/
https://sheenalsmith.com/

Sheena Smith is a Certified Mental Wellness Coach specializing in gut-brain axis wellness, with over 45 years of experience helping families thrive—and a love for popcorn and licorice (together, naturally). As a trusted consultant, she's been a special education assistant for 23 years and has raised four incredible kids, including two with special needs, giving her firsthand insight into family challenges.

When she's not working at her day job in education or coaching, you might find her riding camels in Africa, swimming in underground caves, or even skydiving. An international best-selling author of All Kids Can Thrive, Brain Gym® Instructor, and speaker, Sheena brings warmth, joy, and a touch of adventure to everything she does. Learn more at sheenalsmith.com.

Surviving the Storm:
Keys to Finding Life Beyond Loss

By Sheena L. Smith

I've discovered grief is a journey, not a destination, and that losing someone you love changes your world forever. Choices you make after such an event determine the way you recover and grieve successfully – if there is such a thing as successful grief.

My hero, my first love, passed away in March 2019, and my life has never been the same. He was the kind of dad who was always full of knowledge and wisdom. His knowledge came from his own life experiences as a steel plant worker, photo lab owner, photographer, building supply store owner and building project estimator. His life experiences growing up gave him additional knowledge and a great deal of resilience.

His unexpected death has caused our family much turmoil and strife. The hardest part was navigating the challenging journey through grief. As I quickly processed my emotions, countless memories seemed to flash through my mind – moments with my dad as a child, a teen and an adult. More than anything, I felt like the little girl I've always been at heart, leaning on her dad and feeling like I'd be lost without him.

He always had a listening ear and sometimes advice I didn't take. He took things to heart and often wanted to solve my problems. I know he felt terrible when he couldn't help me at times.

He was the happiest being as a dad and a papa who would do anything for his kids and grandkids. His greatest pleasure was making every one of us feel special. He got the best laughs from the funny things we would say or do.

In the last years of his life, he had a major health battle with cancer. I couldn't see him as much as I wanted during the times that he dealt with chemo and radiation. My job working with children exposed me to cold and flu viruses. I couldn't risk being with my dad with his weakened immune system. Our communication was limited to phone conversations. Not only did he suffer immensely from the horrific and brutal treatments, which haven't changed in many years, but he developed painful shingles as well. He had seemingly survived cancer a few times over the previous 5 years, but life threw him another health curveball.

About a week before he died, he required an hour-long ambulance ride and had emergency surgery for a life-threatening blocked bowel. I was away on a cruise with my childhood girlfriends at the time. My family did not want to tell me so I wouldn't worry. They were right! When I found out, of course, I worried. I prayed he would be fine and that I would make it in time if it were as bad as it sounded. I could hardly wait to see him when I got home.

The surgery was successful, and he was on the mend. We were so grateful for that. I was thankful to be able to visit him and have some quality conversations. More importantly, I had the opportunity to tell him I loved him a few more times.

On the day that he was to be released from the hospital, he discovered in the shower that the stitches were bleeding. He required a second emergency surgery to close him up properly.

The second surgery was tough on him, but he made it through. He was so grateful! I could tell that he had been very scared of that second surgery. He was so emotional and relieved to be alive.

The following day he was discovered in his hospital room after suffering a massive stroke. The nurses were uncertain as to how long he was in that state of cardiac arrest.

I was shocked to be called into the hospital because he had taken a turn for the worse. I couldn't comprehend the change from how he was so good when I last saw him. I thought he was through the worst and going to be able to go home. Yet we were called in together by the doctor to make decisions we as a family did not want to make. However, we knew in our hearts he was already gone. Not knowing how long he had been without oxygen and seeing the stone gaze in his eyes, it seemed like we had already lost him.

Without continuing into other details, we knew an additional stroke was imminent, and we made the heart-breaking choice of what would happen next. We agreed to the 'Do Not Resuscitate' order. He would not have wanted to live in the condition that would result from another stroke.

We were asked to leave the room while they put a cooling pad under him to see if that would lower his body temperature to prevent another stroke. Everything happened so fast, and we were called back to say goodbye. He was already gone.

I leaned in, kissed him, and whispered, "I love you, Daddy," one last time. I instantly felt the unbearable heaviness of grief. I immediately became that little girl from my childhood.

As a little girl, I always counted on my dad to make everything better. He was my safe place when the storms of life hit, the one who teased me about birds landing on my pouty lip when I sulked and reassured me whenever I had a bad dream. He carried me into the house when I pretended to be sleeping after a long drive home, and the guy who was surprised at how astonished I was when I got my first pair of glasses in grade one. He laughed when he realized that I was amazed to discover that trees had individual branches and leaves. Before that, I thought they were clumps of leaves on sticks. Yes, I certainly did need glasses.

Here I was, in one of the hardest moments of my life, getting knocked down by life, the loss of his life. It was heartbreaking. I just wanted him to remind me that everything would be okay and that he would be okay. I wanted this to just be a bad dream, but it wasn't.

After the kiss and last goodbye, I stepped away from his bed and backed up to let others say goodbye too. In a moment that could only be described as self-preservation, I crossed my arms to hold others back and create my own space. It seemed like a way to shield the world from my brokenness and to hold myself together. I had no strength for anyone else at that moment, let alone myself. We were all devastated and shocked at the same time.

Grief has many stages. It wasn't long before I felt angry at the doctor for not taking precautions. She should have known his history and how weak he was from having two surgeries so close together. I was resentful, feeling that he didn't receive the proper medical care. Knowing that he was susceptible to having a stroke (the doctor had mentioned it to me), he could have been on a machine to notify nursing staff if something was wrong. Instead, he was deprived of oxygen for an undetermined amount of time. It breaks my heart. I felt it was so unfair for him.

We were all too broken to fight the system or try to prove they were negligent in his care. We were thrown into survival mode, and we knew it wouldn't change the outcome.

We were all experiencing the stages of grief as Elizabeth Kubler Ross describes the emotional process of getting through the loss of a loved one. The first stage began immediately for me: denial. I put my mind and heart into self-preservation.

I believe we come here in human form, and we choose our path and our lessons beforehand. My bargaining stage was short. I didn't have a choice. He was gone!

It's hard to process such a profound and unexpected loss in the 5 short days of leave from work.

The days were spent planning his celebration of life with my family. It became a blur as we focused our plan around his favourite holiday, St. Patrick's Day.

In my eulogy, I told everyone some of his wisdom. One of his favourites was what to do if you were ever lost in the woods. Always carry a deck of cards with you. Sit down and start playing solitaire. Sure enough, sooner or later, someone is going to lean over your shoulder and tell you what card to play.

He taught us many things, but he didn't teach my brothers and me, or any of the family, how to live without him.

Back at work, seemingly having had no time to grieve or be sad, I felt divinely protected by my denial frame of mind. Then, onto the new stage of missing him, wanting to call him, hoping the phone would ring. Daily, new memories flashed through my mind. He was my "go-to" guy, long before "google." When I had a question about anything, he always had an answer.

The hardest part of the grief journey was acceptance. Acceptance that he was never coming back, that there would be no new memories, no new pictures with him, no new videos. He, like me, treasured memories captured on film.

Grief is a journey, not a destination. I had to take a path of self-compassion and self-care, mentally and emotionally. It took a few months to process the grief I felt as I moved through the shock.

My advice to others going through the same brokenness, permit yourself to feel sad. Start a journal when you remember special times. Keep traditions and memories alive with your children and grandchildren. Laugh together! Tell the stories!

For over 30 years, my dad read "The Night Before Christmas" to my children on Christmas Eve. Two years before he passed away, I recorded his voice reading the storybook. Now, I am so grateful for that because whenever I'm missing him, I can hear him read that story to me.

I love to take pictures and videos to freeze moments forever. I'm so grateful to have many pictures of my kids with my dad, especially since he was usually a behind-the-scenes kind of person. Just like me, he was usually behind the camera. We even had a photo lab in our apartment when I was growing up, where I learned how to develop pictures. That gave me a deep love for photography, just like he had.

If you are currently grieving, remember this: When you're weary and tired, rest and sleep. Make yourself a priority. Stay nourished and stay hydrated with plenty of water. I didn't follow that advice, so do as I say, not as I did. I consumed too much comfort food, aka junk food. I justified to myself that it was okay to eat anything that I felt made me feel better, but it never truly made me feel better. I was stress eating, and I gained over 15 pounds. If you're strong enough, eat small balanced meals and include things that support your gut health and mental health. Salty and sugary foods are not nourishing and can destroy your health. That is what happened to me in my survival mode, and the result was devastating. I had many health issues going deeper and deeper. Inflammation was rampant in my body. Everything was painful. Then one day, I realized, "Yes, it was painful." Grief was my pain! I had to name it to understand it.

Tips for surviving all "the firsts" and beyond were:

- Talk to others, especially those who've been through the loss of a parent. They'll have a better connection and understanding of your sadness.
- Spend time in nature to ground yourself. I craved it. I craved being alone. Having quiet noise was a trigger for me because my nervous system was so dysregulated.
- Move your body. Exercising helps your mood, muscles and mind.
- Practice mindfulness, practice gratitude. I had so many memories with him. My kids got to know him.
- Honour your loved one and your memory of them by fulfilling your dreams. Move forward in life, do not stay stuck, forgive (if necessary), let go and live!

- Use your creative outlets to process your feelings. For me, it's drawing, creating artwork, writing and continuing the search for our ancestry that my dad had started.
- Meditate. Spend time in the silence of your thoughts.
- Write letters to them so you can store them or burn them once feelings are released.
- Create a memory corner if you don't have a gravesite to visit.

As I stated earlier, I believe we all come here for a reason. I also believe that our loved ones are never more than a thought away. It's like they are behind an invisible curtain. We can't see them, but we know and believe they are there and can hear us. I find comfort in "talking" to him and looking for signs.

Do you look for signs from your loved ones? Which ones?

I find comfort in messages from him. I'll often say, "Ok, Dad, give me a song!" Then I select a random radio station to see what comes up. Sometimes it's a song by a singer or group he loved, like Creedence Clearwater Revival, or a song with lyrics I needed to hear.

Another common way our loved ones attempt to console us is through the appearance of feathers and/or dimes in strange and unexpected places. The appearance of butterflies, repeated numbers, or seeing someone who looks like or is dressed how they did.

Dreams: Often, they will reach out to you in your dreams. You must ask your angels to appear, to help them to come to you in your dreams. One day, when talking to a friend of mine, she said that it had been months since her dad had passed, and she had never dreamt about him yet. I said to her, "Well, did you ask him to come to you in your dreams?" Her response was, "No." The next time I saw her, she happily told me that her dad visited her that night. "He was wearing his old fishing hat, and he had the biggest smile ever." She was so comforted by this.

Birds & animals: Do you notice a particular bird or animal often? Many find comfort in seeing the appearance of a red cardinal or blue jay. Whenever I see a seagull, I think of my dad. He must be feeling so free. One of his favourite books was *Jonathan Livingston Seagull*.

Smells & scents: Another friend and I were talking about her mom, who has passed away, and when she was on her way home, she smelled her mom's favourite perfume in her car. Her mom had never been in that car (when she was, anyhow).

Electrical disturbances: Sometimes your loved ones try to reach you through flashing lights, televisions going off and on, or through home phones ringing and no one being there. Years ago, I lived in a house where the phone would ring in the middle of the night. When I answered, no one was there, but by the background noise, it seemed far away. I heard later that an elderly lady lived there and that she said it happened to her a few times after her husband passed away. He must have been welcoming me as the new owner of his home.

Intuition: Breathe and get yourself calm and centered in a quiet place. When you feel calm ask the loved one to show you their presence by standing behind you, left or right side, you choose. As you stay calm and breathe gently, notice what you feel. Do you feel warmth on the side that you've asked her/him to stand? Feel the love!

Know that they are near. One time I was feeling very sad and alone because my spouse couldn't accompany me for our daughter's surgery that was 8 hours away from home. She woke up from surgery and said, "Who are all those people behind you?"

Trying not to show I was shocked, I nonchalantly said, "Oh, there's people behind me?"

"Yes, she exclaimed, "Three ladies and two men."

I smiled from that moment on. I did not feel so all alone. When I told a nurse about what she said, she commented that she often hears children say things like that when they wake up from surgery. Angels are around us everywhere.

Sadly, not only did our family change, but our world changed. Nothing has ever been the same since.

A more recent and collective experience of grief was during the 2020 pandemic. Grief touched everyone in some shape or form, whether through the physical loss of loved ones, the loss of familiar routines or restrictions of personal freedoms.

We weren't alone in this. Many of us cycled through the stages of grief – shock, denial, anger, bargaining and depression. Ultimately, we needed to find acceptance. Acceptance of our circumstances, acceptance of other viewpoints and acceptance that we still can make a difference and make the best of an unprecedented situation.

When you experience your journey of grief, as everyone will at some point, may you know that it's okay to set boundaries, it's okay to say no and focus on what you can handle. Have patience with yourself! There's no set time for grief. Honour your loved one by finding your happiness so that one day you can smile and remember them through your happiest memories.

Staying broken, lost or even punishing yourself after a loved one's death is not the intent of our journey on earth. Another piece of wisdom my dad used to say was, "Things always work out."

I like to add, "It may not be how we want it to be, but it's how it was meant to be."

May your path be filled with wonder and comfort, and may your journey bring you hope and healing. One day, one step, and one breath at a time. Love is forever!

Sherry Vinson

Founder of Kendi Bella Bouquet's & Thing's LLC

https://www.linkedin.com/in/sherry-vinson-ba9565ab
https://www.facebook.com/profile.php?id=61569448508496
https://www.instagram.com/Mrs_S_Vinson
https://www.kendibella.com/

Sherry Vinson is a devoted wife, mother, and grandmother whose love for family fuels her passion for life. As the creator and founder of Kendi Bella Bouquets & Things LLC, she has turned her creativity into a thriving small business that brings joy and beauty to her community. Beyond her entrepreneurial spirit, Sherry is an aspiring author, seeking to share her journey and inspire others through the written word. She believes in honoring God in all aspects of her life and is dedicated to empowering women to recognize and embrace their own strength. Through her work and writing, she aims to uplift and encourage others, reminding them that they are capable of achieving greatness. With a heart full of love and a mission to inspire, Sherry continues to make a positive impact on those around her.

She Grows Stronger: She Will Not Fail

By Sherry Vinson

In the quiet moments of my life, when grief and stress threatened to overwhelm me, I was feeling broken and alone. I found myself on my knees, in the middle of the floor, crying out to God like I had never done before. It was in these depths of despair that I discovered a wellspring of strength within me, a strength I never knew existed. Somehow I knew God was answering my cries, and I would never be the same. This is my testament to that journey, a story of how I grew stronger through faith, and how you, too, can find empowerment in your own life's challenges.

Like many women, I have many roles in life. I am a loving wife, mother, grandmother, daughter, friend, dedicated church member, entrepreneur, and employee. But most importantly, I am a believer in the almighty God. I am not perfect in any way; however, I do my best to be found pleasing to the Father. In other words, I'm just a girl trying to conquer the maze of life. So far what I have concluded is that I need nothing or no one as much as I need God walking with me and showing me the way.

That's it. That's the secret to life's journey. Whether surviving or thriving, we need God! No matter the trial or the situation, He is the answer. Whatever you may be going through, seek God. I promise if you choose to listen to Him, you will make it. I can say this because I have had to make that choice while not truly knowing if God could even hear me, let alone bless me, especially feeling as unworthy as I did. Unfortunately, I had been there time and time again. I can now proudly say I will never have to make that choice again. My decision is final and I am never looking back. I refuse to let go of my belief that God has saved me, and He will continue to keep me covered with His blessings as long as I hold on to His hand.

Life has thrown some heavy punches my way. For starters, my parents divorced when I was just a kid. From what I understand, my sister suffered abuse at the hands of my mom's boyfriend, which led to a court case. Eventually, my brother, sister, and I were placed in my dad's care.

My father didn't have much money, but he worked hard and did his best to raise us. Meanwhile, my mom moved from Florida to New York and started a new family, having my two younger brothers. So, we did not get to have that mother-daughter relationship that I had craved. For years, I believed that if she had lived closer, my life would have been better. But God knew best. About ten years ago, she moved back to Florida, and even now, I sometimes find myself longing for the kind of relationship that we have yet to create.

Although I did not enjoy the most ideal childhood, I do believe my parents did the best they could with what they knew and what they had.

As a young teen, I survived rape and molestation. I have dealt with teenage pregnancy, the devastating loss of my baby boy, and my own near-death experience that left me questioning if I'd even make it to see adulthood. Before I even turned 16, I had already faced more heartbreak than most people experience in a lifetime. These are just some of the things, minus some of the sad details. Each of these moments left scars, but they also became the groundwork for a strength I didn't know I had.

By the age of 23, I had 3 daughters. They became my world. I had missed my chances for the college campus experience, which I always wanted. However, my three angels have been a constant source of motivation for me. For years they were my only reason for wanting to live. I will never forget the look on their little faces when I had to be rushed to the hospital to have my stomach pumped because I had chosen the easy way out and swallowed a bottle of pills. It was an instant regret for me. I promised God and them that no matter how bad things felt I would never ever do that to them again. I have to say God did bless me with 3 of the most beautiful, intelligent, loving young ladies to care for. To think God trusted me with His children and I almost blew it. I just thank God for second and third chances.

From then on, I wanted to be a living example of strength for my daughters, so I made it my mission to shield them from the worries that weighed so heavily on me. Bills, rent, food—I carried those burdens quietly, determined that they would never feel the struggles I faced. I wanted them to enjoy their childhood, to have the joys and opportunities other kids had, without the shadow of hardship clouding their days.

There were countless moments when I wanted to break down, when the pressure felt unbearable. But I couldn't let them see my fear. I refused to let my struggles become theirs. So, I stood tall, even when it hurt, doing everything in my power to create a life for them, filled with hope and possibility.

I couldn't always give my kids everything they wanted, but I made sure they had what they needed. As they grew older, I noticed how they began finding ways to ease the burden on me when it came to the things they wanted. While I was proud of their resourcefulness, it broke my heart that I couldn't provide more for them.

But through it all, I am deeply grateful for the moments when they witnessed God's hand at work in their lives. It's one thing to tell your children to pray and trust God—it's something else entirely different when they see Him show up for themselves.

One unforgettable example was when my oldest was heading to college, and we didn't have enough money for her tuition. We prayed, trusting God to make a way, and He did. She received the money she needed just in time. While others were sent home in tears, she stayed. And not only did she stay, but she also went on to complete all four years and graduate.

Moments like that weren't isolated—they happened with my other daughters too. Time and time again, God provided in ways that reminded us all it wasn't "Mommy making it happen," but God. Those experiences became life lessons for my girls that no amount of money could ever buy. They have grown up to be some pretty strong young ladies themselves.

They have their own children now, and they are the best mothers a kid could ever have. They are part of the reason I began to go to church so faithfully and learn more about the word of God. We visited the church with a friend, and they fell in love with the youth ministry and wanted to go every week. It did not take long, and I was excited about the word of God too. I had been to church before, but this time, it was finally starting to click. The Bible was actually making sense to me, and I was locked in.

As the world continued to turn, life kept unfolding. I had compounded stress from a failed marriage that ended in divorce, years of financial struggles, unhappiness with my career, and concerns for a new grandbaby. And the conflict in my new marriage just about caused me to lose my mind. I found myself questioning God all of the time, asking God, "Why?" and "Where are you? What am I supposed to learn from this?" Slowly my commitment began to wane.

I am ashamed to say that I was disappointed in God. I was angry with Him and did not trust Him. Wow, some nerve I had...right. I mean all those times He had blessed me and my children, and I had the nerve to be mad at God! Let me just thank God for the grace and mercy He allowed me.

But honestly, I was hurt and confused. I felt like God did not hear my prayers or just chose not to answer my prayers, and my thinking was that he had let me down like everyone else in my life, and it was a waste of time to attend church or pray. So, I stopped praying as much, and I started missing church services, and before I knew it, I had missed months. At the time, I was not admitting it, not even to myself, that I was upset with God. I blamed it on the church, hurt and just not connecting with the church anymore. The pastor's message was just not moving me. I would sit in church and just murmur against everything the pastors said.

It was the loss of my stepsister Dee Dee, which awakened something deep within me but also triggered my deep disappointment. Somehow because I prayed, and she didn't live, I claimed her death as another failure for myself. And I blamed God for not coming through for us like He had done before.

Dee Dee was just one year older than me—our birthdays shared the same special day, April 30th. Despite that bond, we were never as close as I wanted us to be. I always thought that as we grew older, life would naturally bring us closer together. I pictured her and I, along with my younger sister Angie, as grey haired old ladies, but still fly, lol, sitting on a porch somewhere, reminiscing about our childhood and bragging about our grandkids. But that won't ever happen.

We lived opposite lifestyles, rarely crossing paths as adults. Still, I loved her. What I didn't realize was just how much—until she was gone.

For years, I believed she and my stepmother didn't like me. At times, I didn't like them, either. There were moments when their words or actions hurt me deeply, leaving me feeling rejected, judged, and not good enough. Yet, those painful memories are balanced by the joyful ones.

One of my favorite memories is of her teaching me a church song that became so dear to me. Moments like that remind me of the good we shared as a family, and it's a memory I will carry with me forever. I remember going out to a club with her one night; it was just us two because everyone else canceled. I was a bit nervous because I never went out much, but we had more fun in the car on the way there. I don't remember much about the club, but I do remember laughing so much with her in the car that night. I smile now when I think about it. Her passing brought clarity to my feelings, revealing a love that I hadn't fully understood before.

I still remember the moment everything began to change. It was a busy day, filled with errands, when my dad called to tell me my sister was in the hospital. Something in his voice told me it was serious. I asked if I should head to the hospital, but he told me not to rush—she was undergoing a procedure. He promised to call back with more information.

I tried to go about my day, continuing my errands, but the call weighed heavily on my mind. I couldn't shake the unease. After calling my dad back a few times for updates, I finally decided to just head to the hospital. When I arrived, the situation was worse than I had imagined. My sister had suffered a ruptured brain aneurysm, causing extensive bleeding and pressure on her brain.

The doctors were hopeful, and so was I. I convinced myself she would recover fully, with a renewed appreciation for life. I just knew the God I served would not allow my sister to die. While my family believes in God, I was the only one in the immediate family who attended church or prayed regularly. Even then, I was shy about praying in front of others. I felt my prayers weren't long or eloquent enough, but I prayed for her anyway, sensing that everyone was counting on me to reach God on her behalf.

For 21 days, she remained in the ICU. I visited her almost every day, talked to her, and prayed, fully believing she would walk out of that hospital. However, I began to have dreams warning me of what was coming. I refused to believe them, clinging to the hope that she would recover. Even when the doctors started suggesting she might need long-term care in a nursing facility, I held on to my faith.

One day, a nurse tried explaining the gravity of the situation, hoping that I could help my stepmother understand what was happening and make the right decisions. But I couldn't accept it myself. I wasn't ready to give up, and I would not accept what she was saying. The next day my stepmother called to tell me the decision had been made to take my sister off life support. Turns out she knew exactly what they were saying. I commend her for the strength it took to make that decision. I don't think I would be able to.

I was devastated when they moved her to the hospice unit. Still, I held out hope, believing that God would show up at the eleventh hour and work a miracle for Dee Dee. On the day they were to remove life support, I ended up being the only one with her for most of the day. I sat by her side, talking to her, singing to her, and praying with her. I apologized for anything I had done to hurt her and forgave her for anything she had done to hurt me. I even apologized that my prayers hadn't saved her yet.

I held on to hope until her final breath. As the moment drew closer, my family members left the room, overcome by the pain. But God equipped me with the strength I needed. Holding her hand, I told her how much she was loved, assuring her that she would never be forgotten. Watching her take her last breath was the hardest thing I have ever done.

Still, I couldn't let her leave this world without feeling the love of her family surrounding her. I stood strong that night, shedding only a few tears, though I'm still not sure how I managed to drive myself home from the hospital that night.

Over the next few years, I wrestled with questions for God. Why? Had I done something wrong? Were my prayers not enough? What good could possibly come from this? What did He want from me? I was so confused, lost in the silence that followed. But why would I expect answers to those questions when He hadn't answered my prayer to save her life? I felt abandoned. I was a mess, walking around like nothing was wrong.

On top of that, my job was relentless. My previous supervisor was harsh, seemingly determined to make me fail. She had succeeded in driving almost everyone she targeted out of the company, and I feared I would be next. Somehow, though, I held on and even earned a promotion to an elite team. But instead of celebrating, I was consumed by imposter syndrome. My new teammates were brilliant, and I constantly felt like I was struggling just to keep up. It was demanding and stressful, with every day feeling like a battle to prove I deserved my place on the team.

As if work wasn't hard enough, my emotions—grief, anger, and sadness—began to spill over into every aspect of my life, including the office. I wasn't the person I used to be.

And then there was home. My new blended family was anything but harmonious. My husband and I couldn't seem to see eye to eye on anything. Every time we tried to fix things, they only seemed to get worse. Our communication was awful—strained, defensive, and unkind. What should have been a home filled with the joy of newlywed bliss felt more like a silent war zone.

The pain was unbearable. I wanted to hold on, but I couldn't keep living that way. Eventually, I decided to move out, hoping the separation would give us space to reflect and see things more clearly. Deep down, I still believed that if we truly loved each other, we would find a way to work things out. But I also knew that if we didn't, I didn't want to stay long enough for that love to turn into bitterness or hate.

Just before our wedding, I had given up almost everything I owned—everything except my clothes—to move in with my husband. I let go of my little house, believing it was the start of a new chapter. But now, here I was, leaving again, moving into a two-bedroom apartment with my daughter, who was a young adult.

At the same time, I was helping my parents purchase their home, which brought its own set of challenges and anxiety. It was an incredibly stressful process, and I felt the weight of it all. I wanted to do as much as I could to support them, but the burden felt overwhelming at times. Still, I couldn't bring myself to let them down.

Helping my stepmother was particularly complicated. For years, I had felt like she didn't like me or even love me. But now, I was deeply concerned for her. Losing her only biological child was a pain I couldn't begin to imagine. Despite the tension we had in the past, I did everything I could to help, putting aside my own hurt to show her I cared.

Even so, I couldn't shake my own confusion. Everything felt so heavy, so out of place. While I had pushed my pride aside to support my family, I still wrestled with the whirlwind of emotions brought on by everything that was happening.

Because of everything I was going through, I decided to start seeing a counselor. Soon after, I took a leave of absence from work to focus on my mental health. During that time, my supervisor suggested I revisit a creative project I had once done—a brooch bouquet. I had made one as a gift for a coworker, and everyone raved about my talent. They encouraged me to turn it into a business, and my supervisor thought I would be wasting talent if I did not try.

She was right. Crafting those bouquets became my escape. It was soothing, almost like therapy in itself, and it turned out I was really good at it. I loved the process, the artistry, and the joy it brought to others. Eventually, I took the leap and started a business: Kendi Bella Bouquets and Things, LLC, named after my granddaughter, Kendi. I'm incredibly proud of that business. I refuse to let it go or let it die completely.

I had high hopes for my business. I really wanted to be creating bouquets full-time. I received lots of compliments and plenty of praise for my work but not nearly enough well-paying customers. I was working a call center job from home since the pandemic, but my hours began to dwindle until the job eventually ended. Suddenly, I was uncertain about what to do next. I had no savings and no place to get more money quickly.

At the same time, my separation dragged on much longer than I had hoped. The longer it lasted, the more I started to lose hope that we would ever reconcile. I began to believe we were headed for divorce. The thought was heartbreaking—here I was, staring down the end of my second marriage. I couldn't stop thinking, "Why can't I ever get it right?" I felt like a failure, not just in my marriage, but in everything I touched.

I was exhausted. Tired of trying and failing. Tired of giving everything I had, only to watch it crumble. At some point, I stopped praying altogether. I couldn't hear God, and I wasn't even sure I wanted to. But every so often, I would talk to God and beg Him to show me what to do to bring some peace to my mind. I felt like a crazy person wanting to curse the name of God and wishing He would help me at the same time

There were countless other challenges I faced, each one leading me to a pivotal moment. After two years in an apartment with my daughter, I finally found a house for rent. It wasn't in the best shape and needed a lot of work and care. The landlord and my dad promised to help fix it up, so I moved in alone, ready to put in the effort. I spent countless hours painting and fixing things, making the house livable. But there were still a couple of major problems, one being the air conditioning. A few months after moving in, the weather changed, and the house became unbearably hot. A 95-degree heat inside a house with no cooled air was pure hell. It was as if everything I was going through emotionally and spiritually was manifested physically.

I talked to my daughters on the phone often, and I spoke to my husband, too, trying to figure out if we could work things out. But there were still so many unresolved issues between us. Most of the time, I was alone in the house, overwhelmed by my intrusive, negative thoughts. They clouded my mind, and I found myself once again considering ending it all. But then, I remembered the promise I made to my daughters—I couldn't do that to them.

I was stuck in a relentless cycle of "Why me?" and the haunting refrain of "God doesn't care about me." I had hit rock bottom, and deep down,

I knew something had to change. My thoughts spiraled: "Why is my life such a mess? When will I catch a break?" Amid the chaos, a quiet but persistent voice whispered, "You know what you need to do. You know why things aren't working out."

At first, I ignored it. Day after day, I wrestled with my frustration and despair, until finally, I broke. Desperate and exhausted, I reached for the one thing that had always brought me peace—gospel music. There's something about those melodies that speaks straight to my soul. Every time I listened, especially when I was stressed or overwhelmed, the songs seemed to carry me to a place of calm.

This time was no different. As I let the music fill the house, I felt the familiar stirrings of peace. But then, a few songs hit me differently. I remember listening to Jekalyn Carr, and suddenly, the floodgates opened. I broke down in tears, raw and vulnerable, and through the sobs, I began to pray—not a casual, rehearsed prayer, but a deep, heartfelt cry to God.

I asked for forgiveness. I asked for help. I poured out my heart in a way I never had before. Somewhere in the midst of it all, the Holy Spirit met me there. I can't tell you how long I was on the floor, but when I finally stood up, though tears still streamed down my face, I felt a weight lift off of me. There was a shift in my spirit, a quiet assurance that everything was going to be okay.

From that moment, I started praising God and praying with renewed purpose. And almost immediately, things began to change. Phone calls started coming in. Opportunities appeared out of nowhere. My husband and I reconciled, and I moved back in. One of my customers even became a close friend and led me to the church I now call home.

Joining that church has been one of the greatest blessings of my life. I've grown so much in my understanding of God's Word and His love. Serving there has given me purpose, and I'm grateful every day for both my pastors and the incredible community of brothers and sisters in Christ I've found.

Looking back, I realize that breaking down wasn't the end—it was the beginning. Since that moment on my knees, I've had other times where I've knelt in prayer. But now, it's not out of desperation or despair. It's out of reverence and gratitude. I willingly bow to honor my Father because I never want to forget where He brought me from and how far He's taken me. That moment changed everything, and for that, I will always praise Him.

Life is full of lessons—some small, some monumental, and others so life-changing they leave scars that tell stories of survival. Many don't make it through those trials, and for those who do, the evidence of their journey is often visible. But there are a few who emerge stronger, untouched by bitterness, their strength a testimony not of denial or pretense, but of God's transformative power. These are the ones He brings through the fire, not just surviving, but thriving, with lessons etched into their souls and faith as their foundation.

I believe I am one of those people. God carried me through trials that could have broken me, and instead, He built me up. Now, I pray that my journey glorifies Him, and that the lessons I've learned—even the ones born out of pain—become a beacon of hope for others walking similar paths. My prayer is that these lessons guide others to the Father's loving embrace, especially when life feels too hard to bear.

As children, we may face circumstances beyond our control, but God watches over us. Even when bad things happen—and we may not understand why—He has a purpose. He takes what's meant to harm us and turns it for our good. As adults, we are given the gift of free will, and with that comes the responsibility to choose wisely. Yet even when we falter, God is there, ready to guide us if we seek Him. His angels, His Holy Spirit, and His Word are our constant companions, lighting our way and lifting us up when the weight of life feels unbearable.

The key is this: Don't stop. Don't give up. Even if you have to start over, keep moving forward. Keeping God at the center of your life doesn't mean the storms won't come, but it makes navigating them possible. It helps you learn quicker, grow faster, and avoid the endless cycles of repeated mistakes.

I've made plenty of missteps, faced terrifying moments, and endured heartache that felt unbearable. Yet, by God's grace, I've survived it all—and not just survived, but emerged stronger. Looking back, I can confidently say I don't look like what I've been through. That's the power of God's love, mercy, and purpose working in my life.

And if He did it for me, He can do it for you too. Don't give up—your testimony is still being written.

Shirin Lakhani

MSR CLEANING AND PROFESSIONAL SERVICES PTY LTD
Director

https://www.linkedin.com/in/shirin-lakhani-a1730757/
https://www.facebook.com/shirin.lakhani2
https://www.instagram.com/shirin_lakhani/
https://msrcare.com.au/
https://yscleaningservices.com.au/

Shirin Lakhani is a resilient business entrepreneur, women's mentor, and fierce cancer fighter who has spent the last 17 years in Australia. As a mother to a five-year-old, Shirin's life has been shaped by both profound chalenges and hard-earned wisdom. Having endured the loss of nine organs and six miscarriages, she has navigated life with a tenacity born from her experiences

Through the trials she has faced, Shirin learned an invaluable lesson; you are your own strength. No one else can carry you through life's hardships-- you must be the one to fight, to feed yourself, to care for your child, and to rise every day on your own. Despite giving so much of herself to others, she discovered that betrayal and backstabbing are inevitable parts of life. This reality has taught her the importance of living without expectations and finding peace in giving without the need for return.

Shirin's journey has made her fiercely independent and determined to help others who are facing their own struggles. She believes in the power of self-reliance, in supporting others without expecting anything in return, and in building a life grounded in the strength and wisdom that only comes from facing adversity.

Her story serves as a powerful reminder: no matter what life throws your wav you have the inner strength to keep moving forward and live your life on your own terms.

Ray of Hope

By Shirin Lakhani

The dawn broke over the horizon, painting the sky with hues of orange and pink. As the first rays of sunlight kissed the earth, they also touched the heart of a young woman standing at a crossroads of her life.

Her name was Maya, which meant "illusion" but felt more like destiny. With each sunrise, she battled the shadows of her past, determined to step into the light of a new day. Today was different. Today, hope was not just a distant glimmer; it was a tangible force, urging her forward.

In the quiet stillness of the morning, Maya remembered the words of her mother: "Strength isn't just about how much you can handle before you break. It's about how much you can endure after you've been broken." Those words had carried her through many storms, and now, they propelled her towards a future filled with possibilities.

Maya took a deep breath, feeling the crisp morning air fill her lungs. She looked out over the city from her small apartment balcony, watching as people below began their daily routines. Each person had their own story, their own struggles and triumphs. Maya wondered how many of them, like her, carried the weight of the past, yet moved forward with hope.

Her thoughts drifted to her younger self, a girl full of dreams but encumbered by circumstances beyond her control. The journey had not been easy. She had faced betrayal, loss, and moments of sheer despair. Yet, each challenge had forged her spirit, making her stronger and more resilient. It was in these moments of darkness that she found her inner light, a spark of hope that refused to be extinguished.

As she stood there, lost in thought, the morning sun grew brighter, casting long shadows that slowly receded. Maya felt a surge of determination. She was ready to embrace her future, to chase her dreams with unwavering resolve. She would be the architect of her own destiny, a beacon of hope not just for herself, but for others who struggled to find their way.

With a final glance at the rising sun, Maya turned back inside, ready to take the first steps towards her new journey. Today, she would begin the next chapter of her life, fueled by the lessons of the past and the endless possibilities of the future. Today, she would grow stronger.

As she entered her small apartment, she glanced at the framed photograph on her desk. It was a picture of her and her mother, taken on the last family vacation before everything changed. Her mother's eyes sparkled with the same light of hope that Maya felt now. It was as if her mother's spirit was guiding her, whispering words of encouragement in the silence.

Maya sat down at her desk and opened her journal. The blank pages stared back at her, waiting to be filled with her thoughts, dreams, and plans. She picked up her pen, feeling a sense of purpose and clarity she hadn't felt in a long time. She began to write, pouring her heart onto the pages, capturing the essence of her journey and the strength she had found within.

The hours passed quickly as Maya wrote, her pen moving swiftly across the pages. She wrote about the pain of her past, the lessons she had learned, and the hope that now filled her heart. She wrote about her dreams for the future and the steps she would take to achieve them. With each word, she felt herself growing stronger, more determined to create a life filled with purpose and joy.

Finally, as the sun reached its zenith, Maya put down her pen and looked at the pages before her. They were filled with her story, a testament to her resilience and strength. She felt a sense of accomplishment, knowing that she had taken the first step towards her new life. She knew that the road ahead would not be easy, but she was ready to face it with courage and hope.

Maya closed her journal and stood up, feeling a renewed sense of energy. She walked to the window and looked out at the city, feeling a deep connection to the world around her. She was part of something bigger, a tapestry of lives interwoven with hope and dreams. She smiled, knowing that she had the power to shape her own destiny and inspire others to do the same.

Today was just the beginning. Maya was ready to embrace her journey, to grow stronger with each step she took. She was a ray of hope, shining brightly in the world, ready to make her mark and create a life filled with purpose, love, and joy.

As the day unfolded, Maya decided to take the first tangible steps towards her new life. She made a list of goals, both big and small, that she wanted to achieve. From learning a new skill to connecting with others who shared her passion, each goal was a stepping stone on her path to personal growth and fulfillment.

She also resolved to volunteer at a local community center, where she could use her experiences to help others facing similar challenges. By giving back, she knew she could find a deeper sense of purpose and continue to build her strength.

Over the next few weeks, Maya's life began to transform. She immersed herself in new experiences, made meaningful connections, and found joy in the simple moments. Each day, she grew a little bit stronger, her hope shining brighter with every step she took.

One evening, after a particularly rewarding day at the community center, Maya received a phone call that would change her life. It was an invitation to speak at a women's empowerment event. The organizers had heard about her work and wanted her to share her story. Maya felt a mix of excitement and nerves, but she knew this was an opportunity to make an impact.

The day of the event arrived, and Maya stood backstage, her heart pounding with anticipation. She took a deep breath and stepped onto the stage, the spotlight illuminating her. As she looked out at the audience, she saw faces filled with curiosity and hope.

With each word, Maya shared her journey—the struggles, the pain, the moments of doubt, and the unwavering hope that had guided her. She spoke from her heart, her voice steady and strong. The audience was captivated and moved by her honesty and resilience.

When she finished, the room erupted in applause. Maya felt a surge of pride and gratitude. She had not only found her strength but had also inspired others to find theirs. She was a ray of hope, shining brightly in a world that often seemed dark.

Maya walked off the stage, her heart full of joy. She knew that this was just the beginning of her journey. She would continue to grow stronger, face each challenge with courage and hope, and inspire others along the way. She was ready to embrace her destiny, to be the star she was always meant to be.

A few months later, Maya met someone who would become a significant part of her life. Alex was an entrepreneur with a passion for social change, and their paths crossed at a networking event for community leaders. They were instantly drawn to each other's energy and shared a vision for making a difference.

Their relationship blossomed quickly. Alex admired Maya's resilience and strength, while Maya found inspiration in Alex's entrepreneurial spirit and dedication to their causes. Together, they supported each other's dreams and ambitions, creating a partnership built on mutual respect and love.

Maya and Alex decided to get married, and their wedding was a celebration of their love and shared purpose. Surrounded by family and friends, they vowed to support each other through all of life's challenges and to continue working towards their goals, both individually and together.

As a newlywed, Maya found herself balancing her roles as a wife and a businesswoman. She was determined to succeed in both areas, driven by her love for Alex and their commitment. She faced new challenges in her business but tackled each one with the same determination and resilience that had always guided her.

Maya's business flourished under her leadership. She became known for her innovative ideas and compassionate approach, and she earned the respect and admiration of her peers. Through her work, she continued to empower others, proving that with hope and determination, anything was possible.

Together, Maya and Alex became a powerhouse couple, making waves in both their personal and professional lives. They supported each other through every obstacle, celebrating their successes and learning from their failures. Their love and partnership were a beacon of hope for many, showing that true strength comes from unity and shared purpose.

However, life was not without its challenges. As Maya and Alex prepared to welcome their first child, the pressures of their personal and professional lives began to take a toll. Alex's behavior changed, and Maya found herself facing a new and terrifying reality—domestic violence.

The once loving and supportive relationship turned into a nightmare. Maya endured physical and emotional abuse, feeling trapped and isolated. The fear for her unborn child's safety gave her the strength to seek help. She reached out to a trusted friend, who helped her find a safe place to stay.

Maya knew she had to protect herself and her baby. She filed for a restraining order against Alex and began the process of rebuilding her life once again. The journey was arduous, filled with moments of doubt and fear, but Maya's resilience and determination never wavered.

With the support of her friends and the community she had once helped, Maya found the strength to move forward. She continued to run her business, using her experiences to advocate for other survivors of domestic violence. Her story became a beacon of hope for many, showing that even in the darkest times, there is always a way to find the light.

As Maya prepared for the birth of her child, she felt a renewed sense of purpose. She was determined to create a safe and loving environment for her baby, filled with hope and strength. The challenges she had faced had only made her stronger, and she was ready to embrace this new chapter of her life.

However, life took another devastating turn. Just weeks before her due date, Maya experienced complications with her pregnancy. Despite the best efforts of the medical team, she lost her baby. The grief was overwhelming, and Maya felt as though her world had collapsed around her. To add to her pain, Alex abandoned her, leaving her to navigate this tragedy alone.

In the wake of this profound loss, Maya was consumed by sorrow. The dreams she had for her child, the hopes and plans she had nurtured, were all shattered. The loneliness and heartbreak threatened to engulf her, but deep within, a small spark of resilience remained.

Maya allowed herself to grieve, to feel the full weight of her pain. She knew that healing would take time and that there was no shortcut through this heartache. Her friends and community rallied around her, offering support and love and reminding her that she was not alone.

Gradually, Maya began to rebuild her life. She sought counseling to help her process the trauma and leaned on her support network. She found solace in her work, throwing herself into her business and advocacy efforts with renewed passion. Helping others became a way to honor the memory of her child and find meaning in her suffering.

One day, while visiting the community center where she volunteered, Maya met a young girl named Lily. Lily had faced her own share of hardships, and Maya saw a reflection of her younger self in the girl's eyes. Determined to make a difference, Maya took Lily under her wing, mentoring her and providing the guidance and support she needed.

Through her bond with Lily and her work at the community center, Maya found a renewed sense of purpose. She realized that her strength lay not only in her ability to endure pain but also in her capacity to transform it into something positive. By helping others, she was healing herself.

As time passed, Maya's business continued to grow. She became a prominent figure in the community, known for her resilience and dedication to empowering others. Her story inspired many, and she was frequently invited to speak at events and workshops, sharing her journey of hope and strength.

Maya also found the courage to reopen her heart to love. She met someone new, someone who treated her with the kindness and respect she deserved. Their relationship blossomed slowly, built on mutual trust and understanding. Together, they created a future filled with love and hope, embracing the challenges and joys that life brought their way.

Maya's journey was far from easy, but she emerged from each trial stronger and more determined. She became a symbol of resilience and hope, a reminder that even in the darkest times, there is always a way to find the light. Her story was a testament to the power of the human spirit, the strength to overcome adversity, and the courage to build a new life from the ashes of the past.

Sonia Rodrigues

Transition to Wellness
Psychotherapist & Life Transition Coach

https://www.linkedin.com/in/sonia-rodrigues-48b87149/
https://www.facebook.com/SoniaRodriguesLPC/
https://www.instagram.com/transition.to.wellness/
https://www.transitiontowellness.com/
https://soniarodriguesmarto.tribesites.com/

Sonia Rodrigues has been a licensed psychotherapist for 20 years. She is the owner of a psychotherapy and coaching practice called Transition to Wellness. She has worked with people of all ages, helping them navigate various challenges in their life. She utilizes a holistic approach and provides a safe and supportive environment where her clients can feel supported on their path towards healing from their traumatic experiences and she guides them towards creating the life they desire. She provides individual therapy and coaching and also offers a variety of presentations and workshops on topics related to trauma, post-traumatic growth and fostering resilience.

Surviving and Thriving: The Power of Resilience

By Sonia Rodrigues

One thing I think we can all agree on is that life is unpredictable. Even when we have a well-designed plan in place or we identify very specific goals that we want to accomplish, there is usually something that happens that throws us off. Life has a way of throwing curveballs at us, doesn't it? No matter how carefully we plan or how clear our goals are, there is always something unexpected that can throw us off track. Whether it is heartbreak, loss, failure, or illness, these moments often hit us when we least expect them, leaving us feeling knocked down and sometimes even hopeless. It is in these moments that we may start to question ourselves—our strength, our worth, and whether we will ever be able to rise again. It is easy to fall into the trap of thinking resilience is simply about surviving these storms, just pushing through until the hard times pass us by. Many will often say, I just need to figure out how to get through the day or the week. But what if resilience is about more than just surviving? What if it is about using these challenges to grow, to become stronger, and to uncover parts of ourselves we never knew existed? Sometimes things happen that force us to deal with the things we have pushed to the side for a long time or ignored and pretended it is not impacting us. What if you could not only survive adversity but thrive because of it?

In this chapter, we are going to explore the deeper layers of resilience—what it really means, how it can transform your life, and how you can start using it to not just cope, but thrive. Together, we'll explore the science, mindset, and practical steps that can help you navigate life's challenges with greater resilience. By the end of this journey, my hope is that you will come to believe that the struggles you face are not just happening to you, but rather happening for you as opportunities for growth and transformation. With each step, you will become stronger, wiser, and more capable than you ever imagined, ready to face whatever comes your way with confidence and grace. My hope is that you will identify the steps you need to take when you feel knocked down by life to get yourself back up feeling excited and hopeful about your life.

Defining Resilience Beyond Survival

So, what is resilience, really? Many people think of it as just "bouncing back" after something difficult happens. And while that is a part of it, resilience is much more than that. The concept of resilience is not just about enduring tough times, it is about using adversity to become a stronger version of yourself. It is about transformation.

Think of resilience like the process of refining gold. The gold is put through intense heat to burn away the impurities, leaving behind something beautiful and pure. In the same way, life's challenges, as painful as they can be, often leave us more refined, more resilient, and more capable of handling whatever comes our way.

But here's the catch: Resilience isn't automatic. It's something that we have to cultivate. It is something we have to nurture, especially when life feels like it's testing us in ways we never expected. The truth is, we are not just here to survive or get through life—we are here to grow and live our best life. For some of you, you may not be able to see past the pain, hurt, or trauma right now, but I can assure you, what you learn about yourself and your situation can serve as the foundation to build a stronger, more resilient version of who you are. I know it may feel overwhelming or even impossible to imagine a time when the pain will feel like less of a weight, but the truth is, the struggles you are facing right now are not the end of your story—they are a part of the process that can shape you in ways you may not yet be able to understand. Every challenge holds lessons about your strength, your values, and your capacity for growth. Though it may take time to see it, this experience is planting seeds for a future where you stand more grounded, more self-aware, and more capable of handling life's twists and turns. Trust that, even in the darkest moments, you are laying the groundwork for the person you're becoming.

The Foundations of Resilience

At the heart of resilience, there are qualities that each of us can nurture and grow, no matter where we are in our journey. Take a moment to think about someone you admire for their strength—someone who seems to face life's challenges with grace, no matter how tough things get. What is it about them that stands out to you? Chances are, the resilient people you admire share certain traits. These qualities are not fixed or unchangeable—they are within all of us, waiting to be cultivated, especially when we need them the most. These are some traits that resilient people have been known to embody, and they're qualities that can help you navigate even the toughest of times. Resilient individuals tend to have a strong sense of emotional regulation, allowing them to face challenges without being overwhelmed by their feelings. They also cultivate optimism and hope, trusting that even in dark times, there's a way forward. Adaptability is another key trait—they're able to adjust when life takes unexpected turns, seeing change as an opportunity to grow rather than something to fear. A deep sense of purpose often grounds them, helping them find meaning and direction even in adversity. And perhaps most importantly, resilient people aren't afraid to seek support when they need it—they understand that asking for help is a strength, not a weakness. These traits are not something only a few people are born with; they can be developed by anyone willing to learn, practice, and grow through life's challenges. Some of these traits include:

1. **Emotional Regulation** – Resilient people do not let their emotions dictate their actions. They understand that emotions, while important, are temporary. They can feel pain, frustration, or anger without allowing it to control their next move.

2. **Optimism and Hope** – A resilient person does not give up when things look bleak. Instead, they trust that better days are ahead. This doesn't mean ignoring the reality of the situation—it means believing in the possibility of improvement, no matter how difficult the journey.

3. **Adaptability** – Life is full of change. Resilient people embrace it, even when it is uncomfortable. They see change as a natural part of life and figure out how to adjust their sails when the winds shift.

4. **A Strong Sense of Purpose** – Resilience is not just about surviving for survival's sake. People who thrive through adversity often have a deeper reason for pushing through. It could be their family, their dreams, their sense of responsibility, or a desire to make a difference.

5. **Support-Seeking Behavior** – Resilient people understand they do not have to face challenges alone. They reach out to others when they need help, whether it's for advice, support, or simply someone to listen. We heal and thrive through connections.

But these traits do not come naturally to everyone. They can be cultivated. Building resilience is a journey that takes time, patience, and a willingness to grow through the tough moments. But here's the hopeful part: our brains are incredibly adaptable. Neuroscientists refer to this process as neuroplasticity—the brain's ability to reorganize itself and form new connections, even in the aftermath of hardship. What this means for you is that, despite the pain and challenges you face, your brain has the remarkable ability to heal, adapt, and grow stronger over time. Each experience, no matter how difficult, helps you build the inner resources and skills needed to face future challenges with more confidence and resilience. Healing may take time, but know that every step forward is a sign of growth, even when it doesn't feel that way in the moment.

The Role of Mindset in Resilience

Let's take a moment to talk about mindset. One of the most powerful tools we have for building resilience is how we choose to view challenges. This is where the idea of a growth mindset comes in. Carol Dweck, a renowned psychologist, explains that people with a growth mindset believe that their abilities and intelligence can be developed with time, effort, and perseverance. They don't see challenges as barriers, but as opportunities to learn, grow, and become better.

Think about Sarah for a moment. Sarah had a job in marketing at a tech company, and she loved what she did. But when the company went through a major restructure, she was laid off. Initially, she was devastated. She felt like it was a personal failure. But instead of letting that moment define her, she shifted her perspective. Sarah began to see the setback not as an ending, but as a chance to gain new skills, explore new opportunities, and ultimately start her own business. That change in mindset—viewing a challenge as a stepping stone—allowed her to grow in ways she hadn't imagined.

So, when you're facing your own challenges, I encourage you to ask yourself: *How can I turn this into an opportunity to grow?* Can you see adversity as part of your evolution, a chance to become stronger, wiser, and more resilient, rather than something to just endure? It's not always easy, but with each shift in perspective, you're building the resilience that will carry you forward**Turning Setbacks Into Stepping Stones**

The truth is, setbacks are inevitable. But what if those setbacks were actually invitations to grow stronger? Think of moments when you've faced an obstacle—something that made you question your own strength. Now, imagine how you could reframe that challenge. Could it be a lesson in patience? A chance to learn resilience? A way to discover hidden strengths within yourself?

Consider Maria, who faced the sudden death of her mother. For months, she struggled to navigate her grief. But as time passed, she realized something profound: her grief had taught her a depth of empathy she never knew she had. She became a counselor for others who had experienced similar losses, using her pain to guide others through theirs. Her setback became the stepping stone that led her to a deeper sense of purpose and fulfillment.

Turning adversity into strength isn't always easy. But one powerful tool for reframing challenges is practicing self-compassion. It's so easy to be hard on ourselves when things go wrong. We often think, *I should have done better, I should have been stronger*. But self-compassion is about being gentle with yourself. It's about recognizing that you're doing the best you can and giving yourself grace as you grow through hardship.

Practical Strategies for Building Resilience

Resilience isn't just a quality—it's a practice. And like any skill, it gets stronger the more you use it. Let's talk about some practical ways to build resilience in your daily life.

1. **Create a Resilient Routine:** Habits like regular exercise, mindfulness, and sufficient sleep are essential for maintaining mental and physical strength. Even small things like a morning routine or taking time to write down your thoughts can make a huge difference in your ability to face stress with clarity and calm.

2. **Build a Strong Support Network:** Surround yourself with people who lift you up. Whether it's a close friend, a mentor, or a community group, having a support system is one of the most powerful ways to build resilience. People who understand you, encourage you, and challenge you to grow are essential for thriving through tough times.

3. **Reflect and Learn from the Past:** Take time to reflect on past challenges. What did you learn? How did you grow? Each challenge contains wisdom that can help you build greater resilience for the future.

Thriving Through Resilience

Resilience isn't just about bouncing back to where you were before—it's about going beyond survival and unlocking your full potential. Resilience leads to deeper self-awareness, confidence, and the strength to embrace whatever life brings your way. And remember, resilience is a lifelong practice. It's not something you "get" and then leave behind—it's a journey that evolves as you do.

You are capable of far more than you realize. Resilience is a muscle, and just like any other muscle, it gets stronger with use. You don't just have to survive your challenges—you have the power to thrive through them.

So, what's one small step you can take today to begin cultivating resilience in your own life? Maybe it's starting a daily meditation practice, or reaching out to a friend for support. Whatever it is, remember that resilience is not about perfection—it's about progress. You've got this.

Conclusion: Your Path to Thriving

I want you to take a moment and really hear this: *You are stronger than you think.* The challenges you face, no matter how overwhelming they may seem, do not define you. You are not just someone who survives—they are the very experiences that can propel you toward becoming the person you're meant to be.

Resilience is about embracing the truth that life will bring difficult moments, but those moments do not have to break you. They are opportunities—sometimes buried under pain and struggle, yes—but opportunities nonetheless. Opportunities to grow, to learn, and to ultimately find parts of yourself you never knew existed. Your strength doesn't lie in avoiding hardship—it lies in how you choose to respond when it knocks at your door.

But this isn't about instant transformation. It's not about snapping your fingers and magically feeling resilient overnight. This is a practice—a lifetime commitment to yourself. It's about taking small steps every day to build your inner strength, to nourish your mind, body, and soul, and to create a life that can withstand the storms while also thriving in their wake.

Here's the beautiful truth: Your journey of resilience is uniquely yours. No one else has walked your path, faced your exact struggles, or felt the way you feel in this very moment. That's what makes your strength so powerful. It's born from the rawness of your experiences, from the depth of your heart, and from the unspoken courage that rises within you when the world feels too heavy. You have everything you need to not just survive but to flourish.

So, I encourage you to take a step today, no matter how small. Maybe it's acknowledging the strength you already have, or perhaps it's choosing one small habit to start building resilience. If it's reaching out to a friend or taking a few minutes to journal your thoughts, just take that first step. It's not about perfection. It's about showing up for yourself in ways you never have before.

I know there will be days when the weight of the world feels unbearable, when you question if you're enough, if you can keep going. And on those days, remember: you don't have to do it all alone. You don't have to carry it all by yourself. Resilience doesn't mean you don't lean on others or ask for help—it means you know you're worth it. You are worthy of support, of rest, and of kindness.

Above all, believe in the potential within you to rise, again and again, with more strength, more wisdom, and more grace. This is your journey, and each step forward, no matter how small, is a victory. You are not just surviving. You are becoming the best version of yourself through every hardship, every tear, every triumph. You are a testament to the power of resilience.

And now, it's time to live it.

Stéphane-Laure Caubet, PhD

Founder and CEO of 8S2BUSINESS PTE LTD

https://www.linkedin.com/in/st%C3%A9phane-laure-caubet/
https://www.facebook.com/stephanelaure.caubet/
https://www.instagram.com/8s2business_fr/
https://www.8s2businessonline.com/
https://8s2business.com/

After completing a doctorate in international business law and gaining over 10 years of experience in management, recruitment, and legal advisory leadership positions in Paris, Stéphane began questioning her true calling. Passionate about travel and human sciences, she shifted her focus to entrepreneurship. Her desire for positive social impact led her to Vietnam, where she collaborates with NGOs, universities, and international firms. There, she founded 8S2Business, a consulting firm, and published A Business Planner for the Business Starter. Today, Stéphane lectures, mentors, and trains professionals, guiding entrepreneurial leaders in overcoming challenges and turning uncertainty into growth opportunities. Convinced that change is driven by action, she empowers others to take the necessary steps to transform their entrepreneurial journeys into meaningful and exciting achievements.

Beyond Boundaries

By Stéphane-Laure Caubet, PhD

I have always been an outsider. Rarely in my life have I felt like I was in the right place...

My parents named me Stéphane-Laure. The name was very long, so I went by Stéphane, a shorter, but a boy's name.

I was born and raised in France with young parents whose on-again-off-again relationship meant I would alternate between living in one country or another, depending on their status.

Then, beyond visible mixed heritage, cultural mixing also becomes part of my identity.

I inherited this complexity from my mother, who, despite being mixed racially, had blonde hair and blue eyes and grew up in Africa—a situation she often describes as feeling "like a grain of rice in a bag of coffee." For me, having spent more time growing up in France than in Africa, I encountered the opposite.

Behind these anecdotes lies a deeper reality: one that led to my mother being abandoned by her own mother, for the reasons I've just described: She did not look like the others.

I spent my early years between Europe and Africa, moving from one homeland to another without much of a challenge. This experience gave me a love for travel, discovery, and challenges, along with the understanding that **we're all remarkably similar in our differences.**

At 20 years old, I dreamed of bringing education to Africa and meeting Nelson Mandela. Things didn't quite unfold as I had imagined.

I had always tried to be the "good girl" doing all the right things—getting married, buying a flat, having a cat, securing a good job with a good salary, and having kids. But deep down, I yearned to travel, to see the world, to help people, and to make an impact.

A few years ago, I lived in Paris, finishing my studies and working as an in-house lawyer at a pharmaceutical laboratory. Even though I had a good job with a comfortable salary, I wanted something more. That's when my husband and I decided to leave France, with the agreement that whoever found a job first, the other would follow.

We left France, but I lost the bet. Although I became the one who followed, I never wanted to be "just" a housewife following her husband. I was preparing my doctorate at the time and planning to work for international organizations to fulfil my goal of making an impact. Determined to pursue my dream of bringing education to Africa.

I realized the journey would be more complicated, or at least different, than expected.

We had decided to leave France, but nothing had prepared me for landing in Asia, particularly Vietnam. Though I had visited Bali during our honeymoon and found it magnificent, settling in Asia years later came as a complete surprise, one for which I was barely prepared, if at all.

We arrived in Hanoi as a family, my husband, our 2-year-old daughter, our cat, and our suitcases. We found ourselves between a feeling of excitement with the discovery of a new place along with its unknown culture, and the natural anxiety that comes with such uncertainty.

I felt confident about finding work, ready to accept any position that would help me engage with local life. I immediately began learning Vietnamese within my first month.

Learning the language quickly proved essential, first for simple tasks like giving my address to taxi drivers, then for daily life like haggling at the market. In Hanoi, everything was negotiable, from motorcycle rides to mangoes.

I learned enough Vietnamese to understand, make myself understood, and navigate daily life independently. I still call it a survival kit since I'm far from being able to have a real conversation, but I know just enough of the language to manage basic needs.

Then came the challenging part: finding a job...

I struggled to find permanent work, only securing short-term assignments that left me unsatisfied, as I wanted something stable, a "real job."

During this period, I found an institution online while still in Paris that became my first destination upon arrival. Dressed in my suit and heels, CV in hand, I set out to find "La Maison du Droit."

Though the website hadn't been updated in over two years, and its status was uncertain, I had to investigate.

After an hour's journey from home, I arrived at what appeared to be a university under heavy construction. No one at the entrance spoke English, and while most people were students, I searched for an administrative office.

In a courtyard surrounded by buildings, I noticed German text on one building, recognizable from my school years studying German.

I checked that building but found no reception area.

Returning to the courtyard, I entered what looked like a library, where, fortunately, I found a young woman at the reception desk.

Though she didn't speak English, I showed her the logo and address of "La Maison du Droit." She recognized the address but not the institution's name, nor its logo.

I realized she wouldn't be able to help me find a solution, so I thanked her and decided to continue my search.

As I went on to search for an international office, she sent a student to bring me back. At her desk, she opened Google Translate and invited me to type my query, which I did. After the software translated my words into Vietnamese, by the look of her smile and response, though incomprehensible to me, it seemed promising. That's when she asked a passing student to guide me somewhere.

As I was trailing behind that student, we crossed construction areas and wooden planks until we reached a house-like building where the student gestured that this was it and left.

Despite the absence of signs, I entered and climbed upstairs, where I had a remarkable conversation with an international volunteer.

When I explained I was a newly arrived law doctoral student offering my services, she asked if I'd heard about their legal methodology teacher resigning the previous day.

I explained that I had only been in Vietnam for three days and knew no one there yet. This coincidence led to my first teaching position in Vietnam.

Though the pay was modest and the location distant, it felt like a meaningful beginning. But with only two hours weekly for a few months, I needed additional work.

My attempts at partnerships with law firms fell through, one, a failed collaboration, and, another, lost due to visa complications. I continued receiving offers to teach and run employability workshops for Vietnamese youth interested in international careers.

I faced countless rejections from various organizations, usually due to language barriers or complications with hiring foreigners. Even NGOs and development organizations suggested it would have been easier to secure employment from abroad.

The uncertainty crystallized into a harsh reality. Finding work would be difficult.

Self-doubt crept in as I watched my husband thrive professionally, and my daughter was able to speak English and French fluently. I felt stagnant, having lost our original bet, yet refusing to accept defeat.

I decided to channel my energy into completing and defending my doctorate thesis, a goal I could better control.

We could at that moment summarize my mindset in one sentence from John C. Maxwell: **"Why worry about things you can't control when you can keep yourself busy controlling the things that depend on you?"**

For a year, I maintained an unusual schedule: researching and writing day and night, taking advantage of my insomnia to work during sleepless hours, while spending my daytime caring for my daughter, having family dinners, watching movies, and then returning to work.

After defending my doctoral thesis in Paris, I decided to pursue something more aligned with my goals.

An international organization offered me a promising position, but the wait was too long, they wanted me to start in December, and it was only January.

I needed work sooner than that.

Nothing was unfolding as I had hoped. Despite my extensive studies and genuine desire to work in development aid, helping build schools, roads, and airports in countries that needed it, I was facing unexpected resistance.

People insisted I should not work at all; they did not want to pay me, claiming it wasn't my proper role.

"You should stay at home," "Women should not work" … this is the kind of conversation I had on a daily basis.

Everything I had trained for was right there, yet I felt like a complete failure, unable to grasp how things truly operated.

Though I believed I had followed all the right steps, reality had other plans.

I found an NGO position that could start within a month. After two years of job hunting, I took it.

This professional experience reflected everything I had encountered since starting work in this field. For months, colleagues would not even exchange basic greetings like hello or goodbye. Though I maintained my courtesy regardless, my workdays were mostly spent in isolation. This situation gradually changed over time, and I viewed it as a kind of professional initiation.

After taking on all the tasks my boss avoided, I initially viewed it as a chance to develop new skills. However, nearly a year into the job, I discovered that I had been chosen to take the blame for one of his mistakes.

I was summoned to my boss's office, where he claimed I had failed to return an important document for a project validation file, resulting in a denied certification. Surprised, I asked for details since I had no idea what he meant. He then unfolded a story in which every team member had supposedly provided me with materials, including the driver who allegedly hand-delivered documents to my home that I never returned to the office.

When I asked my boss if this was explicitly what he had been told, he called in the entire team. I sat stunned as each member described conversations we'd never had, claimed they'd given me reminders I'd never received, and mentioned documents I'd never seen. I found myself facing a united front, all determined to blame me for a mistake I hadn't committed and hadn't even known existed.

I had never encountered such a situation. I felt not only unjustly accused but trapped, surrounded by people who clearly felt protected by both the system and their boss. While I had learned to tolerate being ignored on their whims and being treated as unsuitable for the position, despite being the project expert and the only one conducting field visits for monitoring reports, I now realized that no amount of competence would ever be enough.

This is how, despite it being a good position, I discovered that my idealized vision of this position was far more romanticized than the reality.

That day, I reached my breaking point.

The self-doubt ran deep. This environment and its constant shifts made me question my entire career path. Had I been wrong about who I was all along? I'd invested so much faith, energy, and time only to end up here. Feeling lost and isolated, I believed I had no right to complain since I'd chosen this path.

But when is enough enough?

I refused to let these false accusations stand. Thanks to my habit of meticulously documenting everything, I needed just 24 hours to trace my actions and prove the physical impossibility of their claims. In an email, I addressed each baseless accusation, including their claim about delivering documents to my home when I wasn't even there. In the same message, I stated my intention to complete my remaining contract months without renewal.

That's when I finally understood there were limits; not everything was acceptable. I realized it was possible to make mistakes and go down the wrong path, and sometimes continuing isn't the best solution.

I had envisioned my life one way, but reality told a different story. I had been wrong. It took countless falls, immense effort, and precious time to see this truth. But then what?

For weeks, I drifted through disappointment and emptiness, unable to imagine my next step or envision any future at all. My dream, and all I had done to achieve it, had died alongside my desire to pursue it.

Through those long months of doubting and self-questioning, I began to see that perhaps not everything was lost. I had no wish to discard all I had accomplished. Instead, I would embrace my entire journey, both the parts I chose and those imposed upon me, because it was my path. Now, it was time to adjust course and move forward.

I understood then that change requires a catalyst, and this catalyst rarely appears on its own. We don't naturally seek change; it's easier to remain in discomfort when it's familiar.

Through this experience, I realized I hadn't changed before because I simply hadn't hurt enough. **Change comes when the pain we endure hurts more than our fear of the unknown.**

This is when I decided it would be my last job working for someone else. I chose to work for myself, focusing on smaller but meaningful projects that would make a real impact. I wanted to help others and contribute to changing lives.

I did not plan to be an entrepreneur; I started my business **when my carefully laid plans took this unexpected turn**.

I did not know if it was possible or if it would work, but I began thinking about what I could do that would make a difference and align with my goals.

This led me to develop my method for helping people become entrepreneurs, based on my knowledge, experience, and aspirations.

I started offering my services and gaining clients, validating that there was a need. When one client followed all the steps of my method and asked for an invoice their company could pay, I registered my company and became officially a business owner.

Since 2015, I've never stopped developing my company. Living internationally presented unique challenges, particularly not knowing where I'd be in two years.

While this uncertainty made life exciting, it complicated business development, especially when relying on physical events and networks. This was my initial business model, as I knew I needed to build a strong network for referrals and visibility.

The first year focused on validating my method, which went well.

Then we moved to another country. The first year of any company is typically the hardest, but I faced my "second first year" in Singapore, a place where no one knew me.

Despite my previous success and visibility, I had to start over.

Although my initial plan was to stay there for the next 10 years, we remained only for one year.

In Singapore, I was quite active, wanting to learn everything I could about the vibrant entrepreneurial ecosystem. I decided to work from a co-working space to meet other entrepreneurs. There, I fortunately met several people, including someone looking for experts to join the board of her social enterprise. She invited me and five others to join this venture, which I accepted. Through this opportunity, I met talented individuals, and one of them became my business partner. With his strong financial expertise and passion for entrepreneurship, our partnership has been incredibly positive. I'm fortunate to still work with him today, even though we're no longer involved in this social enterprise.

Once again, things didn't work out as planned, and we moved back to Vietnam a year after arriving in Singapore as my husband received an offer for a job in Vietnam, but this time in the South. Moving again the following year meant starting my "third first year." It was tough, but I was prepared for it.

One lesson I learned: **You can only predict how challenging something will be once you're experiencing it**.

In this new city, I rebuilt my network and business. Not finding any entrepreneurial organizations, I started one.

Fortunately, others shared this vision, and we joined forces. While it helped with visibility and partnerships, my previous years' work generated more business growth.

However, the partnership we succeeded in having with an international Business Network Organisation took an unexpected turn. After a year of building a network with them, they said we wouldn't succeed; we proved them wrong. It led them to want to absorb it into their organization, which wasn't the original agreement. Four individuals against one institution proved an unfair fight. As the only entrepreneur, losing meant being excluded from the network.

After a year of developing this network and visibility, I felt I'd lost all my work. Even though the network hadn't brought many clients, I knew this wasn't going to be a sprint but a marathon.

Still, the impact initially seemed devastating.

This taught me another lesson: **While a physical network is valuable when you're settled in one place, being international requires an online presence.** Most importantly, **as an entrepreneur, you must build your network and, even better, a community.**

Things became more challenging as I lost clients, and then COVID arrived.

I saw this as an opportunity to pivot to what I'd learned from my experiences, building an online business.

Though I had no experience with digital platforms and wasn't fond of social media, the lockdown gave me time to learn.

I took classes, watched tutorials, and worked to establish an e-shop for my services.

I wanted to create a platform where professionals could offer their expertise, though I recognized my limitations in digital marketing and sales.

During the first year of COVID, I had one client whose company needed support for survival, which helped both of us stay afloat. One of the support services I provided was helping create an online school, which aligned perfectly with what I was implementing myself.

I worked hard to adapt my business to this new digital environment, eager to learn despite its challenges. As an entrepreneur, I knew that continuous learning was essential, so I embraced the opportunity to develop new skills.

Despite my limited marketing expertise, I offered numerous free and paid online workshops.

People somehow found their way to us, though it was challenging. After two years of building my online presence, as life returned to normal, I questioned whether my business was truly viable.

Looking back, I hadn't achieved the explosive growth I was helping other entrepreneurs and companies pursue.

A turning point came when my brother visited. As a business owner in the event industry, his journey was not easy either. He struggled for such a long time in Paris.

He started making music in Paris, but it wasn't working out for him. He couldn't get any gigs. Even though professionals found him talented, they couldn't help him take off.

He clearly couldn't make a living from his music, and things got so hard for him that he decided to move to London, and there... Within a year, he exploded.

The events he was organizing worked well, he was able to make a living from his music and turned it into a business.

While sharing with him about my business, there was this moment when he stopped and said something that changed the trajectory of my company.

His experience led him to understand that: **If there's no market where you are, try to look elsewhere. Things not working here could work there, so be where your clients are**.

I realized that while I'd initially focused on building physical networks and in-person connections, I was in the wrong place. I didn't speak the local language, they didn't speak much English, and there weren't many foreigners. All of which limit my reach and make me overly dependent on others' networks.

While using existing networks initially seemed like a good business model, it had a dark side, being controlled by those networks.

As I said, I have always been an outsider. Rarely in my life have I felt like I was in the right place...

While the reasons I turned to entrepreneurship may not have been what I initially envisioned for my career, over 10 years, I became a professional in the field.

My journey has allowed me to explore, learn, and develop a passion for and within entrepreneurship.

I love doing concrete things, being independent, learning, progressing, and supporting others—this is finally where I feel I belong.

Through this journey, I discovered entrepreneurs as creators of value and positive change, and seeing their impact on the world inspires me.

Having met, interviewed, trained, and supported entrepreneurs from diverse backgrounds, I'm continually moved by the passion in their eyes.

While my path may seem unusual, I've learned that every entrepreneur's journey is unique. This realization has enriched my understanding through countless interactions with innovative minds.

What I've found is that we share a beautiful paradox, we're united in our uniqueness.

I've witnessed firsthand what true courage, humility, resilience, tenacity, and passion look like. **The entrepreneurial journey is rarely straightforward, it's filled with obstacles and setbacks, and success is never guaranteed.**

Yet this path reveals our hidden strengths and courage.

So, in any case, dare to try!

Suzanne Andora Barron

Suzanne Andora Barron LLC
Coach

https://www.linkedin.com/in/suzanne-andora-barron-02536511/
https://www.facebook.com/suzanne.a.barron
https://www.instagram.com/suzanneandorabarron/
https://suzanneabarron.com/
https://christopherbarronlivelife.org/

Suzanne Andora Barron is an adjunct professor at her local college where she teaches Yoga for Stress Management. A certified yoga teacher, Jin Shin Jyutsu practitioner and mindset coach, Suzanne teaches women over 45 how to connect to and process their five core emotions to find emotional and physical well-being. She hosts the podcast, Finding Joy in the Hard and is finishing a memoir of the same name. Suzanne is the founder and president of The Christopher Barron Live Life Foundation dedicated to bringing comic creation programs to underserved kids.

Finding Joy in the Hard

By Suzanne Andora Barron

I stood in front of the display case at our local café on a warm summer evening in July of 2011, waiting for my dinner order. Excitement buzzed within me, lingering energy from our recent trip still fresh. Ryan, our eleven-year-old, and I had just returned from the Jersey Shore yesterday. Mom had rented a house, and my four siblings—two of whom live here in New Jersey—joined with their kids. We spent our days boogie boarding, building sandcastles, and playing games on the beach.

Tomorrow, Ryan, my husband, Rich, and I leave for Utah for a two-week vacation. Some people didn't understand how I could stack vacations like this, leaving just one day to swap out beachwear for hiking gear. But I preferred it this way—summertime at home still felt lonely, even though we were much stronger.

Laughter spilled into the eatery, pulling me from my thoughts. I glanced towards the front glass door. A mother and her son stepped inside, pausing a few feet in front of me to look up at the menu on the back wall. The boy, lanky and lean, was a full head taller than his petite mother. He was likely around thirteen. His mom was no taller than five feet, much like me. She tilted her head back to talk to him, her expression soft and engaged.

Unexpectedly, panic gripped my chest, squeezing tightly. A tear slipped down my cheek, and my limbs began to tremble. Christopher would be about the same age now. Would he be a head taller than me too?

I glanced towards the back door, roughly fifty steps away. My car was parked in the lot behind the restaurant. A lump grew in my throat. I was moments away from breaking into full-on sobbing. *Should I leave and come back? Would I even be able to come back?* Ryan and Rich were waiting for their dinner. I peered over the counter, searching for the owner, dressed in a crisp black shirt and white apron. Our food should be out any minute. I reached for my ring finger and breathed, knowing it helped calm my sadness.

Last week marked four years. Four years since we lost our precious firstborn son, Christopher. He was nine. He had leukemia.

"Suzanne," I heard my name called. Arjuna, the owner's brother, stood behind the counter, holding a large brown bag with handles. He passed it to me. I forced a shaky smile. "Thank you. Have a good night."

I hurried towards the back door, my mouth quivering.

The minivan beeped twice as I clutched the key fob in my palm. Sliding into the driver's seat, I set the brown bag on the center console and slammed the door shut. My head fell against the steering wheel, and my whole body shook with sobs. A wail erupted from deep within me.

Grief was like that. It came out of nowhere and flattened me when I least expected it. When I had been in the depths of grief, it felt long, dark, and all-consuming. Sunlight hurt. Breathing took effort. But even now, as life had settled into a new normal, grief caught me off guard.

It was triggered by moments like tonight. Other triggers included seeing two brothers walking through town, heads together, whispering in their secret language—one only siblings understood. Or watching my siblings' children, families intact. Even the sound of sibling squabbles could cut deep, though not every reminder elicited the same reaction.

Fighting was a normal part of growing up, a way for kids to work through their problems. But Ryan no longer had anyone to fight with. So I let him work out his frustrations with me instead—a concession I never would have allowed in the past.

Before I get too far ahead, let me start at the beginning...

* * * *

We were a regular family: mom, dad, two boys. We lived in a middle-class suburb, 30 minutes outside of New York City. My husband, Rich, and I met in Hoboken in our late twenties and married in our 30s. He was 30; I was 31. We both commuted into the city for work, Rich by train and me by bus. I worked at a midtown PR firm, while he was at a bank in lower Manhattan.

I had planned to return to my job after our first child was born, but Christopher surprised us by arriving nine weeks early. His premature birth left me feeling terrified and unprepared. I had barely begun to imagine myself as a mother when I found myself sitting by his side in the neonatal intensive care unit, petrified we might lose him as he struggled to breathe.

When he finally came home, a month later, weighing only four pounds, a new kind of fear set in. How would I ever care for such a fragile, tiny newborn when I barely even knew how to hold a baby? My inexperience and overwhelming anxiety had me begging Rich not to return to work when his two-week paternity leave ended. "Wait one more week, please," I pleaded.

"One of us has to work," he replied.

As Rich walked out the door, I held our screaming infant, convinced I'd fail him in some way. Those early days were filled with exhaustion and self-doubt. In time, however, I came to cherish being a stay-at-home mom. I loved engaging with Christopher, teaching him colors and words, and telling him about our day.

One morning as I leaned over his baby carrier in the supermarket, explaining our plans to visit a friend after, a cashier stopped me. "I can tell you really love being a mom," she smiled. She was right—I really did.

I came to see the world through Christopher's eyes. Everything was fresh and full of wonder. After his nap, one afternoon, I whispered to him,

"Isn't it a beautiful day?" It wasn't until I was cradling him in my arms that I noticed, it was gray and raining. But to me, holding him close, it was a beautiful day.

Twenty-three months after Christopher was born, Ryan came along. Surprisingly having two children was far easier than one. The adjustment was minor. I was comfortable being a mom. Christopher immediately stepped into his role as big brother, looking out for Ryan, who idolized and copied everything he did.

Christopher would lie next to Ryan on a blanket on the floor, teaching him colors. "Red, black, white," he would say proudly. Christopher also adored reading *Thomas the Tank Engine* to his brother, having memorized the books word for word. He'd squeeze in close to Ryan, who would gaze back at him in wonder. On weekends, the four of us snuggled in bed together, relishing the warmth of our little family.

Our first Christmas with the boys was pure magic. We started playing Christmas music in October, excited to create our own traditions. The week before Christmas, we attended *A Christmas Carol* in Madison Square Garden. Ryan slept on Rich's chest, while I whispered explanations to Christopher, who took it all in. Every night, Christopher would wave goodnight to the Christmas tree.

"Good night, Christmas tree," he'd chirp.

My heart melted as I watched on. These two little boys effortlessly filled our home with love and laughter, making every moment feel extraordinary.

In July 2001, six weeks before Christopher was scheduled to start Pre-K3, he woke up with a cough and seemed unusually tired. I took him to the pediatrician, who prescribed medication and sent us on our way. But by the weekend, his breathing worsened, and we rushed him to the ER.

There, we learned his lung had collapsed. Our baby's lung had collapsed!

Two ambulance rides and a mercy flight later, we were given the devastating news: Christopher had leukemia.

We were completely blindsided. He had been perfectly healthy, having had no residual effects from being a preemie. We stumbled through each day, uncertain how we'd survive if Christopher didn't. Those first weeks were bleak and excruciating. Christopher would beg me not to take him to the clinic, where the nurses stuck him with needles.

"Mommy," he'd scream. "They hurt me."

Meanwhile, his fourteen-month-old brother, who hated being apart from Christopher and me, would yell. "Take me, take me."

My heart shattered every time I carried our screaming three-year-old out the door, leaving his brother behind.

As much as family supported us, cooking dinners and watching Ryan, they couldn't truly understand—their lives carried on while ours fell apart.

And then, at 28 days, Christopher got into remission—our little boy was cancer-free. The treatment, however, was long—two and a half years. By the end, Christopher would be almost six and Ryan nearly four. Despite everything, my husband and I were determined their childhood would not be defined by cancer.

Because we couldn't predict what each day would bring, I decided we would do one fun thing a day. No matter what.

We'd play volleyball with a balloon in the living room, tapping it into the air.

"Get it, Christopher, get it, Ryan," I shouted, my face glowing with excitement, as their giggles filled the room.

They'd yelp and screech with delight, leaping inches off the floor, their little arms stretched up to keep the balloon afloat. In those moments, my anxious mind settled, reminding me that Christopher was winning.

It was my need to focus on the positive, no matter how small, that led me to start a gratitude journal. Friends were surprised I'd taken up this practice during Christopher's chemotherapy. But I recognized that good things would happen during these two and a half years, and I didn't want to miss them.

Still, some days, it was hard to find one thing, let alone five, to be thankful for, especially when Christopher was nauseous and throwing up from chemo and antibiotics.

Those days taught us to notice the minor, often overlooked moments: Ryan running into the kitchen yelling, "Christopher, I'll get you a bowl." The three of us cuddled in bed for hours, lost in the world of *Thomas the Tank Engine*. And the pure joy on the boys' faces as they jumped into Rich's arms when he came home from work. It was these precious moments that carried us through.

One saving grace during this time was that all of Christopher's treatment was outpatient. He was low risk, meaning he required less chemo, and his chances for survival increased from 80 percent to 90 percent. By the fourth month, he transitioned into the maintenance phase—fewer infusions and daily chemo pills. With maintenance, life began to shift. Christopher attended pre-K two days a week and started play dates and library story hour. Slowly, life took on a new color as we adjusted to a different normal.

As challenging as the diagnosis was, it taught us to savor each moment. In doing so, our lives became filled with joy and a kind of ease. Treatment eventually finished, and life returned to an even better normal. On our 17-hour drives to Hilton Head for summer vacations, we'd play tag on grassy rest-area lawns. In winter, we taught the boys to ski. Christopher took to it instantly, skiing with me in rainy weather and late spring when trails were patchy with grass. Rich and Ryan joined us, but preferred diner breakfasts when the conditions were less optimal.

My youngest sister, Camille, often said, "I love hanging out with the Barron's. They know how to have fun."

Life carried on at a usual pace until April 2006 when Christopher, who was now in second grade, and Ryan, in kindergarten, got one fever after another. I didn't think much of the first one. He had been in remission for four and a half years. After the fourth fever, a week after Christopher's eighth birthday, his oncologist ordered a bone marrow tap to rule out leukemia.

That ruling never came.

Christopher had relapsed.

Shock, terror, and overwhelm shrouded our waking moments. Life became a haze—a state of disbelief and fear. This couldn't be happening—we already had our hard times. Our child couldn't have cancer a second time. That kind of thing only happened to other families. But it was real, and this time, the diagnosis was high-risk leukemia. Harsher treatments, most of which were administered in the hospital.

Christopher, now eight, struggled with losing his hair and leaving school to begin treatment, a heartbreaking adjustment for all of us. Determined to preserve a sense of normalcy, Rich and I did our best to keep the boys together as much as possible. Mom dropped Ryan off at the hospital after morning kindergarten ended, and Rich picked him up in the evenings when he came to visit. But no matter how hard we tried to keep things normal, we couldn't hide our fear and uncertainty. Ryan, only six, sensed it all.

But we couldn't afford to fall apart. Rich and I immediately reached out to experts at the top children's hospitals across the country while caring for both of our children.

Then just as before, Christopher got into remission within 28 days. It felt like a miracle. He was cleared to join the American Red Cross swim lessons at the town pool, something he eagerly looked forward to every summer. As a special treat, we purchased lunch at the snack bar, relaxing with friends. The boys and their friends would balance on the railroad tires, pretending to have lightsaber duels with colored push-pops. After, they would run back and forth between the giant slide and the diving board. Days at the pool were more frequent than I could have imagined—another blessing, another moment I added to my gratitude journal.

In September, Ryan attended first grade, and Christopher started third grade, with no hat, no hair, and a wide smile on his face. He was in school three to four days a week. He rejoined town soccer, running up the field with the other kids, his stamina surprisingly strong. His coach would often ask if he was okay to play the whole game. We'd reply, "Ask him, he'll tell you." We made it to the slopes as often as we could, though not as frequently as in past years.

Despite the tougher treatment, Christopher was thriving. He begged us for a dog, even writing a five-page paper on why every kid needed one. "In the summer, when you're in maintenance," we promised him. We had so many dreams for the upcoming summer—his hair would grow back, we'd return to Hilton Head, and life would feel a little more normal again.

Just as we had begun to find a rhythm in our new normal, Christopher caught a fever that was going around school. His blood counts dropped, and though he recovered from the illness and returned to school, his counts never bounced back. Chemo was halted, and we waited. I spiraled, terrified it was happening again.

A bone marrow tap confirmed our worst fears. Only it wasn't a relapse. One of the chemos had caused a more aggressive cancer. I couldn't sleep. I couldn't eat. I was petrified we would lose him. We transferred his treatment to a renowned cancer hospital in New York City, where he started experimental protocols. Thankfully all his treatments were done on an outpatient basis, unless he developed a fever. I begged God to save

Christopher, as one treatment failed after another. A church friend gave me a book on healing prayers for desperate cases—it became my lifeline.

While we fought for a cure, our community rallied around us, helping us bring Christopher's little boy dreams to life. Unable to attend movies in public, a local theater graciously closed its doors one weekday morning for a private screening of *Spider-Man 3*, allowing Christopher and his friends to celebrate his 9th birthday. The day began with arcade games, followed by the movie, and then pizza and cake back at our house. His friends and Ryan even skipped school to be there. These precious moments were added to my gratitude journal, a reminder of the love and support surrounding us.

While I cherished these blessings, we were beside ourselves because the treatment wasn't working. Mentally and emotionally exhausted, I finally surrendered control to God. Letting go helped me be more present to the boys and Rich. Faith, family, and friends became the threads holding me together.

However, the cancer couldn't be stopped.

Christopher passed in July 2007, at just nine years old.

Devastation didn't begin to describe our heartbreak.

My husband said, "Our hearts have been ripped out, and still, we're expected to live."

Leaving the hospital without our child was one of the hardest things we would ever have to do. I quickly learned that grief had a way of piling hard moment upon another, each one heavier than the last. How we survived those early days without our sweet boy, I don't know.

Constant panic consumed me.

People asked me if I was holding it together for Ryan. Any semblance of composure I might have had had long since vanished. I cried all day long, wondering if we had done something different, he could have survived. I only left the house for church and to take Ryan to the pool. As much as it pained me to see others' lives continue on, Ryan needed to know he mattered.

Anger at God consumed me. Guilt gnawed at my heart. As Christopher's mom, I should have been able to save him. On days Ryan was at camp—Rich had insisted he return a week after the funeral—I found myself reliving the past, pouring over journals, and sifting through photo albums.

And then, one day in late August, Rich asked, "Do you want to go on a bike ride with me?"

As an avid cyclist, he had been asking me for years to join him. I always refused. "What if I get hit by a car? Who would take care of the boys?" I had said. This time, however, I said, "Okay."

Worry was a waste. It didn't save Christopher. It changed nothing.

So, I bought a bike—the store owner had to teach me how to get on it—and started riding. When Rich asked where I wanted to go, I answered without hesitation.

"The cemetery."
"That's nine miles," he said.
"That's where our child is."

Cycling became a daily ritual, offering a temporary escape from grief. Tears blurred my vision as I pedaled up hills. While the rides gave me moments of release, I felt myself sinking deeper into a black hole. The anger I once clung to had been replaced by sheer devastation. I didn't know how to survive this.

Eager for guidance, I reached out to other parents who had lost children. Our conversations brought a sense of connection, but it wasn't enough. I still felt hollow and lost. Eventually, I realized I couldn't do this alone—I needed God.

I purchased my first Bible and started a study. Prayer felt impossible—I had no words. Instead, I turned to scripture, and in those verses, I found comfort. In seeking God, I felt closer to Christopher. He visited in my dreams and sent me signs—in the form of hearts—reminding me he was close.

But when Ryan started second grade, and Rich returned to work after his six-week bereavement leave, the silence pulled me into further despair. I'd drive Ryan a quarter mile to school and return home, collapsing on the living room rug, wailing. Fatigue flattened me, and eating felt impossible—every bite seemed to close my throat.

A friend suggested a grief counselor, and that was how I met Kathy at CancerCare. She encouraged me to create an imaginary toolbox filled with anything that had ever brought me joy. I added writing, biking, journaling, yoga, and drawing. Kathy urged me to weave these activities into my routine.

I enrolled in an art class through the community school and signed up for an adult ballet class—something I had always wanted to try. After just one ballet lesson, I quit. I didn't have the capacity to follow the instructions.

The art class, however, reconnected me to my childhood love of drawing. As a ten-year-old, I had filled black sketchbooks with drawings of everyday objects—our backyard swing, a stick of gum, a pumpkin. Moving a pencil across the page again provided a small, comforting respite from my grief.

Resuming yoga was another gift. Stretching my limbs and moving through the poses helped edge out some of the darkness. On the mat, I allowed myself to cry freely without anyone rushing to comfort me. The practice became a space of healing where I could release my pain.

Yoga eventually led me to Jin Shin Jyutsu, an ancient Japanese healing art involving light touch and breathwork. I learned simple practices, like holding my ring finger helped balance sadness. Holding my thumb calmed the worry that every food might cause an allergic reaction. Specific hand placements eased the itchy throat that sometimes followed. Both yoga and Jin Shin Jyutsu became cornerstones of my healing. They gave me a sense of control I never expected to feel again. Over time, I became a certified yoga instructor and certified Jin Shin Jyutsu practitioner, wanting to help others the way these practices had helped me.

For our first Thanksgiving and Christmas without Christopher, Rich, Ryan, and I went away, hoping to create new traditions in unfamiliar surroundings. Slowly, through unwavering love and commitment to one another, we began to navigate life as a family of three instead of four. As the years passed, new rhythms and routines replaced the old ones.

To honor Christopher's memory and help children who might not have the same opportunities my boys had, we started The Christopher Barron Live Life Foundation. Now, in its 15th year, the foundation celebrates Christopher's love of creating comics by hosting comic-creation workshops at underserved schools. It's a way of keeping his vibrant spirit alive while inspiring young imaginations.

When the pandemic hit, it brought a fresh wave of challenges and uncertainty. People who had never experienced anxiety found themselves struggling, overwhelmed by the growing panic of an unpredictable world. Having dealt with worry for much of my life, I leaned on the hundreds of tools I had learned to find calm. To support others, I started a Sunday newsletter called *Staying Strong*, where I offered mindset tips and Jin Shin Jyutsu healing practices that people could use to ease their anxiety. The newsletter quickly gained traction and now reaches close to four hundred readers.

To provide even more support, I launched a live 15-minute online guided Jin Shin Jyutsu meditation via Zoom every Monday, that continues today. These sessions became a shared moment of peace and grounding for many during a time of isolation and fear. I found solace in helping others navigate their struggles, even as I continued to work through my own.

When Ryan left for university, I felt compelled to help young people learn to cope with stress. I became an adjunct professor, teaching Yoga for Stress Management at my local college. One assignment that I included every semester was a gratitude journal where students were asked to write down three to five different things every day for a week and then answer specific questions in a reflection. This encouraged them to notice and appreciate the smaller, often overlooked moments.

Recognizing how suppressing emotions can contribute to discomfort and disease, I developed a seven-week online course called Process What You Feel to Heal, for women over 45. The course teaches participants how to balance their five core emotions and face uncomfortable feelings instead of stuffing them inside.

Last year, I launched a podcast, *Finding Joy in the Hard*, where I interview people who've undergone incredible challenges and emerged with resilience and hope. I'm writing a memoir by the same name.

Seventeen years later, grief still finds its way into my life. When meditation, exercise, or journaling fail to bring relief, I pause and ask myself what's truly going on. A small voice usually whispers, "It's grief." Those moments remind me to slow down, reflect, and give myself grace.

Two things I know for sure: We are so much stronger than we think. And joy can be found in the hard.

<u>Suggested hold to calm worry, find balance and quiet the mind</u>: Gently hold one of your thumbs, either one. Close your eyes and breathe, inhaling through the nose for the count of four and exhaling through the nose for the count of six.

Continue for five to ten rounds. Extended exhales calm the nervous system. Before you begin, notice on a scale of 1-10 how you feel. When you finish, notice again on a scale of 1-10 how you're feeling. Remember don't squeeze or massage your finger. Light touch. As you practice, you might twitch, hear rumbling in your belly or feel sensation elsewhere in the body. This is your energy pathways beginning to balance. This practice can also help you fall asleep at night.

Teri Katzenberger

Live Well Now Academy LLC
Functional Health and Lifestyle Wellness Specialist

https://www.linkedin.com/in/livewellnow/
https://www.facebook.com/TeriKatzenberger/
https://www.instagram.com/terikatzenberger/
https://livewellnow.academy/
http://www.livewellnowacademy.com/

Teri Katzenberger has been a Functional Health and Lifestyle Wellness Specialist since 2003. She is the CEO-Founder of the Live Well Now Academy LLC.

From the age of 19 – 23 Teri became the survivor of a violent marriage, disabling self-image issues, a chronic eating disorder and a life threatening alcohol and drug addiction.

Teri is an incredible overcomer with a deep passion for all people on all walks of life.

Teri began her own personal health journey in 1991—(to save her own life).

She specializes in people, and her specialty is helping you achieve your best life. She teaches and shares hard truths to help you achieve real results.

Teri holds a diploma as a Fitness & Nutrition Specialist, a Medical Fitness Specialization as a Hormone Fitness Specialist and numerous other certifications.

Her Mission: To Help People Live a Healthy, Well, Fit, Strong, Whole Life from the Inside Out.

I Celebrate Recovery

By Teri Katzenberger

As I sit and prepare my message in our amazing book, *She Grows Stronger*, there is only one way that seems to fit me—my life—on how to begin sharing my story.

Hello, my name is Teri Katzenberger, and I celebrate recovery from this thing called My Life!

In this thing called—My Life—I have experienced unending hurt, unbearable pain, heartache, bitterness, belittling, and physical, mental, and emotional abuse. The result decades later? I found myself fighting for this thing called My Life—with disabling depression, paralyzing anxiety, and overwhelming internal torment and anguish. My life was not my own. I was losing the very thing that kept me living—the one thing that kept me fighting forward. I was losing my joy for this thing called Life. I was losing my joy for the people, places, and things that truly mattered.

Here's what I have learned on my life's journey: If we are not mindful, cautious, and plugged into the word of God, our life as we know it can and will be taken from us. We will be robbed of this beautiful thing called Life! We will be living while slowly dying on the inside. Now, I encourage you to drop what you are doing, find a quiet place, and grab your favorite soothing beverage. You know, the one that makes you go "ahh-mmmm" at the very first sip! Kind of like me and my very first sip of morning coffee. I'll begin to unpack what this really means!

Where It All Began

I was born Teresa A. Thompson, one half of a set of twins who arrived weighing just three pounds each. My twin brother went home soon after birth, but I remained in an incubator for three weeks. Nurses lovingly called me "Baby Polly," until my dad intervened to spare me a lifetime of "Polly, wanna cracker?" jokes.

But my beginning wasn't the joyful story most imagined. I was born to a mother who didn't want me. She had dreams for herself and her two older children—her "golden children"—but those dreams were interrupted when she discovered she was pregnant with twins. And so, she stayed with my father, not out of love, but because of circumstances.

January 1968, the "Unwelcome Intruders" were born. From the start, our home was divided: my mother and her golden children on one side, my father and the twins on the other. We were cast as the villains who ruined her life, a narrative we could never escape.

For most, home is a haven of safety and warmth. For me, it was a place of resentment, anger, and hostility. I was told, repeatedly, that I made her life miserable. Branded disappointment from birth, I spent decades chasing her approval—a dream I now know was impossible.

To my mother, I wasn't just unwanted; I was a constant source of bitterness. My existence, my voice—"Stop your screeching!"—even my resemblance to my grandmother seemed to fill her with disgust. I was a living reminder of everything she resented.

I grew up suffocating under abandonment and longing for a family that would welcome me as more than a burden. Instead, I remained the eternal outsider, weighed down by a label I never asked for: the destroyer of dreams, a mistake too big to forgive. A living nightmare.

A Triggered Breakthrough

Reflection has a way of bringing clarity, even to the messy, painful parts of life. On April 9, 2022, at a business conference with hundreds of colleagues, I had an unexpected moment of awakening.

The conference included opportunities for attendees to share breakthroughs or insights over the microphone. On day three, I felt compelled to speak, though the voice in my head urged me to stay seated. After waiting nervously, my turn came.

I began sharing my story—the childhood pain, my mother's resentment, and the profound sense of being unloved. Just as I was about to reveal my breakthrough, the leader interrupted me: "Yeah, yeah, yeah, Teri. Your mother sounds like a horrible person. Did you have a breakthrough? Get to the breakthrough."

His dismissive tone cut like a blade. My heart sank, my mind went blank, and humiliation consumed me. I barely managed to say, "I realized I was born with overwhelming love in my heart, yet I have never felt love," before retreating to my seat.

Later, as I replayed his words, I realized why they stung so deeply—they echoed my mother's voice: "You will never amount to anything." "Stop your screeching." It was as if all her bitterness and rejection had come rushing back through him.

But in that moment of despair, I found my true breakthrough: I am not defined by the words or actions of others. Their pain, their judgments—they belong to them, not me.

That day, I let go of the burden of trying to prove my worth to people who refused to see it. I walked away lighter, knowing I was not an intruder in this thing called Life. I have value, purpose, and love to give—whether others choose to see it or not.

Wounded and Set Free

As a wounded warrior, if you can remove yourself from the attitudes, opinions, and actions of others, you can ultimately set yourself free to heal and grow. You no longer need to wear the heavy cloak called: **no-good;** *having no worth, virtue, use, or chance of success; does nothing <u>useful</u> or <u>helpful</u> and is <u>therefore considered</u> to be of little <u>value</u>.*

I walked away from that conference, a woman who armed herself with strength, confidence, and determination to continue to break through the impossible! Our "Before Story" is a deeply significant part of us. It may even be who we became. Never deny that. However, our "Before Story" is not *who* we are. Allow me to help you begin your "After Story."

You may be wondering about my eye-opening breakthrough. It was: *God created me for one reason—to walk in peace, to love and serve His people. When I was born, He filled my heart with all the love that was poured into that "old house." The Twins soaked up all of God's Love. We received it. Yet we went through every waking day, not ever knowing what it really felt like to* **BE** *loved. We may never know what it means to* **receive** *Love.* However, we lived every moment of our days loving, giving to, walking with, and standing by people. Lifting others up and letting them know they are loved and they matter! My twin passed away very unexpectedly on December 9, 2020. Half of me has gone to heaven, while the other half remains here on earth, continuing to fight for this thing called *Our* Life. Today our "After Story" begins.

When you have been wounded, broken, betrayed, abandoned, and just forgotten, you can either accept the world's view of you or trust the voice in your heart that continues to remind you, "You are so much more than you think you are!"

My Own Living Nightmare

It wasn't until 1991 that I began to truly understand the person I had become. I was born with a heart full of love, kindness, passion, and compassion for others. But at 19, I married an older man who was grossly abusive. What followed was a living nightmare of mental, emotional, and verbal abuse, all intertwined with his chronic, traumatic alcoholism and physical violence.

I, too, turned to alcohol—desperate to kill the pain that was killing me inside. It was the only way I could cope with the bitterness, hate, anger, and disgust that filled my home. Trapped. Alone. Afraid. Completely lost. I couldn't believe what my life had become.

If not for my faith in God, I wouldn't have survived.

I hid it all. The abuse. The disease. The shame. After all, who could I turn to? Gossip, judgment, criticism, and belittling had been the soundtrack of my life. I couldn't risk exposing my truth, so I kept it locked away like a shameful secret.

On April 4, 1990, I entered alcohol treatment for the first time. I remember that day vividly as if it happened yesterday. Drunk and desperate, I finally broke. My husband had called my parents, and they arrived at our house, stunned as I laid bare all the torment I had bottled up for so long. That night, they took me to a local treatment center. Kicking. Screaming. Completely sick—sick of my life and sick of living it.

But 28 days later, nothing had changed. My abuser was the one who picked me up from the treatment center. On the way home, he stopped at the liquor store, bought a 6 pack of tall boys, and waved it in my face as he told me, "I'm not quitting drinking." Two weeks later, I was drunk again. The abuse continued—beatings, rape, and verbal assaults. I couldn't survive my life sober.

On April 4, 1991, I entered treatment again—this time at a hospital over an hour away. This would be the day I learned just how deep my family's "secret mold" ran. My mother, the master of appearances, hadn't told anyone about my struggles. As I prepared to leave, she said to me, "Let this be the last time you go on vacation."

Vacation?

I was stunned. "I'm not going on vacation," I said, confused.

"That's what I tell people," she replied. "If anyone asks about you, I just say you're on vacation."

My heart sank. Her words cut me to the core. She was embarrassed. Ashamed of me. To her, my struggle wasn't about my pain or survival; it was a reflection of her. Another flaw in her carefully curated image.

By then, I was gravely ill with alcoholism. I couldn't function sober—I could barely walk or even feed myself properly because of the disabling shakes. I desperately needed love, support, and encouragement from the people who claimed to care about me. But I began to wonder if they ever truly did. Who was I to assume I mattered to them?

And yet, it was during this time that something incredible happened: I broke the generational cycle of addiction, lying, and abuse.

Six weeks later, I left that treatment hospital a completely new person. It was as if I had been delivered out of one life and placed into another. I never went back to my abuser—not for one day. I never looked back.

Instead, I found myself at Second Street Manor, a women's halfway house. It wasn't glamorous, but it was safe. It was home. My parents wouldn't let me move back in with them, and there was no way I would return to my abuser.

I still remember the day my mother dropped me off there after an appointment. She looked around in disgust and said, "I don't know how you can stand living in such a horrible place."

Her words stung, but I stood my ground. "It's because of you that I'm here," I told her calmly. "You wouldn't let me come home. This is my home now, and it's a beautiful home. I'd appreciate it if you wouldn't put it down like that."

I got out of the car and walked inside, shutting the door on her negativity.

Looking back now, I realize that not letting me come home was the best thing my parents ever did for me. Second Street Manor wasn't just a halfway house—it was my sanctuary, the foundation for the life I would go on to build. I've thanked them for that decision countless times over the years.

The saddest part of this? When you choose to keep "secrets" from family and close friends, you rob *them* of the chance to express their own caring, nurturing, and loving selves. You think you're protecting your image or avoiding judgment, but in reality, you're depriving others of the opportunity to support and uplift someone they love.

It's heartbreaking for those around you when they eventually learn that someone they deeply care for is struggling, hurting, and alone. Why? Because they don't share the bitterness, hate, or resentment you harbor in your heart. Instead, they would have shown kindness, compassion, and love. Keeping secrets from them is not only unfair—it's cruel.

Then there's this: My mother's selfishness and embarrassment over my struggles didn't just hurt me; it became my relatives' and close family friends' pain. When they eventually learned what I had endured—years later—they were devastated. They felt guilt and sorrow, wishing they could have been there for me. They told me they would have visited me and supported me in ways I desperately needed. But they never had the chance, because she robbed them of it.

And it didn't stop there. My mother resented me even more when others began to see my accomplishments and successes—when they celebrated me, cared for me, or paid me any attention at all. Her resentment grew as my light started to shine.

I've learned a heartbreaking truth on my journey: The people you love deeply may never feel the same for you. They may never hold love in their heart for you as you do for them. They may never think about you with the same care, compassion, or longing that you think of them.

Most people may never face even a fraction of what I've endured in my life, but nothing compares to the pain of realizing this about my mother and my family. The moment I fully awakened to this truth was one of the most painful breakthroughs of my life.

Family doesn't always think of you the way you think of them. They don't always love you the way you love them. I remember the searing pain of that realization as if it were yesterday. For a moment, I truly thought it would be the thing that broke me entirely—because the people who hurt me most weren't strangers. They were my family.

But here's the beautiful part: By October 1991, I had turned my life around. In just six months, I left the halfway house and moved into my own place for the first time in my life.

There was no turning back.

Pain in Freedom

But none of that prepared me for the pain of realizing that: *"The people I longed to love me may never feel the same towards me."*

As unbearable as that revelation was, something remarkable happened when I finally spoke those words out loud. Admitting the truth and allowing myself to feel it—that was the beginning of my freedom. You see, this is the part of my "Before Story" that never fully goes away. But here's the difference: I can choose to live in it, or I can choose to move out of it. In 1996, I chose to move out of it.

Every day since, I've made the choice to give thanks to my family. I thank God for watching over them and for keeping them safe, healthy, strong, and whole. I thank Him for protecting them from harm, even when our relationships are fractured. I choose love.

I share my personal story—my truth—to give hope to others and remind myself of the person I was becoming. I was empowered. On a mission to finally live my life for *me*! I was taking back everything that had been stripped from me by the abuser and others: my confidence, my voice, my well-being, my self-esteem, and my God-given life.

I remember that time as if it were yesterday. Every moment leading up to my graduation from Second Street Manor after six transformative months is etched in my memory. Even now, I still cherish the beautiful vase I received from the staff and the other girls living there. It sits proudly on my desk, a beautiful reminder of how far I've come.

I think about when my divorce was finalized and the pride I had in saving enough money to live on my own for the very first time. I was just 23. Alone, but determined. On a life-changing mission to navigate the real world as an adult.

I was lost. But I *did it*. And I have never looked back.

Yet, over the course of the next 30 years—reclaiming and redesigning my life—I forgot something crucial. Something that is foundational to my growth, my strength, and my future self.

I forgot the personal life standards I had set for myself. Those standards guided me for the next 10 years, shaping my decisions and my journey. Somewhere along the way, on my life's journey, I lost sight of them.

It wasn't until recently, as memories of my past self came flooding back, that I realized this loss. Losing those standards was a shift that forever changed my outlook on life, my attitude, and the person I was striving to become.

My Personal Life Standards:

If you don't like the way I look—Don't look at me!
If you don't like the sound of my voice—Don't listen to me!
If you don't like what I have to say—Don't talk to me!
If you don't like who I am—Stay away from me!
I like who I am. Your opinion does not matter to me!

This list of standards helped take back ALL that was taken from me over the first 23 years of my life. I stood by this with confidence, strength, and courage. I was becoming the best version of myself. Why these standards? All through my upbringing, my mother never liked the sound of my voice or how I looked, nor did she like—Me! I was a thorn in her side from the day she got pregnant. I was programmed to believe that I was not good enough. I didn't "look" good enough. My voice wasn't "good" enough. My existence just wasn't "good" enough.

Somewhere along my journey—starting in 2000 and moving forward—I lost the person I had fought so hard to become. Slowly, my voice began to fade. My very existence felt like it was slipping away. I forgot about my Personal Life Standards, which had once guided and grounded me. I let my guard down and began to drift further from who I truly was.

Little did I know, that was when the slow unraveling began. I wasn't just losing sight of myself—I was dying inside, piece by piece.

The fire that once fueled my strength, my confidence, and my mission to live boldly was replaced by a slow burn of pain, disappointment, and betrayal. And the source of that burn? The very people I surrounded myself with.

These were the people I believed would always have my back, stand by me, and stand with me. But they didn't. And for the next 20-plus years, my life was never the same again.

Although the mental, emotional, and verbal abuse from my mother had been happening since the day I was born, it wasn't until around 2015 that my eyes were fully opened to its devastating impact. To this day, I have no idea what triggered the shift or why it happened. All I know is that my mother decided she wanted nothing to do with me ever again.

She made her feelings painfully clear, tearing into me with hateful words. She called me an uneducated, classless human being and tried to convince me that no one was for me.

As I stood there, her words cutting deep, something unexpected happened. Visions of people who truly cared for me flashed before my eyes. It was as if my soul was reminding me that I was not alone.

I looked her in the eye and said calmly, "You and the family don't have to be for me. That's okay. There are so many others who *are* for me."

Her response was pure venom: "No, you don't! No one is for you! No one is for you!"

Those words echoed in my mind as I walked out of her home that day in December 2016, knowing it would be the last time I ever set foot in the house I grew up in.

The visions of those people who flashed before my eyes? *They* are my truth. *They* are *my people*.

Still, the damage had been done. My life, the one I had worked so hard to redesign for myself, was slowly being destroyed, one step at a time. Although I left that house behind, mental and emotional abuse followed me like a shadow, tormenting me for the next six years and causing unimaginable anguish.

I will never say this has been an easy road. Daily, I was losing that strong, confident, courageous woman by allowing the actions and words of others to paralyze me and destroy me from the inside out. And only I knew it. I attended family gatherings based on "how I felt." Little did I know I was slowly being plagued with overwhelming anxiety and depression. My beautiful life was losing its purpose.

From 2016 to 2018, I faced a new kind of torment—this time, a handful of so-called "close" friends turned my life into a living hell. Why? That remains the million-dollar question.

When I finally picked up the phone to call them out on their cruelty, their silence was deafening. No explanations. No apologies.

In 2016, we were approaching milestone birthdays, turning 49 and 50. But instead of celebrating this new chapter together, mind games, pot-stirring, and backstabbing were on their agenda. I loved these women with all my heart. People I thought I'd grow closer to as we entered our

50s and beyond. I truly believed we would be exploring life together, forming unshakable bonds. Instead, my beautiful bridge to friendship was crumbling, becoming more fragile.

The social anxiety became overwhelming; paranoia began weaving its way into the mix of depression. I clung tightly to my Faith. I reminded myself that God still cares for me, AND HE loves me.

In those dark moments, I revisited the vision I had in December 2016, the faces of those who truly love and care for me. *My people.* They are the ones who stand by me and truly matter.

My Thompson Twin went to heaven in December 2020, but his words live on in my heart. Whenever I catch myself letting people live rent-free in my head, I hear him as clear as day. "Don't let the bastards run ya down." And I smile. I chuckle. In that moment, I remember who I am and why their cruelty can never define me.

Although the emotional pain caused me to lose confidence and weaken my strength, these years of mental and emotional anguish at the hands of people I deeply love and care for have taught me a great deal about myself. I'm becoming stronger and more confident. Facing difficulties no longer feels insurmountable. The chaos in my mind has eased, and the overwhelm that once consumed me is beginning to fade.

She Grows Stronger

We've all heard the saying, "Be careful not to burn bridges." It's usually framed as a cautionary warning: "You don't want to burn any bridges!"

The phrase originated from the literal act of destroying a bridge or path behind you, ensuring that no one could follow. Over time, it's come to symbolize intentionally cutting off relationships, opportunities, or connections. Burning bridges is often seen as a last resort, something reckless or irrevocable, leaving no chance for return.

But here's the question I keep asking myself: "Is it really that bad to burn a bridge?"

I mean, let's be honest—we need to guard ourselves against people who aren't truly for us. If someone isn't for you, then by default, they're against you. That doesn't mean they're outwardly hostile, but it does mean they don't contribute positively to your life. People cannot love you and hate you at the same time. That's not how this realm works.

I ask myself again: "To burn or not to burn the bridge?"

It's a big question. One worth exploring. Because maybe, just maybe, burning a bridge isn't always a loss. Sometimes, it's the first step toward building a better one.

Vengeance isn't necessary. I don't believe in karma—I walk in faith and trust in God. I focus on being who He created me to be. We don't have to be on the attack. Let others burn their own paths of hatred and discontent; you don't have to join them.

It's easier to follow the crowd than to chart your own course and live by your Personal Life Standards. Many people don't want to see others succeed or live joyfully—misery loves company. I refuse to hang out with misery. The smaller my circle, the more peace I have.

Words of Wisdom: Don't rebuild the bridges others have burned. If they don't love you, or support you, let the ashes lie. It's natural to want everyone to like us, but you don't need to chase toxic relationships. Trust me—don't waste your energy on bridges that lead back to haters, bullies, or pot stirrers.

I spent years crossing bridges to people who didn't deserve my time. I've had to forgive myself for letting their actions steal so much of my life. But now, I see that my true bridge—the one I'm building—is beautiful and leads to peace and purpose.

The truth is, when we stop crossing back to toxic people, they accuse us of burning bridges. But we aren't responsible for their paths. We're responsible for our own mental and emotional wellness.

So, keep moving forward. Let the haters hate. You have nothing to lose, nothing to prove, and everything to gain by living boldly on your own beautiful bridge.

There are dream stealers in our midst. I challenge you to become a Dream Releaser! Join me in fanning your flames to spark the fire within your spirit. Setting your Soul on fire! You deserve to be set free!

Here is what I have learned on my journey in this thing called life: When it comes to the haters, the pot stirrers, the bullies, they have no desire to be part of my life. Now, they may want to be "in" my life so they can stay in the loop of what I am up to—therefore, having something for the pot stirrers to mix around. Truth be told (by experience), they do not truly care about me. They just want to be in the "know," so they have something to gossip about and hate.

In September 2023, I had another awakening: *"Do not reward bad behavior."* I've learned that people treat you based on their own misery and hate, not your worth. I refuse to conform to their negativity or let them live rent-free in my mind, dim my spirit, or weaken my soul.

Instead, I'm building a brand-new Beautiful Bridge—not "rebuilding." Rebuilding would mean restoring something tainted by hate, bullying, and toxicity. My new bridge is built on fresh foundations and guided by new Personal Life Standards.

I know this sounds daunting. You might think, *"I'm not strong enough to do this,"* but trust me, it wasn't easy for me, either. Since 1991, my journey has been anything but smooth—it's been lonely, scary, and at times, overwhelming.

What finally made it simpler (not easy, but simpler) was my faith in Jesus Christ, who is my strength. The bridge to the haters, bullies, and pot stirrers grew more toxic with time, but I chose to hang on to my faith and keep moving forward.

It's never been easy, but it's been worth it. Living life forward, without turning back, has given me peace and purpose.

The ONE thing that made my journey simpler, that allowed me to finally exhale overwhelm, anxiety, and depression and inhale strength and confidence? When I understood why Jesus left Nazareth. You see, even Jesus had family, relatives, and close friends who were not for Him. In His hometown, He had haters, bullies, and pot stirrers. He refused to stay where He was not wanted. He walked out of Nazareth, wiped his feet, and never looked back!

In October 2023, I had a life-changing realization: I needed to burn and rebuild my beautiful bridge—not to keep others out, but to stop myself from going back to those who abuse me. The awakening came like a whisper from the Holy Spirit: "Burn the bridge that leads you back to toxic people." My response was a resounding, "Dear Lord, YES!"

*There comes a time in life when we must love ourselves **more** than the people who despise us. Don't let their noise drown out your voice.*

It's time to fan the flames within your soul and extinguish the flames of those who've tried to burn you. Stop keeping those tormenting embers alive. I understand the struggle—I spent 30 years fanning the flames of people who continued to hurt me.

I have no regrets. Everything happens in its own time. Today, I am stronger and more confident. Today, they can no longer hurt me.

When I realized I had nothing to lose, I was set free. That's why I share my story—I owe evil nothing, and I have nothing to prove.

I encourage you to wipe your feet from the toxic ashes that carry with you in your mind, body, and spirit. Walk forward onto your own Beautiful Bridge. No looking back!

I help women overcome hurts, habits, and hangups that prevent them from achieving their best, healthy, happy, fulfilled lives. I would be honored to have a personal virtual coffee talk with you!

Reach out to me to receive your own Personal Standards Homework Guide: Building Your Beautiful Bridge.

With Deep Love,
Teri
TeriKatzenberger@msn.com

Tina Fletcher

https://www.linkedin.com/in/tinadfletcher/
https://www.facebook.com/tinafletchercom/
https://www.instagram.com/tinafletcher_com
https://www.tinafletcher.com/
https://www.tinafletcher.com/links

Tina Fletcher knows the feeling of being caught between two yeses, the one you give the world and the one you really want to give.

For years, like so many of us, she filled roles and met expectations, saying yes or no, on autopilot.

Then, one day, she did something radical:

She Paused,
and consciously decided her answer.

And in that quiet, in-between space, she found something unexpected. Herself.

She writes for women who have spent years doing, giving, and achieving, only to wonder, where did I go?

Her message is about reclaiming that space, that voice, that pause where everything shifts.

And allowing the belief that transformation doesn't happen in grand gestures, but in the small, unseen moments where we start choosing differently.

Tina invites you to embrace The Space Between. Not as something to rush through, but as a space to sit, listen, and trust yourself in what comes next.

The Space Between

By Tina Fletcher

The delicious banana and mango smoothie sat cool in my hand as the quiet streets below began to come alive. Sitting on my balcony, overlooking the old city of Chiang Mai, I watched the world wake up. From the outside, my life looked like a dream: freedom, adventure, mornings in paradise.

As a digital nomad, I moved between cities whenever I felt the desire to see something new, each new place promising a fresh start, but my patterns followed me everywhere.

Looking back, I didn't see it, but I felt the weight of something else.

Each yes I'd given,
each demand I'd met,
seemed to draw me away from the life I thought I was creating for myself.

For me, the freedom of being a digital nomad was now filled with deception. Beneath the adventure and constant motion, I felt a weight pressing back, a quiet tug of unseen threads.

The emails waiting in my inbox.
The messages pinging my phone.
The quiet, insidious whispers of all the yeses I had trained myself to give.

I was good at saying yes. It had brought me here, to Asia, to enjoy the freedom and adventure, but as I stared at my reflection in the laptop screen, the irony struck me: I had simply traded one version of yes for another.

Back home, I was the reliable one — the fixer, the helper, the one who could always handle it all. Here, I was still performing, still proving something to someone.

Different location, same pattern.

My yeses had followed me, filling every corner of the life I thought was mine.

For years, I'd been living on autopilot, driven by expectations I hadn't stopped to question. But that morning, something shifted. Not dramatically; there was no lightning bolt or grand epiphany.

Just a pause.
A breath.
A moment when I asked myself a simple, startling question:
What if I didn't?

What if, in that space between request and response, I could find a different way of being?

It showed up in the smallest moments. Like when a potential client reached out, excited about working together, and I felt that familiar rush to prove my worth. "I can make any timeline work," I started to type – my default response, my way of making myself invaluable.

But something made me pause.

The morning sun was warm on my shoulders, the sweetness of mango still lingering from my smoothie, and for once, I let myself sit in that space between request and response.

What would happen if I didn't immediately accommodate?
If I actually checked in with myself first?

The question felt almost dangerous. Years of conditioning whispered that if I didn't say yes immediately, that if I wasn't constantly available, I'd lose everything I'd built. After all, wasn't that what brought me to Thailand in the first place? The need to prove I could do it all, be it all, on my own terms?

But those terms weren't really mine, were they?

I saw it in my daily calls back home too. "How's paradise?" friends would ask, and I'd automatically launch into the highlight reel they expected. The adventures, the freedom, the perfect Instagram moments. I'd gotten so good at telling the story they wanted to hear that I'd almost convinced myself it was the whole truth.

The whole truth was messier.
Yes, I was living a dream, but whose dream was it, really?

In between the moments of genuine joy and discovery, there was also loneliness, uncertainty, and constant pressure to prove I'd made the right choice. I'd swapped one performance for another, still seeking validation, just from a different audience.

That realization could have been crushing.
Instead, it felt like finally setting down a heavy bag I hadn't even realized I was carrying. The weight of always being on, always being available, always being whatever version of myself others needed, had become so familiar I'd stopped noticing it.

This was the first lesson in reclaiming my power: awareness. The simple act of noticing these patterns was itself a form of liberation. Each time I caught myself automatically reaching for the yes, I was building a new memory muscle, the ability to pause, to question, to choose differently.

But now I noticed.

In the space between messages, in the pause before responses, in those quiet moments on my balcony when the city was still waking up, I started to hear something else. Not the voice of expectation or obligation, but my own voice. Quiet at first, like a muscle that had forgotten how to move, but growing stronger each time I dared to listen.

The first time I actually said no – a real, clear no, not wrapped in maybes or apologies – I was shaking. A big opportunity had landed in my inbox, the kind I would have jumped at before.

A collaboration that looked perfect on paper, that the old me would have seen as validation.

My fingers hovered over the keyboard, muscle memory ready to type my usual "Absolutely, I'd love to!"

But in that pause, in that tiny space between stimulus and response, I felt it.

The subtle tightness in my chest,
the slight nausea that I'd always ignored before.
My body had been trying to tell me something all along.
I just hadn't been listening.

Instead I replied, I would love to connect and find out more about your needs and discover how we can work together. I ended up turning down this opportunity because it wasn't the right fit. And that was okay.

And no, another opportunity didn't come, like you hear many times in stories, and I suddenly magically had a major shift.

Instead, changes followed, small but significant. I started taking my morning walks without listening for that ding of the phone, letting myself just be present in the busy streets of Chiang Mai and be in the moment.

The way the morning air held both incense and exhaust fumes. The rhythm of my feet against the ancient stones. The nods of recognition from shop owners who no longer saw me as a tourist, but as someone who had chosen to simply be present in their world.

Each morning became a small act of trust. Trust that I didn't need to prove my experience to anyone, that living it fully was enough.

I began telling friends back home the whole truth about my journey, not just the highlight reel, but the messy, beautiful reality of choosing your own path.

The most surprising change wasn't in the big decisions, though.
It was in the quiet moments,
the everyday choices
that seemed small but actually shaped my entire life.

Like when I stopped forcing myself to network at every digital nomad meetup because that's what you're supposed to do. Instead, I allowed myself to spend evenings talking to both new friends and business associates in quiet settings, online or in person.

I painted, I drew, and I reconnected with parts of myself I'd set aside in the rush to build my business.

One evening, sitting cross-legged on my apartment floor with acrylics spread around me – something I hadn't done since I was too busy being successful, I realized I was crying.

Not from sadness, but from recognition.
This was me.
Not the carefully curated version I showed the world, not the endlessly accommodating one, but just... me.
Messy, creative, imperfect, real.

The real test came during a video call with another potential client.

I remember every detail of that moment, the whir of the ancient ceiling fan in my favourite cafe, the condensation beading on my iced tea, and the familiar flutter of anxiety in my chest as her words filled my screen.

The old patterns were rising up, that instinct to shape myself into whatever she needed. These were the moments that used to define me, the constant readiness to contort myself into the perfect solution for someone else's problem.

But this time, something was different.
As she spoke about her needs and expectations, her issues, where she was at and what she must achieve, I noticed how my body was

responding: the slight tension in my shoulders, the shallow breath in my chest. These weren't just physical sensations anymore; they were signals I'd learned to read in that space between stimulus and response.

They were my inner compass, finally being heard.

She was exactly the type of client I would have bent over backwards to impress before, successful, confident, and always pushing toward the next goal.

"I've been thinking about shifting direction," she said, her words tumbling out as if they had been weighing on her for weeks. "I'm not sure if it's the right move, but staying where I am feels... wrong. I need to decide quickly, though. What do you think?"

The old me would have asked her to tell me where she was and then jumped into solution mode, offering a dozen strategies and trying to map out her next steps before she had even finished speaking. I used to think action — any action — was what was needed for us women to show we were on the ball, driven, focused.

But I knew now that rushing forward without clarity often led to missteps. Sometimes, the most transformative action starts with a pause.

"What's driving the need to act so quickly?" I asked. The question hung in the air for a moment. She blinked, the tension in her shoulders easing just slightly.

"I guess... I feel like I should," she said. "Like if I don't, I'll miss the opportunity. Or worse, fall behind."

I nodded, understanding that feeling all too well.

"What if we paused to look at what you really want from this shift? Not what you think you should do, but what aligns with where you want to go next."

She exhaled, leaning back in her chair. "That sounds... different," she said, but she could see I was coming from a place of authenticity and was willing to take this step. She then continued, "I've heard you're the one who always makes it happen, so explain what you mean."

Together, we took a step back and explored what success meant to her in this moment — not the version defined by market trends or external expectations, but the one rooted in her own vision and values.

By the end of our conversation, she had a clear sense of the direction she wanted to take. It wasn't about doing everything or making a rushed decision to keep up. It was about choosing the path that felt right for her, even if it meant letting go of the urgency she had been carrying.

As for me, I realized then that all those years of bending myself into shapes to please others hadn't just been exhausting – it had been unnecessary.

The right people, the ones who truly valued what I offered, didn't need me to contort myself. They needed me to be real.

That moment was a reminder for both of us, the permission pause isn't about inaction. It's about creating the space to act with intention.

This clarity began seeping into every aspect of my life.

I started setting office hours that actually ended at a reasonable time, even though I was working with clients in different time zones. I learned to say, "I'll get back to you tomorrow," instead of dropping everything to respond instantly. Small choices, but they felt revolutionary.

One morning, as I walked to get my smoothie, I passed a group of digital nomads huddled over their laptops at a café. A few months ago, I would have felt that familiar pressure to run home and start working also, to prove I was "doing it right."

But that day, I just smiled and kept walking. Their path was beautiful, but it didn't have to be mine. I was finally writing my own story, not just playing a role in someone else's.

Back in my apartment one evening, my phone lit up with a message from another entrepreneur I'd met at a local co-working space. "How do you do it?" she wrote. "I saw you turn down that big project last week. I could never…"

I stared at her message, remembering how I used to be the one saying, "I could never." How many times had I watched others set boundaries and thought they possessed some magical confidence I lacked? But sitting there, watching the sunset paint Chiang Mai's sky in shades of purple and gold, I realized something: Strength doesn't always look like we expect it to.

Mine hadn't come in some dramatic moment of standing up for myself. It had grown in those tiny spaces between – between the request and the response, between the expectation and the choice, between who I thought I had to be and who I actually was.

"Want to grab tea?" I wrote back. Not to give advice or solve her problems, but to share space with someone who was wrestling with the same questions I had.

Over Thai tea, at a quiet cafe, she shared her own story of saying yes until she was drowning. As she talked, I recognized every word – the fear of disappointing others, the worry that success would vanish if she wasn't constantly available, the exhaustion of maintaining a perfect facade.

"But how did you start saying no?" she asked, sipping her tea. "Weren't you scared?"

I laughed softly. "I'm still scared sometimes. But I realized something – we think saying no is about being strong enough to disappoint others. It's about being brave enough to listen to ourselves. It's really about saying yes to you, first."

The next morning, I made a list of all the times I'd said yes when my body was screaming no. Client projects that left me drained. Social obligations that felt like performance art. Business strategies that looked good on paper but felt wrong in my bones. It wasn't just a list of decisions - it was a map of all the places I'd abandoned myself.

But then I started a second list: the small moments of reclamation. That time I told a high-profile client I needed a day to think about how I could help them the best. The morning I chose to paint instead of attending another networking breakfast. The afternoon I turned off my notifications and took a nap when my body asked for rest.

These weren't just isolated choices - they were practice rounds for bigger decisions. Each tiny act of listening to myself was strengthening that muscle, teaching me to trust the wisdom that had always been there, waiting in the spaces between.

The words surprised me as they came out. Not because they weren't true, but because they emerged from such a genuine place – not from my old need to have all the answers, but from my own lived experience of finding my way back to myself.

Later that night, I received another message from her: "I just said no to a project that would have drained me. My hands are shaking, but I feel… lighter?"

I smiled, recognizing that feeling. It was the same lightness I'd discovered on my own journey – not from achieving some perfect state of confidence, but from finally giving myself permission to be human, to have limits, to choose differently.

The true depth of what I was learning revealed itself in the most unexpected moments. Like the morning I woke up and realized I hadn't checked my business email in two days – and the world hadn't ended. Instead of my usual panic, I felt something novel: peace with my own rhythm.

I started noticing how this new awareness was changing not just my obvious choices, but the subtle ways I moved through the world. Even my art had shifted. Where I used to paint what I thought would please others or match the current trends, now I found myself reaching for bold colors, making decisive strokes with my acrylics and letting the canvas reflect my truth rather than my careful calculations.

One afternoon, in the middle of painting what would become my most honest work yet, my daughter called.

"You sound different," she said.

"Different how?"

"I don't know... more like you. Like when I was little and you'd tell me to always be true to myself. You're finally taking your own advice."

Her words hit me hard. I had been that person once – the mother who taught authenticity and directness. Somewhere along the way, I'd learned to soften my edges, to round off my sharp corners until I fit neatly into others' expectations. Coming back to myself wasn't about becoming someone new; it was about remembering who I'd been all along.

That conversation stayed with me as I walked through the evening markets later, weaving between food and craft stalls. The air was thick with the scent of grilling satay and fresh lime, motorbikes buzzing past on the narrow streets.

A year ago, I would have been mentally cataloging everything around me, my mind already racing with how to translate these experiences into business insights, missing the simple joy of just being present.

Instead, I just walked. Noticed. Lived. Sometimes, the most radical act of self-permission is simply existing without analyzing, without strategizing, without turning every moment into a lesson or opportunity.

My phone buzzed with a message from a client – one whose message I loved receiving now, because we'd built our relationship on honest communication from the start. "Got time for a quick call?"

A year ago, "a quick call" would have sent me scrambling to respond immediately. Now, I took a moment to check in with myself. I was in the middle of the Sunday Markets, in the middle of just being. The old guilt tried to creep in – shouldn't I be more available? More professional? More... everything?

But I'd learned to recognize that voice for what it was: the echo of old permissions I no longer needed to seek. I wrote back: "I'm at the markets right now, just about to eat Pad Thai followed by a banana pancake. Can we connect tomorrow at 10am, your time?"

Her response came quickly: "Of course! Enjoy yourself and send me a picture. That sounds delicious."

Simple. Easy. Real.

Standing there in the bustling market, I felt a quiet joy, not from anything profound, by most people's standards, but from a recognition of how far I'd come.

Each small choice to honor myself, each tiny moment of choosing differently, had accumulated into something powerful: the ability to stand firmly in my own truth without apology or explanation.

One morning, facing an unusually full inbox, I felt myself slipping. A long-term client needed an emergency consultation, and multiple time zones were demanding immediate responses. Without thinking, I found myself falling into old patterns – responding rapidly, saying "of course" to impossible timelines and pushing my morning walk aside.

It wasn't until I noticed the familiar tightness in my chest had returned, that sensation I now knew so well. But this time, something was different. Instead of pushing through, I stopped.

I closed my laptop.
I took a deep breath.
I stepped out onto my balcony.

The morning air still held its coolness, and temple bells were ringing in the distance. This was exactly why I'd come here – not to recreate my old patterns in a new location, but to live differently.

I reopened my laptop and wrote gentle but firm emails rescheduling the meetings. The responses were all understanding. In that moment, I realized how far I'd come. The old patterns might still surface, but now I could recognize them faster and redirect them more gracefully.

The real victory wasn't in never slipping – it was in knowing how to find my way back.

What surprised me most wasn't the big changes – it was how this new way of being started showing up in the smallest moments. Like when a client would ask me what they "should" do, and instead of offering quick solutions, I found myself creating space for them to find their own answers.

"What would it feel like," I'd ask, "if you didn't need anyone's permission to choose?"

The question usually met with silence first. The same kind of loaded silence I'd sat with on my own balcony months ago, when I first started questioning who I was trying to be.

During one particularly powerful session, as the fan whirred overhead, a client broke down crying. "I've spent my whole life," she said, "waiting for someone to tell me it's okay to want what I want."

I felt that truth in my bones. Here we were, worlds apart – her in her corporate office in London, me in my sun-drenched apartment in Vietnam – yet connected by the same fundamental struggle.

The constant seeking of permission.
The endless quest for validation.
The exhausting performance of being who we thought we needed to be.

But something beautiful was happening in my work now. Instead of trying to be the expert with all the answers, I was sharing my own journey of stumbling toward authenticity.

Not as a perfect roadmap, but as proof that it was possible to choose differently, and start with a simple pause.

One day, after a particularly powerful group session where everyone had shared their struggles with saying yes to themselves first, for taking that important moment to pause, reflect and decide, I headed down to meet up with some friends. The evening air was thick with possibility, the way it often is in Chiang Mai.

Returning to Chiang Mai, a place I love so much, the lady who ran the small restaurant I frequented waved me over as I was passing. "You have found your balance," she said in our usual friendly exchange.

"I have," I replied, realizing it was true in a way that went beyond the surface level of happiness. This was something deeper – a quiet contentment that came from finally feeling at home in my own skin.

She nodded sagely as if she could see the journey I'd been on. "Sometimes," she said, "we travel far to find what was inside us all along."

I carried her words with me as I jumped on a Grab bike to head home. How far had I come – not just in physical distance, but in the journey back to myself?

Each step had been both an ending and a beginning.
An ending of old patterns,
old permissions sought,
old versions of myself I'd outgrown.
And a beginning of something more authentic, more real, more true.

Back in my apartment, I started laying out my paints differently. Instead of organizing them by what I thought I should use, I arranged them by what called to me in the moment. It was a small change, but it represented everything I was learning about trust – trust in my choices, my instincts, and my right to choose differently.

One evening, as I worked on some marketing, my phone lit up with a message from a previous client. She'd made a big decision – turning down a promotion that looked perfect on paper but felt wrong in her gut. "I kept thinking about what you said," she wrote, "about how sometimes the bravest thing is just listening to yourself."

I stopped working and really let that sink in.

How many of us spend our lives searching for permission in all the wrong places? Looking for validation in the next achievement, the next destination, the next reinvention of ourselves?

The irony wasn't lost on me.
I'd come to Thailand seeking freedom,
thinking it was something I had to find outside myself.

Instead, I'd discovered that real freedom wasn't about location at all – it was about those tiny moments of choice, those small acts of listening to your own voice above the noise of expectations.

During my morning walks now, I started noticing other people like me – digital nomads, entrepreneurs, travelers – all of us searching for something. Some are still rushing from meetup to meetup, trying to network their way to success. Others sitting quietly in cafes, perhaps coming to their own realizations about what freedom really meant.

I thought about how we often mistake movement for progress and busyness for purpose. How easy it is to trade one form of performance for another, thinking we're breaking free when we're really just changing costumes.

One morning, I sat down to write an email to my audience. Not just our usual quick updates, but a real email about everything I was learning.

"Freedom," I wrote, "isn't about being somewhere else or someone else. It's about being brave enough to be exactly who you are, wherever you are."

As I wrote and rewrote these words throughout the day, coming back between other tasks as I couldn't find the words, I realized they were an echo of what I'd been discovering all along. Each small pause between reaction and response, each tiny moment of choosing differently, had been teaching me this truth. It wasn't about grand gestures or dramatic changes. It was about those microscopic moments of choice – to listen, to trust, to be real.

The sun was setting over the mountains, painting the sky in shades of pink and gold, as I finished the email. From my balcony, I could hear the evening prayers, mixing with the sounds of traffic below.

This city and so many I had journeyed to, had given me so much, but its greatest gift hadn't been what I expected.

Instead of finding a new version of myself,
I'd found my way back to who I'd been all along
– just braver now,
more willing to trust my own voice.

Because that's what I finally understood: Our power to choose isn't something we need to seek or earn.

It's already ours, waiting in those spaces between
– between who we think we should be and who we truly are,
between what others expect and what we actually want,
between the life we're living and the life that calls to us.

Some of my most powerful permissions had nothing to do with saying no. Like the morning I stood in front of my limited travel wardrobe, previously a source of constant anxiety about not having the "right" thing to wear.

That day, looking at my few carefully chosen pieces, I felt something different: appreciation for the simplicity, for the freedom of having less. In that pause between old anxiety and new choice, I gave myself permission to define "put together" on my own terms.

The transformation showed up in unexpected ways. When a potential collaboration came along, instead of automatically scaling up the project to prove my worth, I paused and asked myself what felt authentic. The result? A smaller, more intimate offering that actually brought more joy and better results. It wasn't about turning opportunities down – it was about reshaping them to fit my truth.

Now when I help others navigate their own journeys, I share not just strategies but the simple truth I discovered: The space between stimulus and response is where our freedom lives. It's where we find our voice, our courage, and our way back to ourselves.

We just need to pause long enough to hear it.

In Chiang Mai, they say the temples are built with spaces between the bells so their songs can find their way to heaven. Perhaps we, too, need these spaces – between our thoughts, between our actions, between who we've been and who we're becoming – not just to find our way, but to remember we knew it all along.

Traci Powell

CEO of The Rebuilt Woman
CEO, PMHNP-BC, Certified Trauma Treatment Specialist (CTTS)

https://www.linkedin.com/in/traci-powell-np/
https://facebook.com/TraciPowellNP
https://therebuiltwoman.com/
http://www.thetraumapsychnp.com/

Traci Powell is a Psychiatric-Mental Health Nurse Practitioner (PMHNP) and renowned trauma healing expert, dedicated to helping women overcome deep emotional wounds. Through her signature 3-day intensive therapy retreats, Traci leads women through a powerful journey of trauma resolution, emotional healing, and reconnection to their authentic selves. Her unique approach enables women to break free from the pain of the past, rediscover their inner strength, and embrace a life filled with confidence and purpose. Known for delivering rapid, lasting transformations, Traci has become a leading voice in trauma recovery. In addition to working with clients, she trains fellow PMHNPs in advanced trauma treatment techniques and travels nationwide as a public speaker, sharing a message of hope and empowerment for women ready to move forward.

The Strong Woman Myth: Redefining What It Means to Be Strong

By Traci Powell

For years, I played the part everyone expected of me. I built a successful career, cared for my family, and kept my head down, moving forward as life demanded. As a nurse practitioner, people saw me as someone with all the answers, the one who others turned to for support and guidance. But beneath that polished surface, I was hiding the deepest scars of my life. They ran so deep that I barely acknowledged them to myself, much less to anyone else.

I had spent decades building walls around my heart, protecting myself from the pain I wasn't ready to face. But, like any structure built out of fear, those walls couldn't hold forever. At 46, they came crashing down.

People constantly told me how "strong" I was, and I wore that strength like a badge of honor. I was strong for being a single mom, strong for becoming a nurse practitioner, strong for sharing my story of childhood abuse and PTSD. Strong for standing on stage and speaking about my journey. I believed it, too. I thought being strong meant never letting the cracks show, never asking for help, and carrying the weight of the world on my shoulders with a smile on my face. I was so convinced of my strongness that I bought into it. I believed that to make it through life you had to be strong, but my definition of strong was a bit twisted. For me, strong meant you grin and bear it with a smile, never allowing hurts and vulnerabilities to surface. Strong meant never asking for help, taking on more and more responsibilities without buckling under the weight of it all and never admitting I felt like I was constantly juggling too many things, with a smile plastered on my face, hiding the mental and physical exhaustion that was wearing me down.

My kind of "strong" was hard, though. And lonely. And isolating. The strength everyone else saw felt like a heavy burden to me. I wasn't strong—I was surviving and felt completely broken. The truth is I wasn't strong. I was bruised, bullied, and mentally beaten into believing life was about showing up for everyone else and leaving myself behind. It was about never saying no, pleasing everyone, and never knowing I was allowed to take the time to think about the choices I was making and if they were right for me.

Turns out, what everyone else saw as me being so independently strong was actually me being anti-dependent. Years of sexual abuse as a child, as well as growing up in a home with an alcoholic parent who used their words like weapons, slicing me with criticism and anger, caused me to abandon myself. My child's mind grew to believe I was the problem, the black sheep, the reason I was treated so poorly. Surely, I was so terrible that I must have deserved it. So, I did what many of us do—I survived by compartmentalizing. As I grew, I told myself I was fine, that I was strong enough to handle it on my own. I didn't need help and I would never put myself in a position to allow someone to hurt me again.

Except I did.

I stayed with men who reinforced the messages of my childhood. Men who had zero ability to support me emotionally. Men who were miserable, made cutting remarks, and always found the worst in me, convinced it was their job to educate me about my many imperfections. Men who were in my comfort zone. Feeling less than, broken, and worthless was what I knew. Wasn't that the comfort zone I belonged in?

Though my relationships were hard, I was still convinced of my strongness. I was strong to be able to put up with the relationship. Strong for "making it work" and not giving up on the men who I just knew were great guys who just needed to be loved right. If only I loved them the way they needed, they wouldn't treat me so poorly. Right? You know—just like my dad. Maybe if I had been a better daughter, cuter, sweeter, someone he would be proud to show off his Daddy's Girl to the world, he would love me the way I needed. Except it was never enough. Being me wasn't enough. So why would I ever believe that just being me would be enough for the men who darkened my door?

I had separated from the abuse that I endured. I left the wounded little girl in me, who needed my strongness more than anyone, behind. I was terrified of her. Strong is not terrified. The two cannot exist together. I had to be one or the other. I had lived through enough terror, so I shut it down and sided with strong. We often think that being strong is the thing that will help us move forward. That it takes that kind of strength to stand up for what's right or meet some challenge. But what if we have it all wrong?

For years, my incorrect idea of what strong was kept me stuck in the lie that I was not allowed to feel the unbearable pain that comes with years of childhood abuse. Stuck in the lies of self-worthlessness, shame, and blame. Stuck in the belief that I had to appear strong and "fine," never needing anyone.

The little girl in me was weary of my nonstop strong-arming my way through life. She needed me to be strong for her, but I had long since separated myself from her. The trouble was she still very much lived inside me. One wrong look from someone that felt like judgement caused her to convince me to isolate myself. A compliment or kindness from someone caused her to feel self-conscious and underserving. The threat of someone leaving her life caused her to become terrified she would be alone forever.

As the decades passed, a battle waged within me. I needed to keep the facade going of the nurse practitioner who was rising above it all. Yet, I was ripping at the seams. As my anxiety and depression grew worse, I considered ending my life as I sat soaked in shame, asking how someone so supposedly "strong" could be terrified of reaching out for help. And if I did reach out for help, would my peers see me as incompetent?

Would my kids think the mom they knew was gone? I had to stay strong, convincing myself there was no way anyone could know what I was living with. I told myself I was too strong to need help.

Until I did.

Years of internal battling against depression and anxiety had finally caused my nervous system to give up. I no longer had the strength or desire to fight. I felt broken beyond repair. Believed I was a bad mom, bad nurse practitioner, bad daughter, bad friend and I was just so freaking tired. Tired of trying to rise above. Tired of trying to be strong. Tired of trying to prove my worth. Tired of trying to keep everyone around me happy. Nothing worked—no academic degrees, no amount of volunteerism, no spending endless hours entertaining my kids and their friends. There was a gaping void in me that nothing would fill, and I was done trying.

But finally, I couldn't do it anymore. After a particularly dark night, I finally sought therapy. I thought this was going to be the solution. After all, isn't that what you do when you break down? You get help. But my first attempts at therapy left me feeling stuck, confused, and hopeless. I spent years in sessions that didn't touch the core of what I was going through. I didn't heal. In fact, I felt worse at times. I was constantly fighting against my deepest wish to end it all, but I couldn't if for no other reason than the two children I had chosen to create on my own. They deserved so much better, even if I believed that I didn't.

The problem was the weight of my unprocessed trauma, the broken pieces of my past, felt too heavy to carry any longer. I couldn't see a way out and therapy was only making it worse for me. Showing up on that couch for weekly sessions helped some, but eventually for the most part, only served to pull me back to the terrified, sad little girl I was and kept me stuck in the past with her.

I didn't want to be stuck in the past feeling like a helpless little girl. I wanted to be a rock star mom who raised confident kids with good self-esteem. I wanted to feel like the skilled, friendly, and helpful nurse practitioner that everyone else saw me as. I wanted to like myself, and more than anything, I wanted to start living rather than constantly trying just to survive.

Something deep inside me refused to give up. Maybe it was the fighter in me. Maybe it was the desire to be there for my family. Whatever it was, I kept searching, kept digging, until I found someone who could meet me where I was. Someone who helped me go beyond just talking about my trauma and dive into my subconscious mind to understand the child inside me who had been frozen in time, waiting for love, compassion, and attention. It was only when I started to connect with that little girl, meeting the needs she had been longing to be met that the healing began.

I had spent a lifetime searching endlessly for something to fill the ache she had to feel accepted, wanted, and to be enough. The problem was that everything I was trying was external to me—relationships, work, school, and even therapy. All of it was me giving someone or something else the power in my life to help me feel better. As a child, there is no choice. We need people external to us to meet our emotional needs, but when that doesn't happen and we are left with childhood wounds, as adults, the only true healing must come from within, and that's a mighty tall order for a girl who spent her whole life avoiding the hurt inside.

This was the most terrifying yet liberating part of my journey. To sit with that pain, to nurture those unmet needs, and to process the darkness I had avoided for so long required a level of vulnerability I wasn't used to. But it also gave me a strength I had never known. As I peeled back the layers of my hurt, I began to reconnect with myself, the real me—the me that had been silenced by trauma and fear for so long.

As I connected with the little girl and gave her messages that told her she was no longer stuck in the past, and that she was loved and free, I was able to pull her forward to live in my present awesome life with me, rather than her constantly pulling me back to the hard times of the past. In the present with me, she felt accepted, wanted, loved, empowered, and yes, STRONG.

It turns out true strength is not about pushing through, refusing help, and constantly trying to prove my worth. To be strong is to be willing to do what is right for me. To align with myself, regardless of whether or not others like it. True strength is to have compassion for the wounds in others, but to recognize I do not have to allow their wounds to bleed onto me. That I deserve respect and kindness and love that is gracious and accepting, and to know that not staying in a relationship with someone who can't do that doesn't make me a bitch, but rather someone who respects and loves herself.

Strength, I learned, isn't about being perfect or unbreakable. It's about owning your story, every messy, painful, and beautiful part of it. It's about learning to stand tall, not because you've never fallen, but because you've picked yourself back up. My journey from that midlife mental mess to where I stand today is one of the hardest things I've ever experienced, but it was also the most transformational journey that brought me back to me.

Today, I am free. Not because my past has disappeared, but because I've embraced it, made peace with it, and learned to grow from it. The woman I am now is stronger than I ever imagined possible. She is a professional who helps others heal. She is a nurturer who loves her family with a fierce heart. She is a warrior who doesn't shy away from her own truth.

But most of all, she is me. A rebuilt woman. A woman who has loved, healed, and nurtured the parts of her that were stuck in the past and brought them into the present. Authentically, unapologetically, beautifully me.

Experiencing how powerful and life-changing healing the wound parts of myself was led me to return to school one last time. This time, I was stepping into what I was born to do—become a psychiatric/mental health nurse practitioner who is a Certified Trauma Treatment Specialist. I knew that I wanted to help other women, the way I had been helped, especially professional women who have felt they have to live in silence about their inner struggles. I wanted to guide them through the process of healing their own wounds, to show them that they, too, could rebuild their lives and step into their authenticity, not defined by past experiences.

I am dedicated to helping women break free from the weight of depression, anxiety, and PTSD by healing the root causes that often stem from emotional and trauma wounds that were created long ago. Old wounds often reside deep within the subconscious mind, hidden from our daily awareness, yet they shape how we experience life. These unhealed emotional wounds, often rooted in past trauma or unmet childhood needs, manifest as symptoms like anxiety, depression, or feelings of unworthiness. Women may find themselves trapped in cycles of self-doubt, convinced they are broken when in reality, it's these buried wounds driving their pain. These subconscious patterns act like invisible chains, holding them back from fully living. Healing begins when we recognize that these symptoms are not signs of brokenness but messages from within, calling for love, healing, and release.

At my private practice, The Rebuilt Woman, I provide a transformative 3-day intensive therapy process that heals the body, mind, and spirit using the most cutting-edge and effective techniques. This unique experience empowers women to break free from the pain of their past and embrace their true selves. Rather than taking years, my clients undergo a deep, lasting transformation as they reconnect with their inner strength. I watch them shift from feeling anxious and burdened to becoming rebuilt women—radiating peace, power, and the confidence to live boldly as the remarkable women they were always meant to be.

And that's the message I want to leave you with, the message that burns at the core of this book: You have the power to overcome whatever challenges life has thrown your way. You can heal, grow, and rebuild the wounded parts of yourself into one authentic, free, and whole woman. Everything you need is already within you—you might just need someone to guide you in the process of rebuilding and becoming who you truly are.

No matter how broken you feel, no matter how dark your past, there is always a way forward. And when you choose to walk that path, you will find that with each step, you grow stronger. Not the fake kind of strong that says, "Live to please others, reject help, and go it alone," but rather the genuine kind of strong that says, "I am enough, and I am free."

Valarie Harris

Founder of Varris Marketing
President, CMO, Coach

https://www.linkedin.com/in/varrismarketing
https://www.facebook.com/varrism
https://www.instagram.com/coachvalygrl1
https://www.varrismarketing.com/
https://www.timefreedomfreak.com/

Valarie L. Harris, also known as Coach Valygrl, is a certified Business, Branding, Marketing Strategy, and Time Freedom Coach. As the Founder, President, and CMO of Varris Marketing for nearly 13 years, she has dedicated her career to helping entrepreneurs master the art of marketing and time freedom. Valarie is also a keynote speaker and soon-to-be-published author of her first book, 'Becoming a Time Freedom Freak ~ Mastering The Art of Thriving Through Outsourcing.' She is passionate about helping others achieve success without sacrificing their time. Valarie enjoys living life to the fullest in the beautiful Pacific Northwest with her retired sailor of 31 years, their 3 adult children, and 1 grandson. Excited to connect with you all!

Flipping the Script: Prioritizing Passion, Purpose, and Time Freedom

By Valarie Harris

Time—The Commodity We Can't Afford to Waste

Other than air, food, and water, time is our greatest commodity. Unlike money, we can't earn more of it. Once it's gone, it's gone. I know this firsthand because I almost let my business consume the very thing I believe in the most—**Time Freedom.**

Back in 2012, when I started my entrepreneurial journey, I was full of ambition but had no boundaries. My days were spent managing a corporate retail career, coming home to my family for a few hours, and then diving headfirst into my business until the early hours of the morning. I thought I was doing what was necessary to succeed, but instead, I was sacrificing my health, my family, and my sanity. It wasn't until I faced a health crisis and an ultimatum from my husband that I realized I was wasting the one thing I couldn't afford to lose—time.

Here is a strategy for you. Recognizing time as your most valuable resource means creating boundaries, delegating tasks, and prioritizing what truly matters. If your business consumes your life, it's time to reassess.

Your Why—The Foundation of Everything

Why did I start my business? The answer is simple: I wanted to give my family a better life. I dreamed of financial stability, flexibility, and the freedom to be present for my loved ones. But my why didn't stop there.

I also started focusing on **Time Freedom** because I witnessed firsthand what happens when you don't have it. My corporate job demanded my time, my energy, and my focus, leaving little for my family or myself.

The irony? My business, meant to set me free, was doing the same thing. It was only when I reconnected with my why—my family and my purpose—that I began to make real changes.

What you need to do is anchor every decision you make in your why. Whether it's your family, financial independence, or creating a legacy, let your why guide your business and personal life.

Outsourcing—Your Ticket to Freedom

Outsourcing is freeing, liberating, and transformative. It's not just about delegating tasks; it's about creating space in your life for what truly matters. For years, I resisted outsourcing, thinking, *Why pay someone else when I can do it myself?* But that mindset kept me stuck, stressed, and barely breaking even.

Once I embraced outsourcing, everything changed. I let go of tasks that drained my time and energy and focused on what I loved—coaching, teaching, and connecting with others. Outsourcing brought order to the chaos, allowed me to scale my business, and, most importantly, gave me my life back.

So, you want to start small. Identify one task you can outsource and test the waters. Choose partners who align with your values and mission to ensure the work reflects your vision.

Frameworks—The Key to Freedom

Stress is a silent killer, and it nearly killed me. I didn't have a framework or plan for my business or life, resulting in chaos. I was overwhelmed, unorganized, and constantly playing catch-up. The stress started manifesting in my health, leading to a serious wake-up call that left my life hanging in the balance.

A framework became my saving grace. It gave me clarity, direction, and a roadmap for building a business that aligned with my life. With a solid plan, I no longer felt like I was drowning. Instead, I had a structure that allowed me to thrive.

You need to build a framework for your business, and believe it or not, this also works for your life. Set clear goals, develop systems, and regularly evaluate your progress. A solid foundation will reduce stress and increase sustainability.

Time Management—Take Control

There was a time when my time managed me, not the other way around. I had no control over the 24 hours of my day, and it was destroying everything I cared about. My husband knocked on my office door one night and said, *"Val, something's got to give, or this isn't going to work."* That was a moment I'll never forget.

When your kids ask why you're always working, and your spouse feels like they've taken a backseat, it's a gut check. I realized I wasn't just losing control of my time—I was losing my family. That's when I decided to reclaim my time and my priorities.

Try this. Time block your day set boundaries, and say no to tasks that don't align with your goals. Use tools and automation to free up your schedule for what truly matters.

Mindset—The Game Changer

For the longest time, I had the wrong mindset. I believed that because I was educated, I could do it all myself. I thought outsourcing was a waste of money and that I could learn whatever I didn't already know. That mentality cost me dearly.

It wasn't until I shifted my mindset and started seeing time as an investment, not just money, that things began to change. I realized that hiring experts didn't mean I was failing—it meant I was growing. That mindset shift unlocked doors I didn't even know existed.

You want to embrace the idea that you don't have to do it all. Invest in help, trust others, and focus on your zone of genius.

Community—Your Secret Weapon

I used to think I could go it alone. I didn't realize how much I was missing until I found communities of like-minded women who lifted and supported each other. Groups like She Rises and partnerships with other entrepreneurs opened a brighter, more collaborative world for me.

When you surround yourself with people who understand your struggles and celebrate your wins, your potential expands. Community and collaboration are powerful tools that can take your business to new heights.

Here is a great idea for you to try. Join communities that align with your values. Build partnerships and collaborate with others to expand your reach and grow your network.

My Passion for Helping Others

I've been where you are. I've made the mistakes, felt the burnout, and questioned if it was all worth it. But I've also experienced the breakthroughs, the wins, and the freedom that comes from flipping the script.

My passion and purpose are to teach effective and efficient business and marketing strategies so you can achieve what I believe is the number one goal in life: **Time Freedom.** I'm here to help you avoid the pitfalls I faced and guide you toward a business and life you love. Let's connect.

Contact Info:
- www.VarrisMarketing.com
- valarieharris@varrismarketing.com
- 360-559-2383

Wendy Harmon, PhD

Founder of Volitionary Coaching

https://www.linkedin.com/in/wendy-harmon-phd-9292864/
https://www.instagram.com/wendyharmon_coach/
https://www.vitalitylifemap.com
https://www.coachwendyharmon.com

Wendy Harmon, PhD, is a business success coach, creator of the Vitality Life Map, and a champion of sustainable growth in both business and wellness. With a PhD in education, an MBA, and over 18 years as a corporate process improvement leader, Wendy has helped countless entrepreneurs and professionals uncover hidden opportunities, streamline operations, and achieve lasting success. Her journey has shaped her mission. At 47, Wendy was diagnosed with metastatic breast cancer while navigating the demands of single motherhood, a corporate career, and building her own business. This experience inspired the creation of the Vitality Life Map, a system designed to help others reclaim energy, health, and balance—one intentional step at a time. Through her work, Wendy empowers individuals to achieve their goals with practical, science-based strategies that deliver results. She's passionate about helping others build a life where vitality fuels their success.

Why Me, What Now

By Wendy Harmon, PhD

In October 2017, I was in the best shape of my life, my corporate career was at an all-time high, and I was flying home from an amazing business trip when my phone rang. It was my doctor. "I wish I had better news," he said, "but the result of your biopsy indicates you have stage 2 metastatic breast cancer." I hung up the phone and boarded my flight in total disbelief. I was 47 years old, a single mom with a 12-year-old daughter. I always worked out, ate well, and took good care of my body. There was no fucking way I had cancer.

After takeoff, as I replayed the doctor's words over and over in my head, my disbelief turned into despair and fear. What was I going to do? How would I work and take care of my daughter while battling metastatic breast cancer? I started fast-forwarding through my future, wondering if I'd get to see her graduate high school, go to college, meet the love of her life, and maybe start her own family. Even worse, I worried about how I was going to tell my daughter that her mom has cancer.

By the time I landed, I was pissed and full of self-pity. I was mad at God and everyone I knew who smoked, drank, never exercised, ate like crap, and did not have cancer. I kept thinking, "Why me, and not them?" Then, it simply became, "Why me." That question haunted me as I moved from a double mastectomy to chemo to radiation and one surgery after another. Why me?

My cancer journey included chemotherapy, radiation, going into medical menopause overnight, taking estrogen suppression drugs, and 14 surgeries over 4 years. Yes, it was a grueling battle, yet in hindsight, every hurdle became a stepping stone drawing me closer to where I am today.

In the "cancer community," there's a website called "I Had Cancer," where people with cancer and their loved ones can write a letter to cancer as part of the healing process. When the time came to write my letter, I opened a post with "Dear Cancer" at the top of the page and waited for the thoughts to come because I had no idea what I wanted to say. After a few minutes, I looked at the screen, and the words read, "Dear Cancer, I forgive you. Love, Wendy."

I forgive cancer. Those three little words changed my life. Looking back, that letter to cancer held the answer to the question that haunted me...

Why me?

We've all had that moment—the one that knocks the wind out of you, leaves you spinning, and brings you to your knees. It might come as a diagnosis you never saw coming, the sudden loss of someone you love, or the end of a relationship you thought would last forever. Maybe it's reaching a milestone age and realizing life doesn't look the way you thought it would. Or perhaps it's something subtler but no less powerful, like scuba diving in the ocean and feeling, for the first time, the vastness and mystery of a world so much larger than yourself. No matter how it comes, there's one question that almost always follows: Why me?

It's a question that feels impossible to answer, but that doesn't stop us from asking it. When I first started wrestling with my "why me," I did what many of us do—I went searching for answers in my past. I was convinced that if I could just uncover all those limiting beliefs I developed before I was six years old, I'd find my answer. I mean, how many times have you read or heard that what's holding you back now is something you probably internalized before you even started kindergarten?

Self-Assessment: Your Current Systems

Before reading further, take stock of your current systems:

1. What daily routines do you rely on?
2. Which of these serves you well?
3. Which ones might need updating?

This limiting belief journey wasn't something I planned or even wanted at first. Take my childhood Barbie dream house, for example. All I wanted for Christmas was that dream house I'd seen in stores and on TV. On Christmas morning, I ran downstairs to find that Santa had brought me a rather large box made into a two-story home, furnished with hand-made items from more cardboard, tinfoil for mirrors, and various household items forming furniture, appliances, and decorations.

I honestly can't remember exactly how I felt in that moment—whether I was elated to have my dream house or disappointed because it wasn't the store-bought version. But somewhere along the line, I translated that moment into a story about not having enough money, about scarcity, about not having enough.

(By the way, Dad—if you're reading this, I now look back and cherish the work, love, and ingenuity you and Mom put into building my dream house.)

While exploring my limiting beliefs to find "my why" for about 6 months, I went deep into doing the work. I spent time learning different meditation practices and hypnosis, journaled religiously, listened to self-help podcasts, and read self-help books—all because I believed that to find the answer to "why me," I had to fix the beliefs and stories I'd learned to tell myself from a very early age.

Was this journey helpful? Probably. Did I learn an enormous amount about how powerful your subconscious mind is? Yes. Did I learn that your gut knows what's right or wrong before your brain does? Yes. Did

I discover a wealth of information and tools to start reshaping my life? Absolutely. The thing is, none of the information I now carried in my head provided an answer to the "why me" question. They were good theories and plausible explanations, but that wasn't what I needed. I needed answers, not theories. I needed a road map, an instruction manual to know how to move forward and live this new life.

And then, it hit me.

While searching for that how-to manual, that process I could follow to move forward, the answer was in the search itself. Systems. I needed a better system. There it was—that simple. When you research systems as they relate to self-help, get ready for the information floodgates to open! But among all the podcasts, articles, and books, did you know there's an actual systems theory? When I stumbled onto systems, I found something that changed everything.

In *The Power of Systems* by Steve Chandler, I read something so powerful, so liberating, that I still get chills when I think about it. Here's the nugget of information I want you to know, remember, and use for your own "why me" moments: There is nothing wrong with you, there never was, and there never will be; you just need a better system.

Read it again and say it out loud: There is nothing wrong with me, there never was, and there never will be; I just need a better system.

Let that sink in for a moment. As women, we're constantly told we need fixing. Maybe we're gaining weight without changing our diet or exercise routine and believe something is wrong with us. Nope. It's not you, it's your system. By system, I mean your actions. By system, I mean your body's system—hello, perimenopause. By system, I mean your daily habits or routines. There is nothing wrong with you; there is only something wrong with your system.

This revelation changed everything. Instead of asking, "Why me," I started asking, "What now." What system do I need now? When I reflected on how I'd navigated my cancer journey with energy and vibrant health while working and taking care of my daughter, I realized I'd already created powerful systems. I'd endured chemotherapy by providing my body with the nutrients it needed. I'd maintained a positive mindset thanks to different meditation practices and embracing the be-do-have growth mindset. I'd recovered my strength after each surgery with my fitness routine.

And suddenly, the answer to "why me" became crystal clear. Cancer happened to me so I could discover the power of systems, create the Vitality Life Map, and help other women navigate their own health journeys. It wasn't about fixing myself—it was about creating better systems that would serve not just me, but countless other women facing their own challenges.

The Beauty of Systems

The beauty of systems is that it frees you from the burden of self-blame and the exhausting pursuit of "fixing" yourself. Instead of asking, "What's wrong with me?" you can ask, "What system needs adjusting?" Instead of feeling broken, you can feel empowered to create change. Instead of being stuck in "Why me," you can move forward with "What now?"

For me, it's not just about living a good life anymore—it's about having a good death. Do you want to be in a nursing home, dependent on others to feed you, bathe you, and tend to your every need before you physically leave this earth? Or do you want to be tying your own shoes, carrying your own groceries, taking care of your own hygiene until the end? The latter is what I refer to as a good death, and guess what? It's all about having the right systems in place.

Quick Implementation Guide: Getting Started with Systems Thinking

1. Identify one area where you've been self-critical
2. List the current system (or lack thereof) in place
3. Brainstorm three potential system improvements
4. Choose one small change to implement this week

So, the next time you find yourself asking, "Why me," remember that there's nothing wrong with you. You don't need fixing. You just need a better system. And that realization is where true transformation begins.

Discovering there was never anything wrong with me and a look back on the systems I had in place while battling cancer, led me to create the Vitality Life Map—a framework born from my own journey and refined through helping other women reclaim their health and vibrancy. The Vitality Life Map is not just another wellness program; it's a system designed specifically for women navigating the challenging phases of, well, being a woman.

You know those moments when your body seems to have a mind of its own? Maybe you've noticed a few extra pounds hanging around even though you haven't changed your diet or exercise routine. Or perhaps you're experiencing those lovely night sweats (or day sweats, or any-time sweats). Maybe you're using the "one foot out of the covers" technique to regulate your body temperature so you can get a decent night's sleep. If you're nodding your head right now, I see you and I've been there.

The Vitality Life Map framework stands on three essential pillars: Health, Wellness, and Fitness. Now, I know what you're thinking—"this does sound like another health and wellness program." Well, okay, it does have a health and wellness component, but here's where it's different: It's an integrated system that focuses on incorporating all three components instead of focusing on just one or two.

VITALITY LIFE MAP FRAMEWORK

Mindset | Resilience | Clarity
Strength | Stamina | Flexibility

WELLNESS — REVITALIZE
FITNESS — THRIVE
HEALTH — ENERGIZE

VITALITY

Nutrition | Weight | Healing

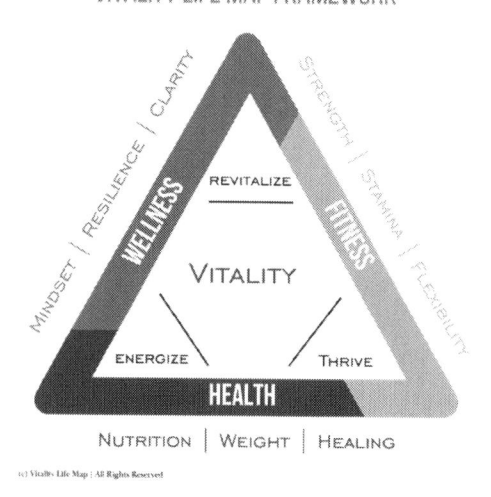

(c) Vitality Life Map | All Rights Reserved

Think silos, if you are only focusing on health or your diet, you are probably losing strength and muscle mass and carrying around a lot of stress. If you are only focusing on wellness and meditation, you are probably not increasing your flexibility or nourishing your body with the right nutrients.

Let me take a minute to define a concept you might not use in your vocabulary. The concept is called having a good death. Having a good death is defined as a death that is void of long, ailing illnesses; a death where you are active and independent until you physically leave this earth. A good death requires applying all three pillars of the framework health, wellness, and fitness and its nine focus areas.

Remember what we learned about systems? Systems are the key to creating the results you desire. You can have a health system like following a keto diet, a fitness system like hiring a personal trainer, or a wellness system with daily meditation or gratitude journaling. If you want to carry your own groceries when you are older, tie your own shoes, or travel and play around on the floor with your grand or great-grandchildren, you need an integrated system, one that focuses on all three pillars.

When I was going through my cancer journey—which included chemotherapy, radiation, and 14 surgeries in 4 years—I discovered something fascinating. The three pillars overlap and work together, and you don't have to master them all at once. During my battle with cancer, I focused primarily on health and Living WILDFIT to nourish my body with the right nutrients. Later, I could turn my attention to mindset and strength building.

While doing a little research on the amount of nutritional education general practitioners receive in medical school, I discovered only 27% of U.S. medical schools offer students the recommended 25 hours of nutritional training. Yes, you read that right, only 27% of the schools offer 25 hours of training. No wonder your doctor's prescribed solution to weight gain is "eat less, exercise more" or take this pill or administer this shot.

Let's use the above example to apply my concept of systems. You could easily blame the doctor for the absence of nutritional knowledge. Looking at this from a system perspective, maybe there's nothing wrong with the doctor and something wrong with our system if less than one-third of our medical schools offer 25 hours of nutritional training.

Quick Implementation Guide: Getting Started with Systems

Identify one area where you've been self-critical:

1. List the current system (or lack thereof) in place
2. Brainstorm three potential system improvements
3. Choose one small change to implement this week

This is why the Health pillar of the Vitality Life Map is so crucial. It teaches you the nutritional foundation you need to maintain or improve your health. When I completed my WILDFIT 90 Challenge in February 2017, I had no idea that just months later, I'd be diagnosed with cancer.

But having that nutritional foundation helped me get through my cancer journey with the nutrients my body needed to heal and stay No Evidence Detected (NED) almost 8 years later.

The Wellness pillar focuses heavily on mindset because let's face it—what good is a healthy body if your mind is chaos? Through the 6-phase meditation technique, I learned to shift from a have-do-be mindset to a be-do-have mindset. I know, I know—what does that even mean? Stick with me here. Instead of waiting to be happy until you have something, you learn to do the things that will give you what you want to have. It's a subtle shift from a fixed to a growth mindset with powerful results.

And then there's the Fitness pillar, which might surprise you. Through the 10X program, I discovered that you could achieve remarkable results with just 30 minutes of strength training per week, with or without a gym membership. When I implemented the 10X program while I was recovering from surgeries, I noticed that I only lost 10% of my strength and regained it within 6 weeks of returning to training. This isn't about spending hours in the gym; it's about having the right system.

The beauty of the Vitality Life Map is that it's not just theory—it's a battle-tested system that emerged from real struggles and real victories. It's designed for women who are tired of being told there's something wrong with them when their bodies change, women who are frustrated with one-size-fits-all solutions, and women who are ready to embrace a system that works.

"Why Me" Moments

Remember those "why me" moments we talked about earlier? My answer to why I was diagnosed with metastatic breast cancer became crystal clear: so I could create this system, this map for other women to follow because they deserve a system that works with their bodies instead of against them.

As you navigate your own journey—whether you're dealing with health challenges, hormonal changes, or just the natural evolution of life—remember this: there's nothing wrong with you. You don't need fixing. You just need the right system. And sometimes, that system looks like putting one foot out of the covers at night or spending just 30 minutes a week on strength training or learning to feed your body what it needs rather than what our food industry says you should eat.

The Vitality Life Map is about creating systems that support you through every phase of life, from the subtle changes of perimenopause to the dramatic shifts of serious health challenges. Because at the end of the day, it's not about fixing what's broken—it's about building something better.

And that's the real answer to "why me." Sometimes, life's biggest challenges become our greatest gifts to others. My cancer journey led me to create a system that now helps women navigate their own health and wellness journeys. So, the next time life throws you a curveball, and you find yourself asking, "Why me," remember, there is nothing wrong with you; there's only something wrong with your system, and maybe, just maybe, it's about the system you're about to create that will help others find their way. It's okay to ask "Why me" but now you are armed with "What now."

Yulia Drummond

High-Level Mindset & Transformation

https://www.linkedin.com/in/yulia-drummond/
https://www.facebook.com/YuliaDrummondOfficial
https://www.instagram.com/yuliadrummond/
https://www.yuliadrummond.com/
https://www.yuliadrummond.com/book-your-session

Yulia Drummond is a transformation powerhouse. She is passionate about elevating women to live confident, empowered and fulfilled lives. Yulia helps women elevate from stress and fear into inner harmony, from limiting beliefs to confidence and strength. Her approach is gentle, effective, unapologetically powerful, and rooted in real transformation—because she's been there. Yulia's journey began at her own breaking point. After building a multi-million dollar business, buying a beach front house and the luxury dream lifestyle that went with it, she felt drained, disconnected and lost. Behind the glossy exterior, her 15-year marriage was falling apart, leaving her riddled with stress and anxiety. Refusing to settle, Yulia shattered her own barriers and rewrote her story. Today, she helps women do the same - shatter invisible blocks and live an empowered life, all while 10X-ing their joy, abundance and fulfillment. Ready to harmonize your world and live an extraordinary life? Visit www.YuliaDrummond.com

Lettuce Talk About My Breaking Point

By Yulia Drummond

It was the first time I had ever experienced a panic attack. I was standing in the vegetable aisle of a grocery store, clutching a head of lettuce, feeling both numb and trembling all at once, when the overwhelming weight of my reality finally hit me. My head spun in circles, and the buzzing of the store around me faded into the background. I had always seen myself as strong, a woman who could carry the weight of the world on her shoulders without ever faltering. But in that moment, I felt like I was unraveling, dissolving from the inside out. A tidal wave of emotions: grief, anger, despair and helplessness washed over me, and I could barely contain them. In that moment, I felt like I was breaking into a million pieces, and I couldn't stop it. My chest felt tight, and the weight of my emotional pain was unbearable. I stood there, trying desperately to hold it together while every part of me felt like it was falling apart. It was as if my emotional system had short-circuited. My body was overloaded. My mind was overwhelmed. And in that moment, I felt completely and utterly broken.

From the outside, I had built what many would call a dream life. I had multiple thriving careers, a multi-million-dollar women's fashion business, and a stunning beachfront home. Yet, in the middle of that grocery store, none of it mattered. I felt lost, anxious, and deeply unhappy. My marriage of 15 years was on the brink of collapse. What once felt like love, had dissolved over the years into disconnect and constant arguments. It seemed that we were pretending to the world that everything was fine when, in reality, neither of us were happy. At the same time, my mother, who was my guide and my inspiration, was losing her battle with cancer. She had always been my source of strength, and now I was helpless to save her. The weight of losing her, the disintegration of my marriage, and the gnawing emptiness I felt in my own heart crushed me from every direction. I had worked so hard to build the life I thought would make me happy, but it all felt meaningless in the face of such profound loss.

Looking back, I wouldn't wish that level of pain and helplessness on anyone. But I also know now that it was one of the greatest gifts of my life. That moment forced me to confront truths about myself and my choices that I had been avoiding for years. It stripped away every illusion I had built around my life, exposing the ways I had been living on autopilot, chasing a version of happiness that was unsustainable. It was a brutal awakening, but it was also the start of something transformative. It was the beginning of my journey to rebuild—not just my life, but myself.

The Burden of Success

For years, I had convinced myself that success, wealth, and external validation were the ultimate goals. I believed that achieving them would shield me from pain and bring lasting happiness. But standing in that grocery store, clutching that head of lettuce, I realized that none of it could protect me from the storm inside. It wasn't just my external world that was breaking, it was me. And I could no longer outrun it.

At 18, I left my home in Bishkek, Kyrgyzstan, to move to America with my American fiancé. It was a leap into the unknown: a foreign country, a different culture, and a language I barely spoke. Despite the fear and uncertainty, I saw myself as tough, resilient, and ready to take on anything. I believed that my determination and emotional strength would carry me through whatever challenges lay ahead.

For years, I poured myself into building a life that focused on success. I worked tirelessly, creating thriving businesses, owning a beautiful home, and crafting a life that looked extraordinary from the outside. But over time, I realized that the happiness I thought these things would bring wasn't lasting. It was conditional and dependent on external achievements and fleeting moments. Yes, there were moments of happiness. I shared beautiful times with friends and family, and my businesses thrived. But the truth was, I wasn't always thriving. My days were consumed by work, relentless deadlines, and an ever-growing list of responsibilities. I told myself I could handle it all, but the cracks were beginning to show.

My mother ended up passing away from cancer, a disease fueled by years of stress, overwork, and a relentless schedule. She spent so much of her life putting herself last, always giving, always doing. And though I didn't want to admit it at the time, I was following the same path. I was burning the candle at both ends, believing I could outpace the toll it was taking on my body and mind.

Even when I allowed myself to take breaks: traveling to over 50 countries and enjoying luxurious vacations, my mind was never truly at rest. I lived in overdrive, always doing something, and, sometimes, unable to enjoy the present moment. I was chasing a life I thought would bring me joy, but in reality, I was slowly losing myself.

Shattered Connection

For years, I convinced myself that my marriage was fine. I told myself that the arguments, the yelling, and the criticism were just part of a normal relationship. Our love and connection had eroded under the weight of neglect. We presented a picture of happiness to the world, but behind closed doors, we were falling apart.

The moment of truth came when we found ourselves living in a luxurious, multi-million-dollar house but feeling utterly empty. The disconnect between the beauty of our surroundings and the unhappiness in our hearts was undeniable. We were miserable. The constant arguments, the emotional disconnection, the lack of love—it was all too much. It seemed impossible to rebuild what we had spent years unconsciously tearing apart. Divorce felt inevitable, but before making it final, we agreed to try a trial separation. It was our last chance to see if there was anything left to salvage. We cut off communication and focused on rebuilding ourselves individually. It wasn't an easy decision, but it was necessary.

Alone and Awakening

During my healing journey, three pivotal transformations helped me rise to a new level of being. These weren't just steps; they were lifelines. They helped me move from merely surviving to thriving, allowing me to finally feel whole again. Each transformation was a piece of the puzzle that rebuilt the person I am today.

1. Self-Love: Reclaiming My Worth

The first shift came during my mother's final year of life. We were traveling together, and I found myself in a sacred place: a quiet corner of a beautiful church in Jerusalem. As I sat alone in the candlelit stillness, I felt completely disconnected. The chaos of my life had left me drained, and I no longer recognized the person I had become. I was lost in a deep void, unable to feel the joy or light that had once been a part of me.

It was in that silence that two simple words surfaced in my mind: *Self-love*. Those words were a revelation, like a lifeline tossed into the dark waters I was drowning in. I didn't know where they came from—whether from my Higher Self, God, or the depths of my soul—but they struck a chord so deep that I couldn't ignore them. *Self-love*. Tears filled my eyes as the meaning of those words settled into my heart. They were a command, a reminder, and a gift all at once.

I realized that for years, I had been living without giving myself the love, care, and compassion that I so freely gave to others. I had poured every ounce of my energy into work, friendships, and external achievements, leaving nothing for myself. It became clear that without a foundation of self-love, nothing else could truly thrive. From that moment forward, I made a commitment to myself. Filling my cup became my priority. I began asking, "*What does my soul need right now?*" And then, for the first time in years, I listened. Some days, it was a walk on the beach or soaking in a salt bath. Other days, it was watching the sunset, journaling, or allowing myself the space to cry and release what no longer served me.

Two events became especially significant to me: taking myself out to a beautiful dinner all by myself and shopping for luxurious lingerie in New York City. These weren't just indulgences, they were declarations of my worth. They were my way of saying, "*I matter. I deserve beauty, joy, and love.*" Through these acts of self-care, I began to rebuild the love and trust within myself.

Self-love became the cornerstone of my healing. It taught me that I didn't need to rely on anyone else to feel whole. I could stand strong in this world simply because I chose to care for myself. This journey toward self-love wasn't just about indulgence, it was about reclaiming my power and recognizing my worth.

2. Reconnecting with My Inner Power

The second transformation came when I realized that I lacked a strong foundation within myself. For years, I had relied on the support of others—first my parents, and then my husband—for stability and a sense of security. Moving to America had already been a test of my independence, but I had always had someone by my side. Now, I was truly alone, and it terrified me. And now, I needed to go inward and find the well of power within me that no one else could give or take away.

This realization came during a moment of deep reflection. I had hit rock bottom emotionally, and the only way forward was to rebuild from the inside out. Each day, I practiced grounding myself, closing my eyes, and tuning into the energy within my body. It was a quiet but transformative practice. Slowly, I began to feel the immense strength I had always possessed but had forgotten.

I discovered that my inner power wasn't dependent on anything external. It was limitless, rechargeable, and always accessible. It wasn't something I needed to earn or prove, it was simply a part of who I was. This power became my anchor, helping me face challenges with resilience and grace.

We are all born with an inner spring of strength and vitality, but over time, we lose touch with it. Life's demands, expectations, and distractions pull us away from this source. Reconnecting with it isn't complicated—it's about pausing, breathing, and feeling the energy within.

To access this inner power, I would stand firmly on the ground, close my eyes, and focus on the sensations in my body. I'd feel the energy running through my toes, fingers, and heart, and sense my connection to the earth beneath me and the air around me. This practice reminded me of my oneness with the world and the strength that was always flowing through me. Reconnecting with my inner power changed the way I approached life. It gave me the courage to face my fears, the strength to set boundaries, and the clarity to pursue what truly mattered. It reminded me that no matter how chaotic life felt, I had everything I needed within me.

3. Aligning with My Higher Self

The third transformation came when I discovered my Higher Self—the limitless, elevated version of me that existed beyond fear, doubt, and limitation. For so long, I had been making decisions from a place of scarcity and contraction, reacting to life rather than creating it. But when I connected with my Higher Self, everything shifted. My Higher Self showed me that I wasn't alone. It reminded me that I was a part of something greater, and that I didn't have to navigate life from a place of fear. Instead, I could operate from love, expansion, and empowerment. This realization became a daily practice, a ritual of sitting in stillness and imagining the most expansive and elevated version of myself. Daily, I would ask myself, *"What would my Higher Self do?"* The answers that came were profound. They weren't just about the next steps in my journey; they were about how I could align my choices with my highest potential. They helped me see that I wasn't a victim of my circumstances. I was a co-creator of my reality, capable of shaping my life in powerful ways.

Aligning with my Higher Self became my compass. It guided me through uncertainty and helped me rebuild my life with intention and grace. When fear crept in, I returned to the part of me that already knew the answers—the part that was wise, fearless, and whole.

The beauty of this practice is its simplicity. To connect with your Higher Self, all you need is a moment of quiet. Feel the part of you that is already limitless, already free. It's the version of you that operates from love, not fear, and from expansion, not limitation. When you make decisions from this elevated place, your life begins to shift in ways you never thought possible.

When the Dust Settled

As I look back on the last 22 years of my life in America, I see now that every event, no matter how painful or challenging, was happening *for* me—not *to* me. Each moment was shaping me, molding me into the person I am today. It's taken years of reflection, growth, and healing to fully understand this, but now I can say with gratitude: It was all meant to happen just the way it did. There were times when I felt completely broken, as if the pieces of my life would never fit back together. Yet, in those moments of darkness, I found glimpses of hope. Slowly but surely, I began to realize that the guidance I so desperately needed, both internal and external, was always available to me. I just had to learn how to listen.

This journey wasn't about finding salvation outside of myself. It was about discovering wholeness within. It was about learning to trust my inner knowing, rebuilding myself from the ground up, and finding the courage to love myself again. It was about discovering my true inner power, forging a relationship with my Higher Self, and co-creating with the Higher Power. These were the foundations of my transformation, the steps that took me from feeling lost and alone to knowing, with every fiber of my being, that I am always guided and supported.

Returning to wholeness wasn't just about healing—it was about evolving. As I pieced myself back together, I found that I wasn't the same person I had been before. I was stronger, more empowered, and more aligned with my purpose than ever before. As I rebuilt my relationship with myself, I found the strength to rebuild my marriage: a relationship I had once believed was beyond saving. What I thought was destined for divorce became a renewed partnership, built on a foundation of even deeper love, respect, and a shared commitment to growth.

The Gift of Motherhood

Three years ago, I stepped into the most profound chapter of my life: motherhood. The moment I held my son for the first time, I felt a wave of love so pure and unconditional that it took my breath away. In his eyes, I saw a light and joy that I hadn't felt in years. It was as if he was reflecting back to me the part of myself that I had lost along the way. In that moment, I realized: This was my second chance.

Motherhood gave my life a completely new meaning. It wasn't just about caring for my son; it was about rediscovering the light within me so I could guide him with strength, integrity, courage, and love. His presence in my life became a catalyst for transformation, inspiring me to become the best version of myself. I wanted to be the mother he deserved, the kind of mother who leads with authenticity and shows him, through her actions, what it means to live a fulfilled and purposeful life.

Every day, my son teaches me the power of presence. He doesn't care about my accomplishments or the goals I've set for myself. What he needs is *me*—fully present, fully engaged, and fully loving. Through him, I've learned that success isn't about what we achieve; it's about the love, light, and joy we bring into the world. He reminds me that the most important thing I can do is show up with an open heart and a willingness to grow.

Motherhood hasn't just been a role—it's been a transformation. It has grounded me in what truly matters and given me a deeper sense of purpose. It has reminded me that my most important legacy isn't the businesses I have built or the accomplishments I have achieved. It's the love I pour into my family and the example I set for my son. It's the way I teach him to navigate life with integrity, compassion, and courage.

A New Chapter

My journey of rebuilding myself from the ground up is more than a personal story. It's a testament to the power of resilience, courage, and self-belief. It's proof that even when life feels impossibly hard, we have the strength within us to rise, rebuild, and create something extraordinary.

This story isn't just about overcoming challenges, it's about embracing them as opportunities for growth. It's about choosing to see obstacles as stepping stones and trusting that even the hardest moments are a part of a greater plan. It's about believing in yourself, even when it feels like the odds are stacked against you.

The message I want to share is simple yet profound: Never give up on yourself. Build a relationship with yourself where you are your own biggest cheerleader, your fiercest advocate, and your most trusted ally. When you believe in your own strength, others believe in you too. And as you change internally, the world around you begins to change as well.

When you become a strong leader for yourself, you create a ripple effect that touches everything you do. Whether it's running a business, nurturing a family, building relationships, or inspiring the next generation, your inner strength becomes the foundation for success. It's not about perfection—it's about authenticity. It's about showing up as your full, unapologetic self and leading with love.

I am honored to share my journey, my lessons, and my experiences with women around the world. My passion is to inspire others to step into their power, embrace their unique gifts, and lead lives that are both fulfilling and impactful. We all have the ability to create a life we love, and it starts with believing in ourselves.

Today, everything I do is guided by one central mission: to be a loving mother, a caring partner, a supportive friend, and a strong leader. This vision has become my North Star, illuminating my path and reminding me of what truly matters. It's not just about achieving goals, it's about how we show up in the face of challenges. It's about choosing growth, even when it's uncomfortable. It's about leading with love, even when it's hard. Every obstacle is an opportunity to grow. Every challenge is a chance to rise. And every moment is an invitation to become the person we were always meant to be.

My personal transformation fueled a new career path for me. Every day, I help ambitious, purpose-driven female entrepreneurs overcome mental, emotional, and energetic blocks that stand between them and the successful, fulfilling businesses they desire. I specialize in guiding women to conquer limiting beliefs, build magnetic confidence, and align their energy with their vision. My approach empowers them to create profitable, impactful businesses that feel deeply rewarding, without stress, burnout, and self-doubt.

This is my story—a story of resilience, transformation, and empowerment.

I am a trailblazer, an initiator of my own rebirth. I chose not to stay defeated. I chose to rise.

JOIN THE MOVEMENT!
#BAUW

Becoming An Unstoppable Woman With She Rises Studios

She Rises Studios was founded by Hanna Olivas and Adriana Luna Carlos, the mother-daughter duo, in mid-2020 as they saw a need to help empower women worldwide. They are the podcast hosts of the *She Rises Studios Podcast* and Amazon best-selling authors and motivational speakers who travel the world. Hanna and Adriana are the movement creators of #BAUW - Becoming An Unstoppable Woman: The movement has been created to universally impact women of all ages, at whatever stage of life, to overcome insecurities, and adversities, and develop an unstoppable mindset. She Rises Studios educates, celebrates, and empowers women globally.

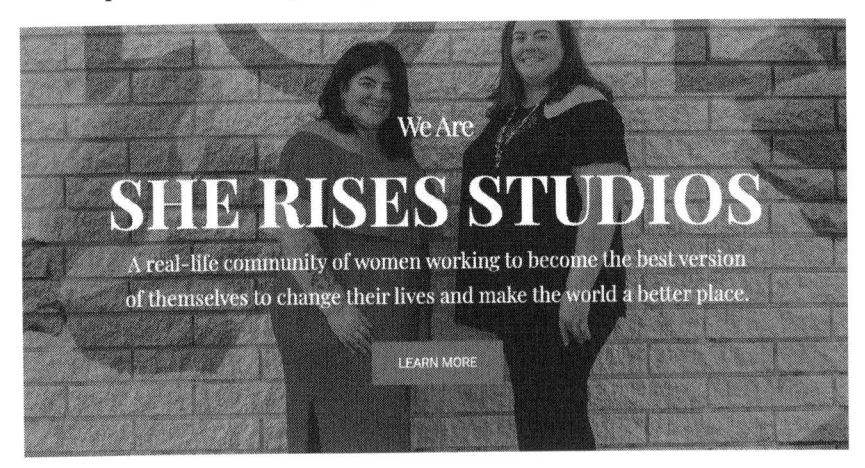

Looking to Join Us in our Next Anthology or Publish YOUR Own?

She Rises Studios Publishing offers full-service publishing, marketing, book tour, and campaign services. For more information, contact info@sherisesstudios.com

We are always looking for women who want to share their stories and expertise and feature their businesses on our podcasts, in our books, and in our magazines.

SEE WHAT WE DO

OUR PODCAST

OUR BOOKS

OUR SERVICES

Be featured in the Becoming An Unstoppable Woman magazine, published in 13 countries and sold in all major retailers. Get the visibility you need to LEVEL UP in your business!

Have your own TV show streamed across major platforms like Roku TV, Amazon Fire Stick, Apple TV and more!

Learn to leverage your expertise. Build your online presence and grow your audience with FENIX TV.

https://fenixtv.sherisesstudios.com/

342 | Women's Stories of Strength and Empowerment

Visit www.SheRisesStudios.com to see how YOU can join the #BAUW movement and help your community to achieve the UNSTOPPABLE mindset.

Have you checked out the *She Rises Studios Podcast?*

Find us on all MAJOR platforms: Spotify, IHeartRadio, Apple Podcasts, Google Podcasts, etc.

Looking to become a sponsor or build a partnership?

Email us at info@sherisesstudios.com

SHE RISES
STUDIOS

Made in the USA
Columbia, SC
28 May 2025